Pictorial History of
TRAINS

Pictorial History of

TRAINS

David S. Hamilton

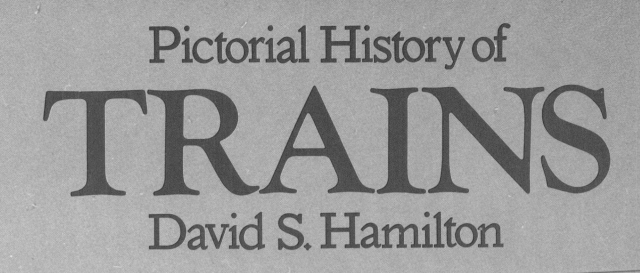

Contents

First published 1977 by
Octopus Books Limited
59 Grosvenor Street
London W1

© 1977 Octopus Books

ISBN 0 7064 0602 8

Produced by Mandarin Publishers Limited
22a Westlands Road
Quarry Bay, Hong Kong

Printed in Hong Kong

Europe

France

From whatever angle one likes to regard them, and at whatever period in their long history, the railways of France provide a vivid and fascinating study. Generally the liveries of locomotives and carriages in the independent days up to 1938 were rather dull though among locomotives there were a few startling exceptions such as the Forquenot 2-4-2s of the Paris–Orleans Railway, with their polished brass jacketed boilers, while the wind-cutter 4-4-0s of the Paris, Lyons and Mediterranean were distinctive enough from their strange external appearance. There was nothing in France to rival the blues, reds and yellows of contemporary British locomotives, not to mention the gay colour schemes to be seen all over Holland.

What French steam lacked aesthetically however, it more than made up for in the soundness, albeit complexity, of its engineering and in the personalities of its men. They copied, with long-sustained enthusiasm, the precepts of the celebrated 'stern-wheelers' of the English designer Thomas Russell Crampton, which had a single pair of large-diameter driving wheels at the extreme rear end, with the driver and fireman ensconced between the wheels. The Northern Railway took another English design, by Archibald Sturrock of the Great Northern Railway, a 2-4-0 of 1866; it was a massively built thing, and after the French had developed it into a 4-4-0 they found it

Right. French National Railways: one of the most famous steam locomotive classes of all time, the Chapelon rebuilt Pacifics, SNCF–G 231–E class, originating on the Paris–Orleans Railway, here seen in the last years of French steam on a Nord express.
Extreme right. One of the former PLM Pacifics—Class '23-K' no. 2, on a 'rapide' from Calais to Paris near Hesdigneul.

would stand thrashing *à l'outrance* and the class became known as the 'Outrance', in other words, the 'all-out engines'. But there is a limit to what even the best-designed machinery will stand, and thrashing *à l'outrance* sometimes led to broken crank axles. This brought about one of the most important technical developments in steam locomotive history.

It was a time when engineers all over the world were seeking ways in which the thermal efficiency might be increased and coal consumption thereby reduced. Two-stage, or compound, expansion was being introduced on many railways, and on the Northern of France, in a fruitful collaboration with Alfred de Glehn, an English

engineer, then practising in Belfort, the compound principle was applied to a locomotive generally of the 'Outrance' type, but with four cylinders instead of two. Instead of thrusting all the power for traction through one axle the drive was divided. The high-pressure cylinders were outside and drove the rear pair of wheels, while the low-pressure cylinders drove the leading pair. Thus the heavy stresses occurring in the Outrance type were avoided and the risk of broken crank axles lessened to a degree that was minimal. From the pioneer engine of the de Glehn four-cylinder compound type, which is fortunately preserved in the French Railway Museum at Mulhouse, Alsace, an entire dynasty of

locomotives followed, leading up to the outstanding Chapelon 'Pacifics' of the Paris–Orleans Railway, dating from 1929, and considered by many connoisseurs of steam locomotive practice to be the finest ever in the entire history of this machine.

Not all the star performers of the steam era in France came from the Northern and the Orleans railways. The Paris, Lyons and Mediterranean Railway had a long and illustrious tradition of locomotive working, and as its main line not only extended from Paris to Marseilles but continued thence along the Cote d'Azur to the Italian frontier at Ventimiglia, the locomotives of the PLM made their running in country of scenic splendour. To reach Marseilles they had to

cross the Rhône delta and in level and very exposed country survive the tremendous force of the Mistral wind. Thick hedges of cypress trees were grown alongside the line, and the powerful four-cylinder compound 4-4-0 and 4-6-0s express locomotives, known as the 'wind-cutters', had semi-streamlined fairings at the front and behind the boiler mountings to lessen the effect of the wind.

Beside the sombre browns, greys, dark greens and blacks of French steam locomotives the modern electric and diesel locomotives are highly colourful. And as with steam practice of old, the modern motive power of the French National railways is second to none in its technical quality. It is since the end of World War II that such remarkable development has taken place. Until then the lines converted to electric traction, notably the Paris–Tours section of the Orleans Railway, presented a rather dull spectacle of uninspiring 'juice boxes', as they were often called, excellent though their technical performance was from the outset. Then came the postwar decision to adopt 25,000 volts alternating current, instead of the 1,500 volts direct current, used on the Orleans, on the first stages of PLM electrification, and in Great Britain and Holland. The 25,000 volt ac system gave promise of getting the work of electrification done much more cheaply.

Much attention has been given to the aesthetic appearance of locomotives and of the luxurious *grand-confort* coaches, so that now, with many trains covering long stretches of the Northern, Eastern and PLM lines at 160 kph (100 mph), and the fastest trains on the former Orleans Railway running regularly at 200 kph (125 mph), the trains themselves and their locomotives are more colourful than any in the long history of French railways. Steam traction is now at an end, and on the lines not yet electrified the trains are hauled by handsomely styled diesel-electric locomotives.

Above left. French National Railways: 'Le Capitole du Matin' – super-speed Electric express train bound for Toulouse, at the Gare d'Austerlitz, Paris. Much of the run between Paris and Limoges is covered at 200 kph (125 mph) by these 8000 hp electric locomotives.
Below left. French National Railways: the Stanislas express from Paris, on arrival at Strasbourg. The electric locomotive of the '1500' class is one of the most advanced technical designs in the world, with automatic regulation of the controls to maintain a constant pre-selected speed.
Above. French National Railways: one of the post-war American-built 2-8-2s 141R class ready to leave Calais-Ville on an evening local train to Boulogne in January 1969.
Right. The prototype ultra-high speed gas-turbine train, which has attained a speed of 317 kph (197 mph) on tests south of Bordeaux.

The change in policy over the system of electric traction to be standardised on French railways brought an interesting problem, and in due course an elegant solution. While lines newly designated for electrification at 25,000 volts ac such as those in the Northern Region, from Paris to Amiens, Lille, and the Belgian frontier, and the Eastern Region main line from Paris to Strasbourg, would be quite separate from the existing 1,500 volt dc lines, some of these latter were marked down for extension, and it was decided to equip them with the newer system. To avoid the inconvenience of changing locomotives at points of demarcation between the two systems new designs were prepared which could operate on either. This project was indeed carried further. On the railways of Western Europe there are four different traction systems on electrified lines:

1,500 volts dc on the older lines in France, and in Holland.
3,000 volts dc in Belgium and Italy.
15,000 volts ac in West Germany, Switzerland and Austria.
25,000 volts ac on the newer electrified lines in France.

French engineers evolved a design of locomotive that could work on all four systems, and which could change from one system to another without stopping. From the early years of the twentieth century it had been traditional to run non-stop express trains between Paris and Brussels, and in steam days the locomotives and crews were French. Introduction of the new quadri-current electric locomotives enabled the tradition to be continued, changing from the French 25,000 volts ac to the Belgian 3,000 volts dc at the frontier, at about 112 kph (70 mph). As the changeover point is approached the pantograph in use is lowered. Then, after passing through a short electrically neutral zone, the driver selects the pantograph for the Belgian system, and raises it. Before power can be re-applied it must be electrically proved that the correct pantograph has been raised. When this has been automatically checked the driver can re-apply power.

Above. SNCF express electric locomotive number BB 25569 at Villefranche-sur-Mer.
Right. A SNCF turbo-train speeds through Bois Colombes (1972).

While it is the policy of the French railways to extend the electrified system wherever possible, elimination of steam traction throughout France was made possible by introduction of a series of new diesel-electric locomotives in various ranges of power. These massive-looking and handsomely-styled units have a strong family likeness, and they are now used in many parts of France in express passenger and mixed traffic service. There are three classes: '67000' of 2,000 horsepower; '68000' of 2,670 horsepower, and the very large '72000' class which, at 4,800 horsepower are the world's most powerful single-engined diesel locomotives. Among other duties they work the Western Region express service between Paris and Nantes, while an interesting duty of the '67000' is to work the 'Catalan–Talgo' service. This operates between Geneva and Barcelona, and at the Spanish frontier there is not only a change of locomotive but of rail gauge. The Spanish-built coaches have a special arrangement of wheels that enables the spacing to be changed to suit the change of rail gauge. They are very low, and when running in France hauled by one of the '67000' class the locomotive positively towers over the coaches following it.

In recent years French rolling stock design has achieved notable comfort, smooth riding and sheer luxury. The *grand confort* coaches used on high-speed express trains in the TEE category, such as the 'Capitole' 'Mistral' and 'Stanislas', in their beautiful grey and red livery and their air smoothed lines, have been designed to provide a high standard of travel at speeds up to 200 kph (125 mph). One is almost unconscious of the speed that is actually being run, so much so that when a train like 'Etendard' or 'Aquitaine' slows down to pass through the great junction of Les Aubrais, Orléans, at about 110 kph (68 mph) it seems that it is stopping!

The latest main line passenger coaches introduced in France are the *voitures corail*, so called from the coral-coloured entrance doors, in a two-tone colour scheme of near-white bodies and blue grey upper panels. These are being introduced on many express services below the TEE category. The initials TEE stand for Trans Europ Express, and were originally applied to certain super class international trains; but the inclusion of a number of purely French trains in the group has made the appellation come to signify a standard of service rather than a necessarily international route.

It is in the South-Western Region that the fastest trains in France are at present operated, with the 581 km (360 miles) between Paris and Bordeaux covered in less than 4 hours. These are not moderately-loaded 'limiteds' but heavy expresses of more than 500 tons, hauled by the powerful 8,000 horsepower 'CC 6500' type locomotives. Nor do the booked times represent the maximum that can be done. The 'Aquitaine', for example, allowed 135 minutes to cover the 332 km (206 miles) from Poitiers to Paris, non-stop, on one journey cut this time by 8 minutes to make an average from start-to-stop of 156·1 kph (97 mph) while for 247.8 km (154 miles) the average was 181 kph (112½ mph).

Yet speeds of this order are not considered enough in France today. On the continuation of this very line, southwards from Bordeaux towards Biarritz, trials have been in progress for more than two years with the revolutionary TGV train (*Très Grande Vitesse*) with regular trial running at 258 kph (160 mph) and more, in readiness for the new high-speed railway upon which construction began in December 1976, from Paris to Lyons.

This is not an instance of a new 'super' railway being built for spectacular prestige purposes to outpace all others in the regular

Right. SNCF diesel-electric locomotive No. 68026 arrives at Angers from Tours (1967).
Below. SNCF railcar set approaching Angers St Laud on the Nantes–Lyon express (1967).

Below left. A SNCF CC 6,500 heads a train
of new *Corail* express coaches.
Right. The Paris-Nice express *Le Mistral* runs
alongside the Mediterranean coast near Anthéor.

day-to-day speed of its passenger trains. It
has been born out of hard operational
necessity. The existing main line from Paris
southwards to Dijon and Lyons serves,
through its numerous connections and
extensions south and east, roughly 40 per
cent of the total population of France, and
its central section, which is only double-
tracked, is saturated with traffic at certain
times of the day. Because of the physical
nature of the route through the Côte d'Or
mountains, provision of extra running lines
would be prohibitively expensive and would
provide little more than a minimal solution
of the problem. The existing route throughout is not suitable for speeds of more than
160 kph (100 mph) and so an entirely new
conception was formed: to construct an
entirely new line that should be capable of

sustaining continuous running at 300 kph
(185 mph), and to carry nothing but high-
speed passenger trains; that *all* long-
distance passenger trains from Paris on the
South-Eastern Region should take the new
route for at least part of their journey, and
diverge from it or continue beyond it as
their ultimate destination required. While
on the new line all trains would run uniformly at *très grande vitesse*.

By this striking project, some almost
sensational accelerations of journey time
are to be made. From Paris to Lyons, for
example, the present fastest time will be cut
from 3 hr 44 min to the even 2 hours; Marseilles, now 6 hr 35 min from Paris, will be
reached in 4 hr 43 min and the time to
Geneva, via Lausanne, will come down
from 5 hr 39 min to 3 hr 19 min. But the

overall conception is not one solely of technical advance and wholesale time-cutting. The philosophy of passenger service is to be radically changed. Hitherto the great trains of France, and those of Western Europe in general, have been operated on a luxury basis. Many of them are first-class only, and the TEE services in particular require substantial supplementary fares. In contrast the new 'TGV' trains will embody what has been called *la democratisation de la vitesse*, in that they will be available to both first and second class passengers and will not involve supplementary fares.

At the same time because of the great curtailment of journey time the style of accommodation is to be quite unlike that of the *grand confort* coaches. In both first and second class the seating will be arranged in the style of a modern airliner, with facilities for serving meals to passengers, airline style, at their seats. There is one difference however. Because the trains will necessarily travel in opposite directions on their outward and inward journeys, half the seats in each carriage will be arranged facing forward, and half backward. The actual spacing between the seats will be much the same as in an airliner, with somewhat wider spacing in first class. There will, however, be through communication from end to end of the new trains, and on the longer journeys a carriage including a bar will be run, in addition to the first and second class seating cars. It is expected that the line will be completed and the new trains in service by 1981.

Europe
West Germany

Above. One of the celebrated Prussian 'P8' class 4-6-0s, design dating from 1906, adapted as a Reichsbahn standard and here shown at Horb, south of Stuttgart, in August 1970.
Right. One of the powerful '44' class 2-10-0s on a freight train in the Moselle valley near Eller.

In the days when the many independent states were brought together by Bismarck in the newly constituted German Empire at the end of the Franco-Prussian war of 1870–1, there were a host of small and largely unconnected railways all over the land. Nowhere did these railways intersect, duplicate one another, and otherwise sprawl out more than in the Rhineland. After 1871 Bismarck tried to nationalize them all; but resistance in the southern states was too strong, even for him, and the railways of Baden and Bavaria in particular remained independent. Most of those in the north were brought under the control of Prussia, but with strong local administrations running them. The only group that was fully nationalized was the unfortunate Alsace–Lorraine system, in the territory annexed from France after the war, which had the prefix 'Imperial' added to its Germanized title. So far as technical developments were concerned it was Prussia and Bavaria that henceforth made the running – each in a way that had influences far beyond the frontiers of Germany.

Of all the railway networks in pre-Imperial days the one in the Rhineland, southwards from Cologne to Frankfurt, is by far the most fascinating. There are, of course, great centres of industrial railway

activity amid the cities of the Ruhr, where notable technological achievements in freight handling and traffic control have been made; but for one of the most interesting and picturesque railway rides he could wish for down the Rhine, the railway enthusiast should make the journey southwards from Cologne.

The principal express trains usually take the left bank of the Rhine, leaving the right bank for the freights. There are, nevertheless, numerous junctions and river crossings, and between high hills, stepped with vineyards, one can switch from one side to the other. There is hardly a valley with its river feeding into the Rhine that does not have its own railway and some of these are far from being country branch lines. One of the most leisurely ways of seeing railway activity in its entirety is to travel by one of the beautiful river steamers; then the trains on both banks can be readily seen, and although one is rarely near enough to see the actual numbers, an enthusiastic 'spotter' could have a busy enough time noting the types of locomotive and the loads they were hauling, whether goods or passenger.

German steam locomotives, whether emanating from Prussia or Bavaria, were functional and efficient. Prussia's greatest contribution to the worldwide development

of the steam locomotive came from a scientist who was not originally a railwayman at all, Dr Wilhelm Schmidt of Berlin, who in the 1890s was developing the use of superheated steam. If steam was used just as it was generated, in the way hitherto accepted on every locomotive that had been built since the days of Richard Trevithick, 90 years earlier, it was *wet* no matter at what pressure it was generated; and there were also problems of condensation. If, after the steam was generated it was heated further, 'superheated', the risk of condensation was lessened; it became much more fluid and its volume was increased. It was on locomotives of the Prussian State railways that Schmidt first applied his superheaters. His early experiments brought no more than moderate success but from 1912 onwards there was hardly a main-line locomotive built anywhere in the world without a superheater.

The development in Bavaria was less obvious at first, but of great importance. In the chapter dealing with the railways of France mention will be made of Alfred de Glehn and his work on the compound locomotive. Now down in Munich, at the famous firm of Maffei, another form of four-cylinder compound was being produced. De Glehn deliberately divided the drive between two axles in order to lessen the stresses in the axles themselves and in the bearings. Maffei arranged his compounds so that all four cylinders drove on to the same axle. There would seem at first to be a contradiction and a recession in practice in this, even though the driving axles themselves were made very strong and generous bearing surfaces were provided. But there was another vital factor involved.

Locomotives were getting large and heavy by the early years of the twentieth century and were reaching the limit which the civil engineer could accept on the track and bridges. These limits had grown up largely as a result of practical experience, not from any very scientific calculations; but at that time the more academically minded of engineers were investigating the effects of unbalanced forces in the moving parts of locomotives, and Maffei's layout with all four cylinders driving on to the same axle gave an almost perfectly balanced machine. Civil engineers on the continent of Europe were prepared to accept heavier

A West German 2-10-0, no. 051 0578 climbing from Neuenmarkt Wirsberg to Marktschorgast on the 07.06 Neuenmarkt-Wirsberg to Hof—one of many locos fitted with tender cabs.

axle loads with engines designed in this way, and this attitude proved of inestimable value to the Netherlands State Railways when they wanted to introduce larger and heavier locomotives in 1910.

After World War I, and the nationalization of all the German railways under the Republic, much attention was devoted to highly spectacular diesel railcar services, such as the 'Flying Hamburger'; but steam remained the solid backbone of the entire operation, and it became even more so during World War II. The emphasis, as everywhere else among the European belligerents, was on freight, and a remarkable feat of locomotive designing and construction was carried out by German engineers. Before the war a very powerful freight engine of the 2-10-0 type had been successfully introduced. This was essentially a heavy main-line engine, and because of its weight there were many important lines over which it could not work. So a lighter version of the same design was produced and construction of both proceeded simultaneously. As the war situation developed, however, and many more locomotives were needed in countries controlled or overrun

by the military campaigns, a decision was taken to produce a general service 'war locomotive', a 'Kriegslok' that would have the widest possible route availability.

Because of the need to conserve supplies of all metals, and particularly the choicer grades needed for aircraft and other direct munitions of war, the design of the lightweight 2-10-0 was examined in the closest detail to see where metal could be saved. The original 'Series 50' was a very powerful engine for its overall weight, with tender, of 144 tons; but by dispensing with everything not absolutely essential in a 'Kriegslok' no less than 27 tons of metal was saved in making the 'Series 52', and eventually more than 10,000 of these locomotives were built – many in Austria and Czechoslovakia. It is not surprising that they are still very familiar objects on the railways of West Germany, and elsewhere in Central Europe. All working steam locomotives in West Germany today are black with red wheels; but the attractive green livery of the Bavarian State railways has been restored on one of the Maffei 'Pacific' engines, now preserved in Munich the Bavarian capital and railway headquarters.

Below. A freight for Trier crosses the Moselle, hauled by one of the heavy '44' class 2-10-0s No. 44-170-9.
Following pages. 044-402-6 52 class southbound freight in the Neckar valley near Horb.

Germany was early in the field in development of diesel traction, and introduction of the twin-car high speed motor coach train, the 'Flying Hamburger' in 1932 cut completely across the then-prevalent European standards both of speed and passenger accommodation. At a time when the fastest trains in Great Britain and France were making averages of 114.9 and 109.5 kph (71.4 and 68.1 mph) respectively, the 'Flying Hamburger' by running the 286 km (178 miles) from Berlin to Hamburg in 138 minutes averaged 124.5 kph (77.4 mph). It provided also a foretaste of what the French railways are now planning for their new TGV trainsets, in that the passenger seating accommodation was much more restricted in space than in normal European express trains. Commercially it was a great success, and similar trains making even higher average speeds were introduced in Germany between 1933 and 1939.

Since the end of World War II, the policy has followed on similar lines to that in France–electrifying wherever possible, and replacing steam by diesel locomotives on the non-electrified routes. German engineers have been to the fore in building locomotives with hydraulic rather than electric transmission, and the Krauss-Maffei 'V 200' class locomotive of 2,000/2,3000 horsepower on the Federal Railway has not only become an acknowledged standard but has proved the prototype for variations and

developments exported to many parts of the world. The 'Warship' class of the Western Region of British Railways was an almost direct equal of the 'V 200'. These locomotives are, however, of somewhat limited capacity by modern standards, having a maximum service speed of no more than 140 kph (87 mph) and they are used on cross-country and connexional routes rather than on trains of the principal TEE network.

Some of the TEE services connecting major centres of population and industry include non-electrified sections in their routes, and an interesting example is the 'Parsifal', running between Paris and Hamburg. It serves Charleroi, Liège, Aachen,

Cologne, Düsseldorf, Essen, Osnabruck and Bremen. This is operated by a self-contained luxury diesel train, with a locomotive unit at each end, and five cars between. The formation includes a restaurant car and a restaurant with bar, with seating for 46 between them; but such is the luxury of the accommodation in the three other cars that these provide seats for no more than 105 passengers, first class only. Except in the lavishness of the seating this type of train, with fixed formation and diesel power at each end, is in some ways a prototype for high-speed diesel trains elsewhere in Europe. The journey time from Paris to Hamburg is about 9 hours, but with the numerous large centres served en route few passengers would make the complete journey. It has proved popular for the shorter city-to-city runs provided by the intermediate stops.

The German system of electrification, at 15,000 volts ac, is the same as that of Switzerland and Austria, and some fine services have been developed on the Federal Railway, particularly on the popular international route following the Rhine from Holland to the Swiss frontier. The celebrated 'Rheingold' express, consisting of through carriages from various northern centres, then running from Cologne to Basle, and there dispersing through carriages to a number of Swiss destinations has proved a very popular train. The northern nucleus has at different times been a restaurant car

Below. DB class 103 Co-Co electric loco No. 103 177–2 pulls a Düsseldorf–Munich car train through Aschaffenburg (1973).
Left. DB class 216 diesel No. 216 014–1 heads the Kohlenz–Paris Est train past Eller (1971).

23

403 005-2
A vüm
58 t
45 Pl
27,45 m
KE-P-A-E-Mg
P · Mg 136 t
P   100 t

section either from the Hook of Holland, or Amsterdam, hauled at first by Dutch electric locomotives, and at one time containing a 'dome' observation car, which was a delightful point of vantage for enjoying the scenic beauty of the Rhine valley between Cologne and Mannheim. The coaching stock is now finished uniformly in the red and cream livery of international TEE trains, and makes a striking sight.

In earlier days 'Rheingold', and other electrically hauled express trains on the German Federal Railway were hauled by the dark blue electric locomotives of the Bo-Bo type Class 'E 10' of 4,400 horsepower, and a few units of this class were specially geared for running at 160 kph (100 mph) with the 'Rheingold' train. It was an impressive experience to ride in the driver's cab and to see the numerous aids to efficient running that were provided. One was a book of oblong shape showing a diagrammatic representation of the line, and on this was shown a speed graph, one part of which showed the maximum speed permitted over each section and the other showing the speed required to be run to keep the scheduled time of the train. One could see at a glance the margin that existed between scheduled and maximum permitted speed. More recently the German Federal Railway have introduced the larger and more powerful '103' class locomotives, which are of the Co-Co wheel arrangement. Those allocated to TEE trains are painted in a red and cream livery to harmonize with the coaching stock.

One very attractive electric vehicle that stands rather apart from the general line of West German motive power is the very picturesque 'Glass' car operating from Munich. It is entirely of glass above the waistline, and is used for making private-hire tours on the picturesque mountain routes south of Munich. Because the German and Austrian railways use the same system of electrification the 'Glass' car used often to penetrate into the Tyrol, to Innsbruck, and elsewhere. It seats 72 passengers on swing-over seats and has a maximum speed of 110 kph (68 mph).

Left. DB's latest high speed train the ET 403.

Europe

Switzerland

In their mechanical, as distinct from their electrical features, the present success of modern non-steam locomotives in France can be traced back to an important Swiss development on the breathtakingly scenic Bern–Lötschberg–Simplon Railway, which in 1944 introduced an express electric locomotive which had all the wheels motor-driven. Hitherto on electric railways all over the world it had been thought essential to have non-powered leading and trailing wheels to provide adequate guiding influence, like the leading bogie of a steam locomotive. The new Lötschberg locomotives, carried on eight wheels, were a great success and the general principle of the mechanical design was adopted by the Swiss Federal Railways, and the authorities in France, to good effect.

On the great Alpine routes, the Gotthard, the Lötschberg and the Simplon, together with the metric-gauge lines traversed by a train like 'The Glacier Express', the Swiss railways make their way through some of the finest scenery in the world. It is often

The two preserved Rhaetian 2-8-0s together on a special train on the south side of the Albula Pass, towards Bevers in the Engadine.

difficult from one train window to appreciate the full grandeur of the country. There is a strong desire to dash from one side to the other! A front seat in one of the special 'Trans-Europ-Express' railcar trains gives a better impression, but best of all is that privileged place the driver's cab. Then the bewildering spiral locations of the Gotthard 'ramps', the amazing descent of the Lötschberg line into the Rhône valley, and the alternations between rack and adhesion on the precipitous inclines of the Brunig Railway, between Interlaken and Lucerne, can be enjoyed to the utmost; they are unique.

It is some time since there was any regular steam working in Switzerland and one had to visit that most beautiful of transport museums on the lake shore at Lucerne to see what some of the principal types of locomotives were like. But in keen appreciation of the tourist value in steam hauled trips, the Swiss Federal Railways have restored to full working order one of the celebrated Series A3/5 4-6-0s that was originally intended to be no more than a static museum piece at Lucerne. This locomotive, No. 705, is of a design originating on the Jura–Simplon Railway and dating back to 1902. The class, which eventually numbered one hundred and eleven, were four-cylinder compounds on the de Glehn system and is probably the oldest working example of that system.

The Rhaetian Railway is the longest and most complex of all the Swiss metre gauge lines. It is well known for its breathtaking electric runs in the High Alps and a train like 'The Glacier Express', and has also not neglected to preserve two of its steam locomotives, in full working order. Unlike the Swiss Federal Railways preserved examples, the Rhaetian 2-8-0s are two-cylinder simples and were built, like very many other Swiss engines, by the SLM Company at Winterthur, in the Rhaetian 2-8-0 case between 1906 and 1915.

Above left. One of the standard electric locomotives of the Rhaetian Railway at Cavadürli, on a train from Davos to Landquart.
Left. On the Swiss Federal Railways: the de Glehn four-cylinder compound 4-6-0 No. 705, of 1902 design, was originated by the Jura Simplon Railway and used on the expresses on the Rhône Valley main line. It is here seen on a special train near Winterthur.
Above right. Rhaetian Railway: one of the two series G 4/5 2-8-0 locomotives now preserved, here seen on the turntable at Landquart. The design, which incorporates a four-wheeled tender, dates from 1906.
Right. On the metre gauge Rhaetian Railway: a rotary snow plough at Klosters, propelled by one of the two preserved 2-8-0 steam locomotives.

Europe

Austria

It is an easy transition from Switzerland into Austria, by the magnificent Arlberg Route, leading into the heart of the Tyrol. In the early years of the twentieth century Austrian steam locomotives were among the most colourful in Europe. But today the most picturesque of Karl Gölsdorf's creations are no more than museum pieces, and only a few of his earlier two-cylinder compounds, designed initially to haul passenger trains over the very severe gradients of the Arlberg route, remain in revenue earning service in Styria. While the student of modernized transport will admire the efficient way in which electric locomotives deal with the mountain gradients of the Tyrol, and of the Semmering Pass, through which the Austrian Southern Railway took the line that was once the main all-Austrian route from Vienna to Trieste, the romance of railways lies in the remaining pockets of steam, mostly on the narrow gauge.

At Jenbach, for example, on the main line westwards into the Tyrol, not one but *two* narrow-gauge lines start away into the mountains. Going north is the Achensee line climbing so steeply up the hillside as to need a rack rail, and coming to the bleak, tree-less lake that gives the railway its name. From the other side of the main line at Jenbach there strikes out the Zillertalbahn, through beautiful Tyrolean valley scenery running mostly at river level and worked by picturesque little steam locomotives. Perhaps the most fascinating of all the Austrian narrow-gauge steam railways are the true mountain climbers. There is the Schafberg, in the Salzkammergut district, easy of access from Salzburg, that starts from the village of St Wolfgang, immortalized in the operetta *White Horse Inn*, and climbs to the summit of the Schafberg, all the time overlooking the beautiful lake, the Wolfgangsee. Then, south of Vienna, from Püchberg, there is the railway climbing to the summit of the Schneeberg, a very busy little rack railway all the year round, on

which there are often five or six steam locomotives in service simultaneously.

One of the most remarkable mountain rack railways in the world is, however, concerned no more than incidentally with passenger tourist traffic. This is the iron-ore carrying line up the Iron Mountain, in Styria. The *Eisenerz* holds enormous deposits of iron ore, which are worked by opencast methods. There is no need for mining, as such, and the railway was built in 1890 to convey the ore down the side of the mountain, on very steep gradients, and the rack system of propulsion is used to obviate slipping. The locomotives have gradually increased in size from the 0-6-2 tank engines of 1900; then came some 0-12-0s, designed by the great Karl Gölsdorf, and finally two enormous 2-12-2s built during World War II, when the Austrian railways were under German control. The station of Prebichl is at the summit of the climb from Donawitz. The iron-ore workings are some distance down the other side. So, the rack locomotives are required not only for the down-grade working of loaded trains but also for working these trains *up* the steep incline from Eisenerz to the summit of Prebichl. Also it certainly would not be practicable to work iron-ore empties up from Donawitz without the rack, especially in winter, as the ruling gradient is 1 in 15. The same applies to the passenger services.

Below. A diverting scene at St. Martin, on the line from Gmünd to Grossgernungs: while the 0-8-0 engine No. 39903 rests and takes water, the crew do the shunting — by muscle power! *Above*. A remarkable rack railway in Styria: to connect the opencast iron ore workings on the Iron Mountain — *Eisenerz* — with the Vienna–Villach main line a railway with gradients up to 1 in 14 was built. Here, on the rack section between Vordernberg and Prebichl summit, a Gölsdorf 0-6-2 hauls a load of hopper wagons. *Page 32 Above*. The fascination of the narrow gauge in Austria: on the Steyertal line an 0-6-2 tank engine No. 298-53 is shunting at Grunberg. *Page 32 Below*. One of the tall and impressive 4-6-4 tank engines of Class '78' of 1931 vintage stopping at Hieflau, in the course of a run from Amstetten to Selztal.

Birth and development 1830-1875

First steps Although the Liverpool and Manchester line in England marks the beginning of the Railway Age, it was by no means the first of the world's railways. A book published in 1550 illustrates a narrow-gauge line in the mines of Alsace, and in Central Europe at about the same time there were mine wagons running with flanged wooden wheels on wooden rails. The idea of mine railways came to England from Germany, and by the middle of the eighteenth century there were about twenty such lines around Newcastle alone. Iron rails appeared in Cumberland in 1738. In 1801 the Surrey Iron Railway, near London, was opened, and was notable in that it was a public railway, not confining its traffic to a particular industry. In 1807 the Oystermouth Railway near Swansea was the first to carry fare-paying passengers. In Bohemia the first section of a public railway was opened in 1827, and the following year France's first public line, from St-Etienne to Andrézieux, was formally opened after a year of unofficial operation.

In America a short wooden rail track had been laid up Beacon Hill in 1795 to transport materials for the new Boston state house. Similar lines, using horse power, were subsequently laid by several mining and manufacturing enterprises. A 14 km (9 mile) line carrying coal to the Lehigh River was opened in 1827; gravity was used for the loaded trip and mules hauled the empty cars back to the pithead. A similar line, but of 47 km (29 miles), was opened in 1829 by the Delaware & Hudson Canal Company to its canal wharf at Honesdale in Pennsylvania. The 5 km (3 mile) Granite Railway was built in 1826 to convey granite for the Bunker Hill monument; its proprietor Gridley Bryant used iron strips to provide a running surface on his wooden rails and these 'strap rails' later became common in the USA; iron rails did appear in America in 1831, but not all companies could afford to import these British products. Bryant also devised a primitive form of swivelling truck, or bogie, for his vehicles; his failure to patent this invention involved him in ruinous litigation with the engineer Ross Winans many years later.

In America and most of Europe, steam locomotives were not used on these early railways, the horse being the preferred tractive power. Although steam locomotives had been successfully used in British mining railways since 1812, it was not until 1825 that Colonel John Stevens built and operated a small demonstration locomotive on a circular track at his estate in New Jersey. Then in 1829 the Delaware & Hudson tried the British-built *Stourbridge Lion* over its track, but found that it was much too heavy for the wooden rails. In continental Europe, France was the first to try steam power when in 1828 the engineer Marc Seguin imported Stephenson locomotives from Britain to be operated on the St-Etienne to Andrézieux railway.

It was another Frenchman, Nicholas Cugnot, who had built the first successful steam-propelled vehicle in 1769. This was a three-wheeler designed to run on roads. It certainly moved, but after it overturned in a Paris street the hostile public reaction was such that Cugnot lost heart. The first railway locomotive was built by Richard Trevithick in 1804. Trevithick had made his reputation by improving the pumping engines supplied by James Watt to the mines of Cornwall. He then built two road carriages. Both of these worked after a fashion, but the better of the two caught fire and was destroyed while its designer was refreshing himself in a tavern. The locomotive that Trevithick designed to run on iron track was to the order of a South Wales ironmaster. This man, impressed by Trevithick's work, wagered that it would be possible to build a locomotive capable of hauling a 10-ton load over his local tramway. Faced with this problem, Trevithick designed a machine that was virtually one of his stationary engines linked up with a four-wheel chassis. This duly hauled the required load over the Penydaren Tramway, and Trevithick's ironmaster won his bet. However, so many of the cast-iron plates of the tramway were broken by the locomotive that it could not be used in regular service.

Trevithick did build other steam locomotives. One, built for the Wylam Colliery in Northumberland, was an improved version of his 1804 machine. However, this was also too heavy for the track and was never used for haulage. A third locomotive ran in London on a circular track for a few weeks; this was an early form of publicity stunt, but failed to achieve the object of attracting financial backing for Trevithick's schemes. After this its designer went to South America and built no more steam locomotives. The first locomotives that showed that steam traction could be a commercial success were those of another colliery line, the Middleton Railway near Leeds. This happened in 1812, when the Napoleonic Wars had continued so long that horse fodder was becoming very expensive. Blenkinsop, the agent for this colliery, decided that what was needed was a lightweight locomotive. He commissioned a local engineer, Matthew Murray, to build steam engines similar to those of Trevithick, weighing only five tons. Since it was believed that with such a light weight the wheels would not grip the rails, a rack system of Blenkinsop's design was employed. Rack teeth were cast on the outside of one set of rails; these were engaged by a rack wheel, driven by the cylinders, on one side of the locomotive. Thus the four carrying wheels of the machine simply bore the weight, without providing traction. Murray improved on Trevithick by having two cylinders instead of one; these were vertical, as with Trevithick's third engine, and because there were two of them they drove much more smoothly. A flywheel (which in any case Trevithick had abandoned in this third design) was no longer needed.

The two engines built by Murray for Blenkinsop's line were a great success; they did the job they were intended to do, and did it cheaper than horses. Two more were built, and they lasted thirty years. Each could haul a load of almost 100 tons at 5 km/h (3 mph), which was roughly equivalent to the work of sixteen horses. Many distinguished visitors made the trip to Leeds to witness these engines at work. One visitor was a future tsar of Russia, Nicholas, who would be responsible decades later for the decision to build railways in Russia. However, for Murray and Blenkinsop there were few orders for their locomotives; one British colliery bought a pair, and so did the Berlin Royal Iron Foundry in 1816, but apparently neither customer was very satisfied. Although the rack system achieved its object, its prospects were dim because speeds were limited to less than 8 km/h (5 mph) by the need for the somewhat crude rack teeth to mesh precisely.

The owner of the Wylam Colliery, undeterred by the failure to make use of Trevithick's engine, persisted in his endeavour to improve on horse traction. His manager, William Hedley, in 1813 put on the rails a steam locomotive of his own design in which the rack system was shown to be unnecessary. Hedley was evidently a methodical man, for he conducted full-scale experiments with a man-powered wagon to determine what weight was necessary to ensure that smooth wheels did not slip on smooth rails. To the surprise of many, he confirmed his own view that a lightly loaded wheel could indeed exert a strong tractive effort on a rail. The locomotives he built embodied this conclusion, and worked well. One of them was the famous *Puffing Billy*, now preserved. The two cylinders of this series of locomotives were set vertically at each side of the boiler and drove two pivoting beams which drove, through connecting rods, a shaft situated between the two sets of wheels, driving the latter through gear wheels. Because the noise of the steam as it was exhausted through the cylinders was very disturbing, Hedley diverted it through the tall chimney. As Trevithick had once noted, letting the exhaust steam pass up the chimney improved the draught enormously, so that Hedley's later engines rarely suffered from lack of boiler pressure.

Not far from Wylam was the Killingworth Colliery, whose owners decided that the steam locomotive had a great future in their business. They had employed George Stephenson as enginewright at Killingworth, and he already was reputed to be a youthful genius in all things concerning steam pumping engines. It was Stephenson who was ordered to construct an experimental steam engine for the Killingworth railway. This, Stephenson's first, appeared in 1814 and was named *Blucher*. It was really a copy of Blenkinsop's locomotives, except that there was no rack arrangement. However, in his second engine (*Wellington*), Stephenson eliminated the gear drive, which was a cause of jerky motion, terrifying noise, and low speed. Instead, the drive from the vertical cylinders was through a connecting rod directly to the wheel, with a crankpin close to the wheel centre receiving the thrust and converting it into rotary motion. Thus a further important step had been taken towards the modern steam locomotive. But the coupling of the driving wheels by

rods was yet to come, *Wellington*'s two sets of wheels being coupled by a chain running on sprocket wheels.

Working for a company that owned several collieries, Stephenson had great opportunities as a locomotive builder. He constructed sixteen locomotives for collieries in this period, which allowed him to introduce successive improvements. Meanwhile, he had educated his son Robert to be his assistant, sending him to private school where he might acquire the learning his father so obviously lacked. In 1825 Stephenson and his associates founded the firm of Robert Stephenson & Co, which Robert was to manage and which was the world's first specialized locomotive-building company. Robert also helped his father plan and survey the Stockton & Darlington Railway, which was opened in 1825. The first steam engine of this 40 km (25 mile) line was the *Locomotion*, designed by George Stephenson and built by Robert Stephenson & Co. This machine and its three sisters were little different from the Killingworth Colliery engines, and it soon became evident that something better was needed. In particular, the long runs of the new line meant that steam needed to be raised faster; there were no longer frequent stops during which steam pressure could be built up.

In his *Experiment* of 1827 Stephenson passed boiler water tubes through the flue, so that hot gases from the fire could impart some extra heat to the water. He also arranged that the exhaust steam should give up some of its heat to the cold water destined for the refilling of the boiler. Both these devices worked, although they were troublesome to make and to maintain, like most ideas for improving locomotives. Another feature of *Experiment* was that for the first time the vertical cylinder concept was abandoned. With horizontal cylinders there was considerably less stress on the track and wheels, largely because it was easier to accommodate a form of springing.

Experiment was virtually George Stephenson's last contribution to locomotive design as such. Henceforth his significance would be more as an initiator of railways, and as a proponent of the railway idea. But his associates, including his son, would continue developing the steam locomotive. These men, like him, were mainly of the trial-and-error school. Having little theoretical inclination, they preferred to progress by intuition and experiment rather than by abstract thought. In general, this approach became the hallmark of the British locomotive engineer and helped to ensure, firstly, that British locomotives were reliable and well-tested but, secondly, that after about 1875 most major advances in steam locomotive design would be made by continental Europeans or by Americans.

George Stephenson and his biographers tended to minimize the contributions made by others. Stephenson's old friend Nicholas Wood, who was exceptional in that he drew theoretical generalizations from experiments, wrote a book that was of great assistance to budding railway engineers throughout the world. He made crucial contributions by his work on laminated springs, thereby alleviating the frequent breakages under stress of wheels and rails. Another hero of his time was Timothy Hackworth, who was in charge of the day-to-day running of the Stockton & Darlington locomotives. Apart from designing some very original locomotives of his own, Hackworth reduced the wheel breakages on Stephenson's engine by casting separate outer and inner wheels, linked by wooden plugs, thus gaining a useful resilience. More important, in order to improve the steam-raising qualities of the Stephenson engines, he experimented with the draughting arrangement. In particular, he learned to constrict the aperture of the exhaust-steam pipe (the 'blastpipe') inside the chimney, making the steam move faster. The draught which Hackworth obtained was sufficient to bring the fire to almost white heat, but it also drew flaming pieces of coal up the chimney. Coal, on a colliery railway, was literally dirt-cheap, but this was a serious problem because in dry weather men had to be regularly employed in beating out lineside fires. How to obtain strong draught while ensuring that coal was fully burned before being drawn up the chimney in the form of smoke or ash was a problem that exercised locomotive engineers right up to the end of the steam era; the best solutions would be found by theorists working on mathematical foundations, not by practical trial-and-error designers.

Meanwhile, Marc Seguin and Robert Stephenson, perhaps prompted by the secretary of the Liverpool & Manchester Railway, were independently making another contribution to effective steam raising. Their idea was to pass the hot gases from the fire through the boiler by means of an array of tubes. Hitherto the exhaust gases had passed through the water space of the boiler to the chimney through a large-diameter flue. In their passage they did transfer some of their heat to the water, but the substitution of

numerous smaller tubes raised the total surface area heated by these gases quite significantly. How far Seguin and Stephenson used each others' ideas is unknown; they may well have come up with their similar solutions simultaneously, but they did know each other at the time (in any case, a primitive multi-tubular vertical boiler had been part of the American Stevens' demonstration locomotive of 1825, but his tubes were water tubes).

The new multi-tubular boiler became the standard type, so convincing was this improvement. Its first use was in the famous *Rocket*. This locomotive was Stephenson's entry in the Rainhill Locomotive Trials, staged by the Liverpool & Manchester Railway to help its directors to decide what kind of motive power to buy. The 5-ton *Rocket* was plainly the best locomotive of the three taking part. It conformed to the strict weight regulations, it finished the tests without a falter (unlike the other contestants) and it reached almost 48 km/h (30 mph) in its final appearance. Part of its success was due to good workmanship, much to its novel boiler, and some to its machinery layout. Like another successful locomotive, the *Lancashire Witch*, which Robert Stephenson had supplied to a colliery in 1828, it had steeply inclined cylinders on each side above the rear axle, imparting a thrust that was only partially vertical and thereby making it possible to fit workable springs on each axle. The *Lancashire Witch* had been so successful that a sister engine, the *America*, was bought by Horatio Allen for the Delaware & Hudson line in America.

The first public steam railway was the Stockton & Darlington, surveyed and built by George Stephen-

Marc Seguin's locomotive for the St. Etienne to Lyon Railway. This pioneer French-built locomotive had a multi-tubular boiler, and a draught for the fire was provided by an axle-driven fan mounted on a special vehicle. Construction of the first two locomotives began in 1829, and they hauled the first French steam trains in 1830.

son at the request of mine owners needing a cheap way of taking coal to the wharf. Although at the hilly inland end haulage was by cables powered by stationary steam engines, the remaining 32 km (20 mile) stretch was operated by locomotives (for freight) and horses (for passenger services). The line proved successful both commercially and technically, and inspired the merchants of Manchester to promote their own line to the sea. Outside Britain, the citizens of Baltimore began a railroad towards the interior in 1828, and in the summer of 1830, apart from the Liverpool & Manchester Railway, three other notable public lines were opened. One was the short Canterbury & Whitstable, a partly locomotive and partly cable worked line in Britain; another was the first section of the St-Etienne–Lyons Railway in France, whose engineer Marc Seguin had designed two steam locomotives to supplement the horses; and the third was the first 21 km (13 mile) section of the Baltimore & Ohio Railroad.

The Liverpool & Manchester Railway is regarded as marking the beginning of the railway age because it brought to public attention the potentialities of inter-city steam-hauled rail transport. It was engineered by George Stephenson, who after making an unsatisfactory survey redeemed himself by successfully passing the line over the formidable Chat Moss bog, laying it on massive piles of brushwood and hurdles. The promoters of the line were largely businessmen who wished to break the monopoly of the existing Manchester to Liverpool canal, which they believed was hindering their business. The project naturally met great opposition from the canal and coaching interests and, as would happen with many subsequent railways, this opposition held up for some months the passage of the necessary railway bill through Parliament. Stephenson also had to struggle with those who preferred to run trains by cable haulage, powered by a succession of stationary steam engines, and it was only the Rainhill Locomotive Trial of 1829 that finally settled this question in favour of the steam locomotive. The 50 km (31 mile) line was opened by the Duke of Wellington in September 1830 and quickly proved a success. Contrary to expectation, passenger traffic was more important than goods; the speed and cheapness of the new form of transport was such that not only did all passengers desert the road coaches, but additional passengers, who otherwise would not have travelled at all, flocked to the railway stations. The financial success of the line inspired projects elsewhere, and promoters used the statistics, such as they were, of this railway to produce estimates of revenue for their own projected railways. It became apparent that railways were a 'good investment'.

Expansion The Railway Age arrived in Britain and America before their governments had found a railway policy. Thus in Britain there was no government guidance to encourage promoters to build lines in accordance with a thought-out plan of construction. The early railways were usually promoted by local interests for the benefit of their trade; the Bristolian's support for the Great Western Railway between Bristol and London is an obvious example. After the Liverpool & Manchester Railway had begun to pay good dividends, other railways were promoted as investment opportunities. These, too, naturally tended to be built where there was a good demand for railway service. But when the funds

seeking investment outpaced the promotion of feasible projects the result was a proliferation of schemes which could never pay a good dividend, or even make a profit. Those of this latter group which passed parliamentary scrutiny and survived to become unprofitable parts of the big railway companies certainly benefited their localities but were, in effect, subsidized by more profitable areas. Railway promotion was so rapid in Britain that by 1840 the shape of the future main lines was clearly discernible. The London & Birmingham had been finished, and Birmingham was connected to the Liverpool & Manchester Railway by the Grand Junction Railway; three companies (which in 1846 would amalgamate to form the London & North Western Railway) thereby collectively provided a London to Lancashire main line. Bristol was about to be joined to London by the Great Western Railway and to Exeter by the Bristol & Exeter. The London & Southampton Railway, the nucleus of the future London & South Western, was being finished, and the shape of the future Midland Railway was discernible in the companies that had laid lines connecting Gloucester with Birmingham, Birmingham with Derby and Nottingham and Derby with Leeds and York. Further north the Edinburgh and Glasgow and the Newcastle & Carlisle railways were almost complete. By 1875 England, and Central Scotland and South Wales, were covered with a dense railway network that included many miles of line that would always run at a loss.

Railway construction in the USA was similarly unplanned, and with similar results. That is, railways were built fast where they were needed, but wasteful competition and duplication, together with lack of coordination, were a high price to pay. After the Baltimore & Ohio, the South Carolina Railroad from Charleston was the next common carrier railway, and was the first to use steam traction in daily service. Both these lines had experimented with sails, and with self-propelled vehicles powered by horses working treadmills, but both soon opted for steam. The Baltimore directors had been impressed by the one-ton *Tom Thumb*, which its builder, Peter Cooper, had demonstrated on their tracks in 1830. Their first regular locomotive was the *York* of Phineas Davis, which won a locomotive contest they staged. The South Carolina's first locomotive was the *Best Friend of Charleston*, built in New York. This locomotive soon came to a violent end, after its fireman had discovered the labour-saving advantages of holding down its safety valve.

Expansion was rapid after 1830, although for the first decades it was achieved by a large number of very small and sometimes under-capitalized companies. Thus it was possible to travel from Washington to New York in 1838, but only by changing from one railway to another at frequent intervals. By 1843, apart from the ferry crossing of the Hudson, there was a continuous line from Boston to Buffalo, formed by the end-on linkage of nine companies. The first single-company link between the Atlantic and the Great Lakes only came in 1851 with the broad-gauge New York & Erie Railroad. Chicago's first train, over a 14 km (9 mile) length of what would later be the Chicago & North Western Railroad, ran in 1848, but it was not until 1854 that a railway traveller, with numerous changes of train and company, could move from the eastern cities to Chicago.

In other parts of the USA isolated lines were being built which would later be absorbed in the big companies. The 8 km (5 mile) Pontchartrain Railroad at New Orleans had a British locomotive in service from 1832. The Pennsylvania Railroad had a line from Philadelphia to Pittsburgh completed in 1854. The first railway in Texas was opened from Harrisburg in 1853, and the first in California, the Sacramento Valley Railroad, in 1856. Such early lines were promoted and financed locally by businessmen confident that traffic would be forthcoming. Gradually, however, railways began to be regarded less as an enhancement of existing commercial activity than as a means of developing and settling virgin territory. Such lines could hardly be financed

railway system. But the parliament intervened; it allocated money for a study of railway problems, decided that its own as well as the King's consent was required for the granting of concessions to build railways, and in 1833 launched itself into a series of debates which eventually resulted in the first nation-wide railway plan, embodied in the Railway Law of 1842. This specified that Paris would be the railway centre, with lines radiating to Calais and Lille, Strasbourg and Nancy, Toulouse and the Spanish frontier, Bordeaux and the Spanish frontier, Rouen and Le Havre, and Nantes and Brest. Only two cross-country lines were envisaged, from Marseilles to Bordeaux and from Dijon to Mulhouse. The government was to provide the land and build the infra-

Robert Stephenson's 'Planet' type locomotive of 1830. This design was a step forward from the *Rocket*, having inside cylinders located at a low level. The first such engine was sold to the Liverpool and Manchester Railway, while others were exported.

by local businessmen, so banks began to act as railroad financiers, collecting money from investors with which to buy shares in railways that looked promising. The Federal government also helped. Anxious especially to develop the West, it gave loans to new railways (thereby sparing them the high rates of interest expected by normal investors) and also made grants of land along the projected routes of new railways. These land grants could be used by the railways as collateral for loans while the lines were building, and could be sold cheaply to settlers afterwards. Between 1850 and 1872 the Federal government and nine states gave land grants equivalent to the combined area of Britain, Spain and Belgium.

France, which was well advanced in steam railway technology, might well have followed the British and American example and created an unplanned

structure (track foundations, bridges and tunnels), while private companies would lay the track and operate trains. The government would supervise rates and safety, and would have its own representatives on company boards. Although the plan was long thought-out, its implementation took even longer. Many companies were formed, but most were soon in financial difficulty. The state began to guarantee a minimum rate of interest to faltering companies, and to operate certain lines for which viable companies could not be found, but by mid-century only about 3,200 km (2,000 miles) were open. The only sparkling results came from the Nord Railway, which was making a success of the Calais and Lille lines. The success of the Nord prompted Napoleon III's government to encourage, by amalgamation, the formation of similarly big companies. Six companies, each with a territorial monopoly, emerged from this

process: the Nord, Est, Ouest, Paris–Lyon–Mediterranée, Paris–Orléans, and Midi companies. All except the last-named (which served the south) radiated from Paris. Helped by government guarantees of interest, the new companies completed their main lines and began to build secondary routes, so that by 1870 the network was largely complete.

The boldest of the European railway plans was that of Belgium. Having won her independence from Holland in 1831, she was only too willing to assert her national spirit by investing in a symbol of a bright future. The commercial basis of the plan was the reward which would be reaped if Belgium could capture the international transit traffic. This she did with her first two lines, a north–south line from Antwerp through Brussels to the French frontier and an east–west line from Ostend through Louvain to Germany. These two state-owned lines, completed by 1844, crossed at Malines, where the workshops were built. A few more lines followed, and then the new organization rested on its laurels; private companies built most of the remaining lines, so that by 1870 the state railways owned less than 900 km (560 miles) of the network of 3,000 km (1,850 miles). The most unusual of the companies was the Société Générale d'Exploitation. This owned rolling stock but no track, and hired locomotives to companies unable to afford their own.

In neighbouring Holland there was very little planning. Dutch capitalists were not keen to invest in railways; in the 1830s the King felt obliged to give a personal guarantee of interest on the shares of a proposed railway. The first line was from Amsterdam to Haarlem, over which a Stephenson locomotive,

Arendt, hauled the inaugural train in 1839. Further progress was slow, largely because canal and coastal shipping already provided a good service (this was one reason why freight revenue was proportionately less important than on other railways; the Netherlands Central Railway never possessed a freight locomotive). The first cross-frontier lines, to Aachen and Antwerp, did not at first link up with the Dutch system; the first main line across the frontier was the Rhenish Railway's line from Amsterdam to Emmerich. A Franco-Belgian company, the Netherlands Central Railway, opened its Utrecht to Zwolle main line in 1864, but was a financial failure. Eventually railways were concentrated, with government encouragement, into two enterprises: the private Holland Railway Company and the Netherlands State Railway. The latter operated mainly in the south and bought most of its locomotives from England whereas the former preferred to use German equipment.

The guarantee system was extensively used by the Russian government to attract both foreign and domestic capital to railway building. The first railway, from St Petersburg to Tsarskoye Selo, was opened in 1837. It was 23 km (14 miles) long, privately built, and intended to attract support for railway construction. Tsar Nicholas I, partly for strategic reasons, did decide to start a carefully planned network; lines from St Petersburg to Moscow, St Petersburg to Warsaw, and Warsaw to the Austrian frontier had first priority. The St Petersburg-Moscow line, opened in 1851, was state-built to very high standards. Under the general direction of the American railway engineer Whistler,

An early 2-4-0 type locomotive. This design was built by Robert Stephenson & Co for the Paris and Versailles Railway in 1837. Others were exported to the USA.

Russian army officers had directed the forced labour of thousands of serfs. However, the state could never find the capital for all the railways it planned, and private companies built many of the subsequent lines.

Spain was unique among the European powers in that its first railway was a colonial line, built in Cuba as early as 1837. George Stephenson visited Spain in 1845 to study railway prospects there and wrote a 29-word report for his British clients: 'I have been a month in the country, but have not seen during the whole of that time enough people of the right sort to fill a single train.' So the first railway in Spain, the Barcelona to Mataró line of 28 km (17½ miles) was opened in 1848 thanks to Spanish businessmen. Because of the mountainous interior and the lack of traffic, railway building in Spain was really beyond the resources of private companies, although they built some substantial early lines (Madrid to Alicante in 1858, Madrid to Barcelona in 1860, Madrid to Cadiz and to Lisbon in 1866). In 1866, following the French example, the government in return for financial aid required companies to amalgamate into larger and more viable concerns.

After the 1840s British participation in the financing and building of Europe's railways diminished; opportunities seemed more inviting in the British Empire and America. French banks and French engineers began to replace the British, so that by mid-century and for long afterwards it was French capital, French locomotives and rolling stock, and French structural engineering that were dominant in many countries. Two French houses struggled for supremacy in this new kind of empire-building: the Rothschilds and the Pereires, the latter usually acting through their Crédit Mobilier. It was the Pereires, who, while the French parliament was endlessly debating how to plan the future railways, decided to speed up the process. They had studied the results of the Liverpool & Manchester Railway and were convinced both of the profitability and the usefulness of railways. Anxious to invest in this promising business, they obtained permission to build a railway right under the noses of the parliamentarians, from Paris to the nearby town of St-Germain. This St-Germain line, opened in 1837, was very successful and helped to stimulate railway construction elsewhere so that when the 1842 Railway Law was passed there were already in existence, on routes which would obviously be a part of the final plan, some 600 km (370 miles) of track already laid. In the following years the Pereires controlled or dominated the Midi, Est and Ouest systems, while their rivals the Rothschilds gained the Nord, Paris–Orléans, and PLé. This balance of power pleased neither group, and each sought to extend its empire abroad. Crédit Mobilier involved itself in building Russian railways and struggled against the Rothschilds to control lines in Austria, Spain, Switzerland and Italy. In this period, European railways were a prototype of the multi-national business.

It was the Rothschilds who had gained the concession for the first Austrian steam railway. This was the Vienna to Brno line, which they cunningly named the Kaiser Ferdinands-Nordbahn, thereby associating the royal name with their enterprise. But the Austrian government decided to build further lines from its own resources, which it did until it found it had no resources left. It then turned back to private enterprise, and the Pereires scored a great victory by forming a new company which bought up most of the state lines; this company, which was managed by French officials and directed from Paris, was called, with misleading delicacy, the Austrian State Railway Company. It was an immediate success; French private enterprise did at least drive out the lethargic, bribe-taking, Austrian bureaucracy. Although it was nationalized in 1909 it continued to have a Pereire on its board until Hitler annexed Austria. The Rothschilds counterattacked in the 1850s, gaining control of the Milan–Venice railway in Austria's Italian territory, of the Sudbahn (linking Vienna with Trieste over the Semmering Pass), and of the Franz Josef Railway from Vienna to Budapest and Belgrade. These acquisitions, with the Rothschilds' other railway interests, meant that that family controlled a sizable railway territory embracing Austria, Hungary, Bohemia and parts of Germany.

In Italy, because of the fragmented political structure, only short lines were built at first. The Kingdom of the Two Sicilies gained the credit for the first Italian railway, an 1838 line skirting the Bay of Naples. Tuscany later built some lines radiating from Florence, and the liberalizations achieved by Pope Pius IX included railway-building in the Papal States: Rome's first railway, to Frascati, was opened in 1856. Piedmont was perhaps the most advanced of the Italian states, and its 166 km (103 mile) line from Turin to Genoa was opened by King Victor Emmanuel II in 1854.

In nearby Switzerland, forbidding terrain for early railway builders, there was a surfeit of promising projects, but little willing capital. Before the new constitution of 1848 the powers of the cantons made it almost impossible to obtain agreement on long routes. Even when the 1848 reform gave more power to the central government, railway building was still considered to be mainly canton business. Nevertheless the first train between Zurich and Baden, hauled by the 'long-boiler' locomotive *Limmat*, ran in 1847. By 1855 there were three large companies and several smaller. All were short of funds, the target of takeover bids by competing French banks, and crippled by the demands of the different cantons. Costs were high, revenues were low, shares were down. The larger companies eventually agreed to coordinate their activities in 1861, but in 1897 they were nationalized. About half the investment in Swiss railways by that time was French; for the Swiss, it had been money well spent, because although the railways had not paid high dividends they had produced enormous benefits for the Swiss economy.

Another nation fragmented by political boundaries was Germany, and here railway building followed a different course. At first the state governments showed little enthusiasm for railways; roads were still very poor and it was thought that they should have priority of investment. However, King Ludwig of Bavaria was a railway enthusiast, and sent men to investigate the British and French railways. It was to his persistence that the first German railway was due. This was the line from Nuremberg to Fürth, 8 km (5 miles) long and opened with the Stephenson locomotive *Adler* in 1835. Another proponent was Friedrich List, enthusing about railways after a visit to America. In 1833 he published a pamphlet that foresaw very accurately the future

German main-line system, and created enough support to launch a line from Leipzig to Dresden. This important and prosperous inter-city railway was opened in 1839. The largest of the German states, Prussia, was cool towards railways, but Crown Prince Frederick William used his influence to permit private ventures to go ahead. The first result was the Magdeburg–Leipzig line in 1840, soon followed by two lines from Berlin. By then, the Prussian government was less suspicious and not only offered guarantees of interest but also bought shares, and even began to construct its own state lines. A railway plan was drawn up and by 1860 5,600 km (3,500 miles) had been opened. States which decided to build their own railways rather than rely on private enterprise included Hanover, Württemberg, and Baden. Even Bavaria turned towards state lines for a decade after private companies faltered. Thus, after a later start, Germany was ahead of France by mid-century. This lead was maintained and would have its appropriate result when France and Prussia went to war in 1870.

Outside Europe and America, early short lines began to appear around mid-century, usually in colonial possessions. First of the colonial railways was Spain's 1837 venture in Cuba; the first British line was in Guiana, opened in 1847. The beginnings of India's substantial network came in the mid-1850s, with the opening of the first line of the Great Indian Peninsula Railway's route from Bombay, and of the East Indian Railway's from Calcutta. In Australia, Victoria's line from Melbourne to Port Melbourne opened in 1854, followed by New South Wales' Sydney to Paramatta line in 1855 and South Australia's Adelaide to Port Adelaide line in 1856. New Zealand's first railway, a 0.9 m (3 ft) gauge mining line at Nelson, was opened in 1862. Canada's first railway was opened in 1836 from La Praire (near Montreal) to St. Johns. Although early Canadian locomotives were British, the trend soon turned towards American-style equipment and operation. In South Africa, apart from an earlier short line at Durban, the first railway was from Capetown to Wellington, opened in 1863 and destined to become part of a busy main line. In the Argentine, no colony but strongly influenced by Britain, the first railway, from Parque to Floresta, was opened in 1857. It was built to the 1.68 m (5 ft 6 in) gauge because, it was said, its first locomotive had been intended for India. Other colonial powers were not slow to build railways. The Dutch began to construct the first line of the subsequently well-developed network in Java in 1864. Among French colonial lines, the Algiers to Oran line, opened in 1871, was interesting in that it was owned and operated by the Paris–Lyons–Mediterranée Railway; a somewhat analogous position was won by Britain's London & North Western Railway in 1873, when it opened its Dundalk, Newry and Greenore Railway in Ireland.

Railways at war The brisk course of American railroad development was enlivened by the Civil War, in which railways played an unexpectedly large role. This was not the first use of railways for military purposes. The Liverpool & Manchester Railway had once been used to accelerate the dispatch of troops from Manchester to a troublesome Ireland, and Tsar Nicholas had used his Warsaw–Vienna line to send troops to help the Austrian emperor defeat the revolutionaries in 1849. A really crucial role had been played by railways in the campaign by the French and the Piedmontese against Austria in 1859. The Paris–Lyons–Mediterranée Railway brought French troops to Marseilles for embarkation, and when they landed in Genoa they were moved into action by Piedmont's railways. The rapid switching of Piedmontese and French troops by rail enabled them to outflank the Austrians and defeat them at the Battle of Magenta. In the post-war settlement France received Savoy, on the French side of the Alps, and the Savoy lines of the Piedmont railways were sold to the PLM. However, Piedmont gained control of most of the Milan–Venice line, because the frontier with the Austrian Empire was pushed back to Verona. This line had merged with the Austrian Sudbahn in 1859, and after hostilities the commercially amalgamated but politically split concern was controlled by an Italian management west of Verona and by the Austrian management elsewhere; these two managements reported to a suitably neutral board in Paris.

In the American Civil War the North relied heavily on its more mature railway network, and soon found that it had to give railway officials freedom from military interference in the war zones, for officers had little understanding of transport organization. Its creation of the US Military Railroads to administer the northern lines, staffed by professional railwaymen holding military rank, largely achieved this. The South was handicapped because most of the locomotive works and rail factories were in the North, so it tried to capture Northern equipment. In the raid on Harper's Ferry it not only destroyed 42 Baltimore & Ohio locomotives, but carried away an additional 14, as well as 58 km (36 miles) of rail. The US Military Railroads succeeded in passing supplies to Sherman's 100,000-man army over a single-track railroad which passed through 580 km (360 miles) of nominally enemy territory. But this achievement was always overshadowed in the popular mind by the 'Great Locomotive Chase' in which the Confederate locomotive *General* was captured by Northern raiders, and then recaptured after a 100-mile chase.

After the Civil War the greatest American railway project could go ahead. Previously, although the idea of a transcontinental railroad had fired many imaginations, a stumbling block had been the insistence of the Southern states that the terminus should be in a city such as New Orleans or Memphis. The Pacific Railway Acts of 1862 and 1864 authorized the Union Pacific Railroad to build westwards from Omaha, and the Central Pacific (later the Southern Pacific) to build eastwards from Sacramento. The latter line faced the worst physical obstacle, the Sierra Nevada Range, which was eventually crossed with the help of specially imported Chinese manual labour. The Union Pacific had no mountain ranges to cross, but was hindered by Indian attacks. In 1869 the two lines met in Utah. This, the first of the world's great transcontinentals, had been largely financed with loans and land grants by the Federal government. In terms of American development as a nation and as an economic system, it was money well spent.

Locomotive development Locomotive development was fast in the decade following the 1829 Rainhill Trials of the Liverpool & Manchester Railway. By 1840 the basic structure of the classic, or 'Stephensonian', steam locomotive had been evolved and further improvements would be more of detail than of fundamentals. The success of Stephenson's *Rocket* at the Trials led the Liverpool & Manchester directors to order similar machines from Robert Stephenson, and the latter took advantage of this successively to enlarge and improve his locomotives. Cylinders were lowered, and took up an almost horizontal position. Proper smokeboxes were provided at the chimney end, making tube-cleaning much easier. The previously separate

provision of a separate frame. Hitherto, the foundation of an engine had been the boiler itself, with the wheels, cylinders and other components fixed to it in one way or another. With increasing size and power, the boiler could no longer carry these stresses, and *Planet* had a stout wooden frame on either side, reinforced by strong iron plates. This type of engine was built for about five years, some being exported to continental Europe and some to America; the best-known of the latter was *John Bull*, sold to the US Mohawk & Hudson line in 1831.

Like the Rockets the Planets tended to grow with each successive unit. With 10 tons carried on just four wheels the axle load was too high; the wrought-iron rails of the Liverpool & Manchester and of

The American locomotive abroad. *Above:* The Norris 4-2-0, the locomotive type which founded the fortunes of that American locomotive builder. The firebox and bar frames are derived from Edward Bury's locomotives exported earlier from Britain to the USA. This unit was built by Norris in 1840 for the British Birmingham and Gloucester Railway. Similar engines were popular in Germany and Austria. *Below:* A 4-4-0 locomotive designed by the American Joseph Harrison for the St. Petersburg to Moscow Railway. This particular unit was built in 1858 to haul the Tsar's train, and an extra axle was added to improve its stability and reduce the axle-load.

firebox was moved to a position in the rear section of the boiler barrel. Weight in working order rose to about 8 tons, and cylinder dimensions rose from the 203 mm × 432 mm (8 in × 17 in) of the *Rocket* to 278 mm × 406 mm (11 in × 16 in). When the Liverpool & Manchester opened, traffic was handled almost exclusively by *Rocket*-type engines. Meanwhile, other firms began to build locomotives and this competition spurred Robert Stephenson to introduce a radically improved design in late 1830. This was the *Planet*, in which the cylinders were brought down to what was to be their conventional position beneath the chimney on the same level as the driving wheels. In this engine the cylinders were placed between rather than outside the wheels; makers of steam road carriages had adopted this arrangement and Stephenson thought it was very neat. Another trend-setting innovation was the

other customers were frequently broken. So, like succeeding generations of locomotive designers, Stephenson was obliged to spread the increasing weight of his locomotives over a greater number of wheels. This was the origin of his *Patentee*. The *Patentee* was a six-wheeler, and carried a larger boiler as well as a new invention, the steam brake. It rode better and was kinder to the track than its predecessors. The first unit was a 2-2-2, but some were 2-4-0s and 0-4-2s, and as early as 1834 an 0-6-0 version appeared which weighed no less than 17 tons.

By no means all the improvements of the 1830s originated in the mind of Stephenson; indeed, some of the ideas credited to him were in fact first suggested by his colleagues or workers. Among outsiders, the locomotives built by Edward Bury were significant because they had a different kind of framing. Instead of the plate frames adopted by Stephenson, Bury devised a structure of bars which served as the foundation of his locomotives. This arrangement was lighter, though perhaps less sturdy, than plate frames. After some of Bury's locomotives had been exported to the USA the bar frame was permanently adopted in that country and moreover, when subsequent US-built engines were exported to Germany and Austria, the bar frame gained a certain popularity in central Europe. Meanwhile George Forrester built some engines for an Irish railway in which the cylinder arrangement of the *Planets* was modified; the cylinders were placed outside the wheels rather than inside. This, again, marked a division between two schools of thought that would last until the end of steam; inside cylinders provided a steadier motion and on railways with severe width restrictions were easier to accommodate; but outside cylinders, were more accessible, and it was easier for the engineers to carry out routine maintenance and repairs on them.

Britain was Johann Schubert, who in 1839 would produce his locomotive *Saxonia* for the Dresden–Leipzig Railway. Schubert was also of very humble origin but, anticipating the academic trend in German locomotive design, he had become a professor in the local technical school before venturing into steam-locomotive construction. Elsewhere in Europe former employees of British locomotive builders were hired by new locomotive works. Among these men was the Scotsman Haswell, who for 45 years would design and build locomotives for the Austrian railways, and would introduce the heavy 0-8-0 freight locomotive to Europe. Another was Joseph Hall, who left the employ of Robert Stephenson in 1839. He then travelled abroad to Germany and in 1841 designed and built the first locomotive of the celebrated firm of Maffei in Munich.

The first locomotive-building concern in continental Europe appeared as early as 1831 at Mulhouse in Alsace; founded by Meyer, it later became the

Meanwhile the technical lead enjoyed by Britain was being eroded by the rise of locomotive builders in other countries. Sometimes, as happened typically in America, British-built locomotives would be the basis on which local mechanics designed their own engines. In other cases overseas mechanics would be sent to Britain by their governments or their employers in order to acquire the new knowledge. Among such mechanics was the Russian serf Cherepanov, who in 1833 would build a Russian steam locomotive at his Urals metal works. Cherepanov spoke no English, and his first locomotive was a remarkable effort, being built on the basis of observation and memory. Another visitor to

celebrated Koechlin Works. In the USA, Matthias Baldwin began to build locomotives at Philadelphia in 1831, at first using British models but later developing his own ideas; his firm, the Baldwin Locomotive Works, eventually became the world's largest. Another influential American was Isaac Dripps, the master mechanic of the Camden & Amboy Railroad, who in 1831 played the leading part in puzzling out the assembly of Stephenson's *John Bull*, which had arrived in a dismantled state. Later he fitted a two-wheel leading truck or bogie to this engine to help guide it round the tortuous curves of his railway and to push away errant cattle (the cowcatcher part had to be altered after an obstinate

European passenger cars of the late 1830s: *Left:* Belgian first-class carriage with two 9-seat compartments and central passage. *Right:* A composite carriage of the Paris to Versailles (Rive Gauche) Railway with a central first-class compartment, a second-class compartment at each end, and seats for third-class passengers on the roof.

bull had been speared by its projecting rods). Dripps also experimented with a spark-catching chimney and in 1836 built a locomotive, appropriately named *Monster*, that had eight driving wheels divided into two groups connected by gearing. One of the best-known of the early American locomotive engineers was Horatio Allen. Allen was sent to England by the Delaware & Hudson Company to acquire locomotives. The *Stourbridge Lion* was one of his purchases, and he drove this on its test trip in 1829, the first run of a steam locomotive on a commercial American railroad. He later helped in the design of the *Best Friend of Charleston*, for his South Carolina Railroad. In 1832 he built three articulated machines for the same railroad. These 2-2 + 2-2 engines with two pairs of narrow boilers back to back, with each pair supplying one cylinder, were by most definitions the world's first articulated locomotives.

Meanwhile in 1841 Robert Stephenson brought out the last of his locomotive layouts. This was the 'long-boiler' type, which was destined to have a

locomotive balancing. It was now realized that unsteadiness was not simply a question of locomotive wheel arrangement and of track standards, but was related to the backwards-and-forwards motion of the heavy iron weights represented by such parts of the mechanism as pistons and connecting rods, as well as the rotary motion of heavy coupling rods. Thus the first attempts were made to induce these dynamic forces to cancel each other out, special balancing weights being added to assist this. Balancing was very complex, ideally needing a scientific rather than a hit-or-miss approach. Two men who helped evolve a workable theory of balancing, and thereby made possible the design of larger and faster locomotives, were the Frenchman le Chatelier and the German Nollau. The latter, who was engineer of the Holstein Railway, went as far as suspending a locomotive from the roof on chains in order to study the forces set up when its mechanism was in operation. Le Chatelier carried out balancing experiments in the late 1840s which showed that

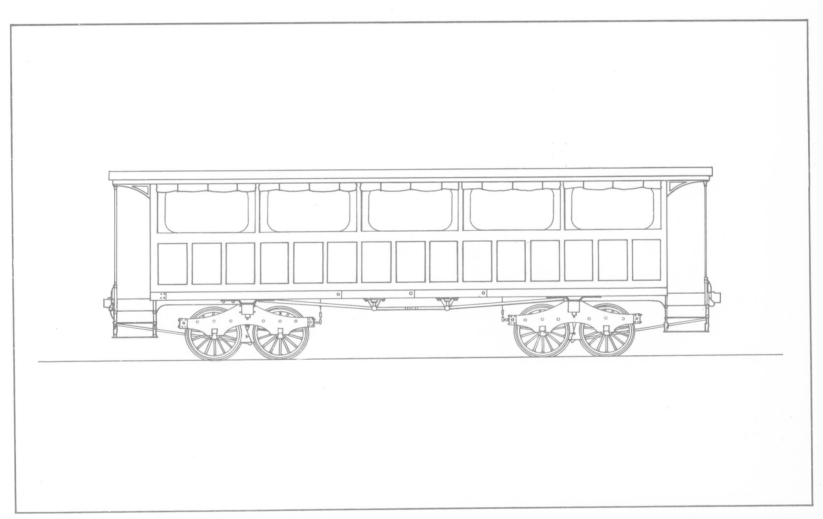

A passenger car design of the early 1840s, as used on the Strasbourg to Basle and Vienna to Brno railways. This is a forerunner of the modern vehicle mounted on two four-wheel trucks, although in this case there was no sideplay. With its central aisle and cross seats the layout is similar to that of the later American 'day coach'.

long life in continental Europe. Really it should have been known as the short-wheelbase type, for what Stephenson did was to mount a longer boiler on the same length of wheelbase. This boiler, having firetubes of greater length, extracted more heat from the exhaust gases before they entered the chimney. However, the type was not really stable at high speeds, which is why it lost popularity in Britain. But in most parts of Western Europe it was very successful, being copied by local engine builders; in its 0-6-0 variant it could be seen in Spain as late as the 1960s.

The instability of the long-boiler engines was one reason why more attention began to be paid to

correct adjustment of the moving parts to achieve better balance not only improved a locomotive's steadiness and durability, but also enhanced speed and fuel economy.

A long-needed achievement of the 1840s was the invention of a locomotive valve gear that could not only put a locomotive into reverse with a minimum of trouble, but could also control the amount of steam admitted to the cylinder in accordance with the ever-changing power demands made on the locomotive in successive stages of its run. By cutting off the steam well before the piston had come to the end of its travel, the expansive energy of that steam could be utilized; exhausting the steam from the

cylinder at close to its original pressure only represented a waste of power, and such 'full cut-off' working could be justified only when maximum power output was required at low speeds. The first successful valve gear that could vary the length of cut-off when the locomotive was in motion was the Stephenson Link Motion, invented by two of Stephenson's mechanics. This invention transformed locomotive driving and was in use on most of the world's railways up to the end of steam traction. However, in the twentieth century it was partially replaced by a somewhat better design, evolved by the Belgian locomotive mechanic Walschaert in the 1840s. An identical solution to the same problem was simultaneously invented by the German Heusinger, with the result that this valve gear is known as the Heusinger gear in central Europe and as the Walschaert gear elsewhere.

Belgians, having an early acquaintance with engineering industry, did much to develop steam-locomotive design, even though it was a Briton, John Cockerill, who founded Belgium's first and biggest locomotive and engineering company. Albert Belpaire, who was the chief mechanical engineer of the Belgian State Railway from 1850, devised the Belpaire firebox, whose distinctive square shape could be seen on most of the world's railways; this firebox presented fewer of the staying and maintenance problems that plagued the cheaper round-top type.

During the 1850s a successful effort was made in several countries to devise fireboxes suitable for burning coal. Hitherto, coke had been the preferred fuel ever since the Liverpool & Manchester directors had specified that a locomotive must 'consume its own smoke'. Coal, if it was not to clog and waste much of its potential energy in the form of thick smoke, required much more air. In America, Baldwin had the idea of fitting locomotives with detachable grates; a train could then stop at intervals to have its clogged coal fire replaced by a brightly burning new one. This appears to have been one of the several Baldwin strokes of invention that were never put into practice, but elsewhere in America there were experiments with extra-wide fireboxes designed to burn the rather small Pennsylvania anthracite. These experiments, which were largely successful, culminated in the wide Wootten firebox of 1877. But the lasting solution was the fitting of a brick arch over the fire at the forward end of the firebox. This forced the exhaust gases, still containing combustible matter, to pass back above the fire on their way to the tubes, and in this passage the smoke was largely burned out. A deflector plate above the firehole forced air downwards on to the fire to speed up this combustion process. A key part in evolving this method was played by Matthew Kirtley of the Midland Railway in Britain.

Two British designs that had a great influence in continental Europe were those of Thomas Crampton and Alexander Allan. The latter, when responsible for the locomotive stock of the Grand Junction Railway, adopted Forrester's layout of outside cylinders, placing them high up by the smokebox and inclined downwards. These engines had sturdy double frames, between which the cylinders were fixed firmly. Allan's aim was to eliminate the frequent crank axle failures then experienced with inside-

cylinder machines; with outside cylinders the connecting rods were merely attached to the outside of the wheels and there was no need for the difficult arrangement with a cranked axle. This layout later became known as the 'Crewe type' in Britain, where it was employed by several railways. Allan's colleague Buddicom took the idea to France, building many of these units for the Paris–Rouen and other lines; these so-called Buddicom engines, which were also built by local locomotive works, became well-known in France and Germany.

Crampton's engines acquired a similarly high reputation. They had the driving wheel axle behind the firebox, enabling the boiler to be kept low even with wheels as large as 2 m (7 ft) in diameter. In fact, the need for a low centre of gravity was much exaggerated at that time, and this arrangement was not really necessary. However, Crampton designed his engines with very generous steam passages, his boilers could be big, and his long wheelbase contributed to easy riding. With these qualities it was not long before the Crampton locomotives used by certain German state railways and in France acquired a justified reputation for high speed and easy running.

In Britain, locomotives grew steadily larger, but after about 1850 the burst of inventiveness that had characterized earlier decades died away. However, in 1863 Adams invented his radial axlebox, which was a primitive but successful attempt to provide side-play for a carrying axle. Perhaps the last of the really resourceful British locomotive engineers was John Ramsbottom, who was locomotive superintendent of the London & North Western Railway

from 1857 to 1871. Among his inventions were the water pick-up apparatus, allowing moving locomotives to take up water from long troughs placed between the rails; a good lubricator (the sight-feed 'displacement' type); the split-ring piston ring, which did much to minimize steam leakage around the edge of the piston; a locomotive speedometer; and a screw reverse system. For high-speed running the British tended to favour the 'single', a locomotive with one pair of large driving wheels. When trains became heavier this type suffered a temporary eclipse from which it was rescued when the invention in 1885 of the steam sanding gear alleviated the problem of wheel slip. Later, the inside cylinder 4-4-0 came into favour, and many of this type were exported.

British engineers still went to work abroad, but their influence became gradually less important as other locomotive-building countries produced their own designers. Nor was this movement entirely one-way. From Dresden came Karl Beyer (later Charles Beyer) to join the British locomotive builder Sharp, Roberts as a draughtsman. The sturdiness of his locomotives, and their bold outline with large rounded domes, set a standard for British-built locomotives, and his influence continued after he founded his own company, Beyer, Peacock, in 1853. Other Germans, who stayed at home, were laying the foundation of the German railway industry. Max von Weber, son of the musician, developed a locomotive speedometer in the hope of reducing accidents to enginemen. His concern for his men was also expressed by providing them with generous protection from the wind. Joseph Trick, an engineer at the Esslingen Works, built the first locomotive specifically for hill-climbing in 1849. He also invented the Trick Port, a supplementary channel for steam entering the cylinder, which in some conditions made efficient valve design easier. In Berlin August Borsig built his first locomotive in 1841, and by the time of his death in 1854 had built 500 more. At first he used British and US models; his first locomotive was based on Norris's type, and his most successful series was a 2-4-0 of British inspiration. However, in later years the Borsig Works followed its own course and became one of the world's greatest builders of locomotives. But possibly the most significant German contribution to locomotive technology came from the Krupp Works, where steel locomotive tyres were manufactured from 1851. The use of steel for this purpose enabled greater axle loads to be used without running the risk of wheel breakages.

Two valuable improvements originated in France. The first practical boiler steam pressure gauge, using a pointer actuated by pressure on a resilient flattened piece of brass tubing, was the work of the Comte de Pambour and was almost universally adopted in the 1850s. Another Frenchman, Henri Giffard, who was trying to build a workable steam-driven airship at the same period, invented an ingenious means of passing feedwater into the boiler. Hitherto a pump had been used, which meant, among other things, that locomotives awaiting duty at depots had periodically to run up and down the line in order to operate the pump, which was worked by the motion of the crosshead. Giffard's injector, which soon became a standard piece of equipment, had no

moving parts, being worked by the impetus of a jet of steam passed through a coned nozzle against a column of feedwater. Elsewhere in France, early locomotive superintendents were steadily founding their own schools of locomotive design. Forquenot, the chief mechanical engineer of the Paris–Orleans Railway from 1860 to 1885, imposed a strict standardization both of locomotive types and of components. He also built about 400 fast passenger engines of the 2-4-2 wheel arrangement. These had outside cylinders to facilitate maintenance and were exceptionally efficient; some survived into the 1950s. Forquenot's predecessor on the Paris–Orléans, Polonceau, is notable as being the first Frenchman to introduce a range of truly French locomotives, with little dependence on the British tradition.

The development of locomotive design in Austria was significant for the future, because the Austrian Empire embraced so much of central Europe. The locomotive trials held in 1851 to determine the motive power for the winding and hilly line over the Semmering Pass did not, at first sight, have much influence because none of the competing locomotives won official approval. However, although the entry of Haswell was placed last it did much to mould central European locomotive policy. In the railway workshops which he managed for the Vienna–Raab Railway, Haswell had built engines that were of the American Norris type, bar-framed machines which had themselves been derived from the British Bury engines. For the Semmering trials Haswell entered his *Vindobona*, the first 0-8-0 in Europe. His development of a sideplay arrangement for his eight-wheeled machines helped to popularize

British railways abroad: the Bombay to Poona mail train of the Great Indian Peninsula Railway in about 1865. The features of British home railways are reproduced, but with modification (the insulated roofs of the passenger car and the extended roof of the locomotive). The leading and last vehicles have brake drums for a continuous chain brake system.

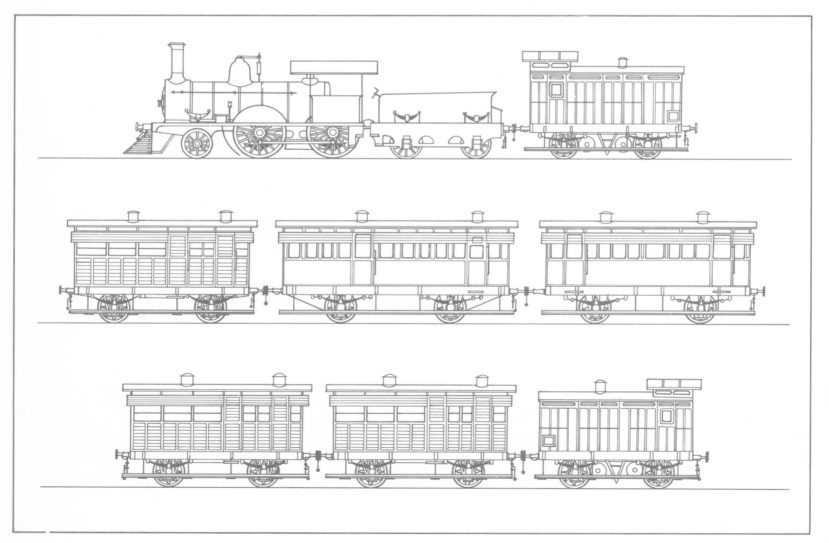

this type in Europe long before it was adopted for heavy freight work in Britain.

Other entrants for the Semmering contest had devised various methods of articulation, breaking up the coupled wheelbase of their locomotives into two units capable of moving independently of each other in order to accommodate themselves to the sharp curves. At the time, these solutions did not appear very promising, but they had their echo in the various types of articulated machine developed towards the end of the century. It was in 1863, however, that the first articulated locomotive to win widespread popularity appeared. Closely reminiscent of one of the Semmering competitors, Robert Fairlie's locomotive had two engine units, which were pivoted and could therefore negotiate very curved track. The Fairlie double-ended locomotive had two boilers, mounted back to back, each carried by one of these power bogies. The cab was in the middle and there was a chimney and smokebox at each end. Although, like all articulated engines, the Fairlie locomotive was prone to steam leakage at the flexible joints of its steam pipes, it was ordered by several of the world's railways, especially those that had a requirement for high power outputs over winding track.

In America, locomotives tended to break away from the European tradition, because conditions were very different. The early adoption of massive oil headlights, like the cowcatcher, was prompted by frequent encounters with animals on the long stretches of unfenced line. During the 1840s the locomotive cab became a standard fitting on some lines; on others the locomotive men built their own

from canvas. (In Britain, where the climate was less extreme, enginemen resented the comfortable cabs which an occasional locomotive superintendent would design, considering such pampering a reflection on their masculine toughness.) Above all, the uneven and sharply curved American track led to the early popularity of the bogie, and it was not long before the 4-4-0 with outside cylinders became the favourite engine for freight as well as passenger and mixed trains. This 4-4-0 became known as the 'American' type and was produced by all the main builders, who competed with one another in the finish and ornamentation of their products. The man most responsible for the success of this wheel arrangement was Joseph Harrison of Philadelphia, who invented the 'equalizing beam' which enabled the coupled wheels to be suspended independently so that each could rise or fall to accommodate bumps in the track. It was Harrison who designed for the Philadelphia & Reading Railroad the 11-ton 4-4-0 *Gowan & Marx* (so named in honour of the London banking company that had heavily invested in the Railway). In 1840 this locomotive succeeded in hauling a 400-ton train over the Railway's fairly level main line. Harrison's reputation was such that he was invited to build the locomotives of the new St Petersburg to Moscow Railway in Russia; he and his partner thereupon closed down their Philadelphia works, transferring much of its equipment and workforce to Russia.

Another powerful locomotive was Norris's *George Washington* of 1836, for which great hill-climbing claims were made. So great was the reputation of this 10-ton 4-2-0 that the Birmingham & Gloucester

Railway in England bought similar engines from Norris. Norris also exported locomotives to central Europe, but this market did not last long, as the Austrian railway workshops soon improved on them. The Norris firm was responsible for the world's first 4-6-0, the 22-ton *Chesapeake*, built in 1847. Because several American railroads faced stiff conditions of grade or load, US builders tended to lead the world in the introduction of new, larger, wheel arrangements. In 1857 James Milholland built an 0-12-0 pusher for the Philadelphia & Reading and in 1883 Stevens of the Central Pacific was to build an impressive but ineffective 4-10-0 for mountain work. An individualist among locomotive designers was Ross Winans, who from 1835 built engines for the Baltimore & Ohio Railroad. Among his innovations was the 'Camel' type 0-8-0, whose two centre pairs of wheels were unflanged, and on which the driver rode in a cab erected on top of the boiler. The tank engine, hitherto not highly popular in America, was boosted by Forney's patent in 1872. An epidemic having killed many of the horses used by city street railways, Forney designed a small tank locomotive in which rear carrying wheels bore the weight of the fuel and the water tank. This type became quite widespread, not for street railways, but for railway suburban services. However, outside America the Forney design was not favoured, and tank engines continued to carry their water in side tanks, or in saddle tanks draped over the boiler.

Rolling stock As with locomotives, the period from 1830 to 1875 witnessed the evolution of almost modern-looking rolling stock from the rather primitive vehicles of the first railways. On the Liverpool & Manchester and other early lines freight traffic, including live animals, was simply carried on flat cars. It was covered with a tarpaulin in rainy weather, but this was inconvenient and never sure. The roofed freight car, nevertheless, was slow to appear in Britain; it was introduced more rapidly in continental Europe and in America. Another peril for freight was breakages caused by shocks in transit; this was alleviated by the application of spring buffers. The latter had been developed earlier in response to the complaints of shaken passengers. Loose coupling of passenger vehicles had also caused bruises, and the screw coupling was invented by an official of the Liverpool & Manchester Railway to remedy this. The essence of this coupling was a central rod, with a left- and right-hand screw thread at either end. By rotating this rod the links of the coupling could be drawn tight after they had been placed on their drawhooks. The British did not use this coupling on ordinary freight vehicles, but the Europeans did, thereby doing much to reduce damage in transit. Another advance, an early example of American practice being adopted in Europe, was oil in place of grease lubrication; this was applied in an axlebox so designed that oil was kept in contact with the bottom surface of the axle by an absorbent pad.

The first railways in Britain and Europe carried their first-class passengers in what were virtually traditional coach bodies mounted on railway wheels. It became the practice to mount three of these bodies on one 4-wheel underframe, thereby creating a three-compartment railway coach. It was from such vehicles that subsequent compartment coaches evolved. The open trucks used to convey early third-class passengers had no descendants, for this comfortless kind of vehicle was soon abandoned. However, the hard wooden seats of the second class were the direct ancestors of the wooden seats still used today in second- and third-class coaches in many parts of the world. The four-wheel passenger vehicle was used in Europe until the twentieth century, although the six-wheeler, which was much more steady-running, grew in popularity after 1850; on Britain's Great Western Railway it had been introduced as early as 1842. The double-deck coach appeared on several early European lines, including the Paris–Versailles (r.g.) Railway, where third-class passengers were given uncovered seats on the roof while second- and first-class travellers sat in compartments below. With refinements (such as protection from the weather) this kind of double-deck stock was perpetuated by several French and Spanish railways for many decades.

Long coaches mounted on four-wheel trucks at each end appeared as early as the 1840s on the Austrian Vienna–Brno and the French Strasbourg–Basle lines, but the trucks did not pivot, and were not true bogies. These coaches had a central aisle and open rather than compartment seating. The open plan had already appeared elsewhere in continental Europe, notably in Belgium, and would coexist with compartment stock.

In America, where distances were long, passenger stock soon overtook European standards of comfort. The first bogie vehicles ran on the Baltimore & Ohio Railroad in 1835, and henceforth not only passenger, but also freight cars, were mounted on bogies. It was the American Pullman Company that was responsible for the first bogie coaches in Britain, those of the Midland Railway in 1873. In America the compartmented coach had a very short life. A central aisle, giving access to a toilet and washroom, and to end platforms where passengers would enter and leave, was so obviously useful that it became the standard. As for sleeping cars, which in a rudimentary form had been offered to passengers between London and Manchester as early as 1838, these too developed fastest in America, especially after George Pullman put his *Pioneer* sleeping coach into service on the Chicago & Alton Railroad in 1864. This vehicle, so large that its purchaser had to increase clearances along its route, set new standards in comfort. However, the upper and lower berth arrangement was not Pullman's invention. For a time there was bitter and litigious competition between the Pullman Palace Car Company and the Wagner Palace Car Company. The latter was backed by the New York Central Railroad, but was eventually bought out by Pullman in 1899, enabling the latter to own and operate almost all the American sleeping cars. In 1867 Pullman built his first dining car, a combined sleeper and kitchen car, with removable tables. This ran on the Great Western Railway of Canada. He soon placed in service the first full-length dining car, and this idea also spread rapidly. For those who could afford it, a railway journey became an interlude of luxury. For the less well-off, there was still the hard-back seat in an ordinary coach.

Europe

Great Britain

I n this chapter on the country which saw the birth and early exploitation of the steam railway engine, we have as on a turntable come full circle. We examine, going clockwise from due North, the route to the North East: the South of England: the sphere of influence of the Great Western Railway; the westerly and central routes to the North West, over Shap and the Settle-Carlisle run respectively; and, finally, we look at the Scottish systems. So much for steam: but, as will be seen, the diesels and electrics, powerful as they are, have not been allowed to have it all their own way, for the public interest in preserving steam has grown constantly since steam, sadly, disappeared from the schedules of British Rail.

Below. Two very famous Gresley 'Pacifics' alongside at York, September 1975: on the left the streamlined No. 4498 *Sir Nigel Gresley* and on the right the well-travelled No. 4472 *Flying Scotsman.*

North-East England On the fringe of the centre of London there stands an imposing though not, it must be admitted, the most colourful part of the world of trains – King's Cross Station. But out of those grimy precincts went some of the most famous trains in history; and they drove north through a countryside that was an epitome of rural, farming England, past the great cathedrals of Peterborough, York and Durham, threading through the industrial North-East, which was the very cradle of the steam locomotive, till they came out on the lonely and fascinating coastline of Northumberland. They climbed no dramatic mountain ranges in the process and crossed no greater river than the Tyne, by the King Edward Bridge at Newcastle. But whatever the country traversed by such trains as the 'Queen of Scots', the 'Aberdonian', and above all the 'Flying Scotsman' may have lacked in spectacular scenery, their glamour was fully provided by the locomotives that hauled them throughout the age of steam.

From 1870 to the very end of steam traction some 95 years later there was never a more colourful range of locomotives than those hauling the Anglo-Scottish expresses out of King's Cross, and those that took them on from York in the days when the Great Northern and North Eastern were separate companies, though close allies in business.

It is fortunate beyond measure that so many examples of this great and picturesque mechanical engineering evolution have been preserved. Many of them can be seen in the National Railway Museum at York, while others are still in full working order and used for hauling special trains. The locomotives of the 1870s were as much *objets d'art* as pieces of hard-working machinery. Patrick Stirling of the Great Northern, who designed the elegant eight-foot single No. 1, refused to try a newer form of valve gear because it would spoil the look of his Eastern, who was an apprentice in Stephenson's works at Newcastle when the ever-famous *Rocket* was built in 1829, designed the supremely decorated 2-4-0 No. 910 of 1872, which was in steam again at the 150th Anniversary parade in August 1975.

The chronology of Great Northern development is complete in preserved loco-

Above. A southbound Anglo-Scottish express is seen here climbing the Cockburnspath bank hauled by one of the powerful 'Deltic' type 3300 hp diesel electric locomotives, the *King's Own Scottish Borderer.*
Below. The LNER 'A4' Pacific named after the designer *Sir Nigel Gresley* here carrying the former *Flying Scotsman* headboard in September 1975.
Below right. The preserved Great Western 4-6-0 No. 4079 *Pendennis Castle,* passing in March 1974 through Gloucester with empty coaching stock en route to Hereford.

motives from 1898 onwards. The legendary large-boilered 'Atlantic' by H. A. Ivatt, No. 251, introduced in 1902, seems now to be finally retired to the quietude of the museum at York. She created something of a sensation, some 70 years ago, and still more so in traffic after she and her kind had been modernized by Sir Nigel Gresley; but that great engineer will always be best remembered for his 'Pacifics', and with three of them still in full working order, and the immortal, record-holding *Mallard* at York, their memory and their distinctive colours will remain for posterity. How *Mallard* attained 203 kph (126 mph), and with it made the world record for steam traction that has not been surpassed, was an epic in itself. Before being retired she was much in demand for special trains and travelled far and wide in Great Britain, though her record in this respect was eclipsed by one of Gresley's earliest 'Pacifics', the *Flying Scotsman*, which made a long tour in Canada and the USA.

Flying Scotsman now carries the beautiful 'apple-green' livery that was standard for express passenger engines on the London and North Eastern Railway; but *Mallard* and the other two streamliners are in garter blue, adopted for this class, when the 'Coronation' high-speed express was put on between King's Cross and Edinburgh in 1937. It was a happy inspiration on the part of the LNER Board to name the hundredth 'Pacific' of Gresley after the designer; and the *Sir Nigel Gresley*, No. 4498, is still an active performer, and has been seen in many areas lately where the garter blue would have been unfamiliar in Sir Nigel's lifetime. The last of this family of locomotives is *Bittern*, one of that series, like *Mallard*, named after the fastest birds of the air. *Bittern* originally worked from Newcastle and was a familiar sight anywhere between London and Edinburgh.

Southern England A holiday on the Kentish coast before World War I would have been enlivened by the sight of colourful trains; for on the boat trains that came sweeping down past the chalk cliffs of the Folkestone Warren and on to the old Admiralty Pier at Dover, were the Wainwright 4-4-0s of the South Eastern and Chatham Railway. However far and wide one has travelled on the railways of the world, it would be impossible to have a more beautifully proportioned, nor more tastefully decorated locomotive than the 'D' class; and to the delight of all Southern enthusiasts one of these has been preserved and restored to all its original glory in the National Railway Museum.

Among many ardent railway enthusiasts William Stroudley was a patriarchal figure. It was he who introduced the famous 'Improved engine green', which was actually a beautiful mid-chrome yellow! It was not only on the Brighton and Portsmouth expresses that Stroudley's engines showed their colours. Local tank engines working through the South London suburbs, or over that unspeakable line through the Thames Tunnel, also sported the famous yellow; and woe betide the driver of those days who had a speck of dirt on his engine! They were all named mostly after stations on the line, though this could be unfortunate for the passenger who mistook the name of the engine for the destination of the train. Perhaps the most famous of all Brighton engines is *Gladstone* which deservedly has a place in the National Railway Museum.

The third constituent of the Southern was the London and South Western which ran through the somnolent Wessex countryside. One of its chief mechanical engineers was that great, though irascible Scotsman, Dugald Drummond who was famous for his bad language to his staff and visitors alike. The beautiful locomotives that remain are mostly of his predecessor's design, that of William Adams, as much a character as Drummond although in a different way, who at one time had been engineer to the Sardinian Navy, before the days of the united Italy. One of Adams' London suburban tank engines works on the Bluebell Line in Sussex, while a magnificent specimen of his 4-4-0 express type is at York.

West of England When that remarkable engineer, I. K. Brunel, built the South Devon Railway beneath the red cliffs of Dawlish and Teignmouth, he certainly provided for all time a backdrop of vivid, majestic colouring that would ennoble the passage of any train, however utilitarian its individual engine and carriages might be on their own. But the Great Western engines of 70 years ago were far from utilitarian in their colouring, as can be seen from the splendid restoration of the *City of Truro* in 1957. This engine made a famous run in May 1904 with an Ocean Mail special from Plymouth, when she became the first engine in the world to reach 160 kph (100 mph).

Her creator, George Jackson Churchward, one of the truly great engine designers of history, was no sentimentalist. Not only did he water down the one-time gay livery of Great Western locomotives, but he scrapped the last remaining express engine of Brunel's broad gauge that his predecessor had preserved – to make more space in Swindon works! Even with the simplified and less colourful livery, engines passing along the Dawlish–Teignmouth sea wall still looked ornate, with their copper-capped chimneys, polished brass safety-valve columns, and a handsome, if restrained, painting style in dark green. The style of Great Western locomotives remained individual and unchanged to the very end of the steam era, and astonishingly so in colour also – even though the nationalized British railways had one spell of painting the largest of them blue and the lesser lights in black. Today *Pendennis Castle*, *Burton Agnes Hall* and several more, up to the giant *King George V*, are in full working order, and can be seen hauling special trains. A little further west on the beautiful branch line from Paignton down to Kingswear the power today is entirely by preserved Great Western steam locomotives, maintained as before.

The home of the *King George V* is now at Hereford, and one of the favourite running grounds for this famous and far-travelled locomotive is over that beautiful route through the Welsh Border country, northwards through Leominster, Ludlow and Church Stretton to Shrewsbury. At that great junction contact is made with a line leading into the heart of Wales, where in the 1930s the Great Western faced something of a problem in locomotive power.

The very picturesque main line of the famous Cambrian Railways had then been incorporated in the GWR, and its track and bridges laid through much wild mountain

country were light, and would not carry the larger standard engines. The 40-year-old 4-4-0s of the 'Duke' class needed replacement, and an ingenious compromise was made by taking the frames of some almost-as-old but serviceable engines which were too heavy as they stood, and putting on 'Duke'-type boilers. These hybrids, using frames from the 'Bulldog' class, became nicknamed the 'Duke-dogs'. They did yeoman work in Central Wales, and one is now preserved on the Bluebell Line.

North West England When the West Coast group of early railways, the London and Birmingham, the Liverpool and Manchester, and the Grand Junction, sought to extend their activities to the Scottish border the

great pioneer George Stephenson was quite deterred by the prospect of having to carry a railway through the Lake District or over the Westmorland fells to get from Lancaster to Carlisle. Instead, he proposed crossing Morecambe Bay, and making a long detour round the Cumberland coast. His one-time pupil, Joseph Locke, was called in to advise and he recommended the great trunk route over the Shap Fells that was actually built.

However, the route was made much more difficult than it might have been as Locke had a great aversion to tunnels. Perhaps it was the ghastly experience he had had in taking over the uncompleted Woodhead tunnel on the line from Manchester to Sheffield, in the building of which many

lives were lost. But on the Lancaster and Carlisle line he could have obtained much easier gradients by going from Kendal up Long Sleddale, tunnelling under the ridge, and coming out beside Haweswater. Instead he took the line in a detour eastwards over an intermediate summit at Grayrigg and into the gorge of the river Lune. And while it was tough going for the locomotives the mountain scenery was sublime. Before it was finished, the great 'West Coast' group to the south had amalgamated to become the London and North Western Railway, the 'Premier Line' of all Britain, and that company operated the Lancaster and Carlisle from the outset and eventually absorbed it.

The engines of the North Western had a fascination that was not surpassed in the days of the old companies. Fortunately there is a very famous example of a nineteenth-century North Western engine preserved in the 2-4-0 loco *Hardwicke*, (see p 56). Until the early 1900s all trains of any weight required two engines to get them over the 280 m (915 ft) Shap Summit, and there the speed would rarely be more than 48 kph (30 mph) with ordinary express trains. But when *Hardwicke* was taking the Highland tourist train on the last night of the great Race to the North it was 'all or nothing'. The load had been cut to no more than three coaches, and she ran the 227 km (141 miles) from Crewe to Carlisle in 126 minutes, an average speed of 108 kph (67 mph)—

Above. A Great Western Society Special from Didcot to Tyseley (Birmingham), leaving Heyford, hauled by the restored 4-6-0 No. 6998 *Burton Agnes Hall*

Below. London-Plymouth express on the Teignmouth sea wall, with the picturesque Parson and Clark Rocks in the distance. The locomotive is a Class 52 diesel-hydraulic No. 1065 *Western Consort*.
Bottom. The British High Speed Train (HST) came into service on the London–Swansea route in autumn 1976. Although advertised as being capable of 125 mph, it can in fact reach a considerably greater speed.

Right. On the one-time broad gauge main line of Brunel: one of the Western Region diesel hydraulic locomotives of the Warship class, *Daring*, passing through Sydney Gardens, Bath, with a London to Bristol express.

Shap included! What that little engine did on the night of 21/22 August 1895 remains one of the greatest epics of railway history.

The great 'gable' of Shap, 50.5 km (31½) miles up from Morecambe Bay and the same down to Carlisle, governed locomotive practice on the West Coast route to the very end of steam days. For the London and North Western Railway Crewe works built larger and larger engines, until in 1913 one of C. J. Bowen Cooke's 'Claughton' 4-6-0s made a record that ranks almost with *Hardwicke's* epic of eighteen years earlier. Tearing through the Lune Gorge and making an all-out charge on Shap there was registered in the dynamometer testing car the highest horsepower of any British locomotive up to the time of grouping in 1923. And what a setting for an outstanding mechanical achievement, in the magnificent scenery of this Lune Gorge, with the railway carried high above the torrent and the fells towering on both sides of the line. Sadly no one thought to take a photograph of the occasion. Only the scientific records remain.

In the 1920s the London and North Western became part of the London Midland and Scottish; 'Claughtons' gave place to 'Royal Scots' and the colour of the express engines became red. But still the majestic scene remained, where the only noise was that of an express running through the gorge or an occasional car making its way up the narrow road over the fells. Today all is changed. The M6 motorway was driven through the valley, at a higher level than the railway, and although much was done after the construction was completed to heal the scars of cutting and embankment the roar of the highway is hardly ever absent. Things have also changed on the railways. There was a transition stage in the first years of nationaliztion, when the 'Britannia' class 'Pacifics' came to supplement the former LMS types, and then came the diesels. Speed did not noticeably increase until the early 1970s when as a foretaste of electrification some greatly accelerated trains were put on which needed *two* diesels to keep time.

The metamorphosis since 1974 has been complete. In former days we would sit by the lineside looking westward towards the ruins of Shap Abbey, and leisurely point

our cameras towards a 'Royal Scot', or a Stanier 'Duchess' struggling up the last four miles at 1 in 75 to Shap Summit. Today the overhead electric wires, carrying 25,000 volts, are remarkably unobtrusive in that vast landscape; but what power they contain! The 'Royal Scot' express of today is of twelve coaches as before, but instead of puffing up that incline at a bare 48 kph (30 mph) its speed is at least 137 kph (85 mph).

The Settle and Carlisle railway Until 1876 the beautiful route over Shap was the only railway from the South and Midlands of England to Carlisle, and the Midland Railway had to send such Scottish traffic as it could over a most unlikely way. It had control of a subsidiary line known as the 'Little North Western' that ran from Skipton, in the West Riding, towards Lancaster and at a wild moorland namesake of London's great Clapham Junction it pioneered a line up the Lune Valley, with the intention of making a junction with the 'big' North Western at Low Gill, and so feeding into the Shap route to Carlisle. But in the 'cut and thrust' of railway politics in mid-Victorian times the 'big' North Western got in first and built a branch line of its own southwards from Low Gill. The result was an end-on junction with the Midland branch at Ingleton. Furthermore it made interchange of traffic so awkward that the Midland determined to have its own line to

Above. The veteran London and North Western 2-4-0 of the 1895 Race to Aberdeen, No. 790 *Hardwicke,* in steam at Carnforth after her restoration to running condition in July 1975.

Below. Early morning on the Shap Incline: an overnight express from London to Glasgow climbing the 1 in 75 gradient, hauled by a Stanier 'Black Five' 4-6-0 with a second engine banking in the rear.

the Scottish border. Thus was conceived the magnificent Settle and Carlisle railway.

It was no easy task to find a way through the dales of North-West Yorkshire and Westmorland. The new route had to be competitive in speed. There was no case for a cheap mountain route: it was to be a fast express route, by which the Midland could match the best London and North Western times to Carlisle, and north west of Skipton was an area of deep valleys, rugged mountain ridges and sedgy moorland, all subject to the worst extremes of weather. From the south there was a possible route up North Ribblesdale, but this ended, after fourteen miles, in the waste of Blea Moor. From Carlisle there was the Eden Valley, extending in all its north-country variations for nearly 80 km (50 miles) to the 355-m (1,167-ft) high Ais Ghyll Moor. But between Blea Moor and Ais Ghyll lay the high Pennines, and C. S. Sharland, the surveyor, had to find an alignment that could be built into a fast express route. The outcome was one of the most dramatic pieces of main-line railway in Britain: tunnels through limestone rock; viaducts so exposed to the winds that stonemasons sometimes had to cease work for fear of being blown off the scaffolding; bog where there seemed to be no solid bottom on which to build an embankment. But all the difficulties were overcome eventually, and in 1876 the line was opened to traffic—a notable advance.

Above. One of the celebrated Stanier 'Black Five' 4-6-0s on a Glasgow-Dundee express near Gleneagles, Perthshire.

Below. On the Settle and Carlisle line: a diesel-hauled Leeds to Glasgow express ascending 'The Long Drag' from Settle to Blea Moor in winter, with the flat-topped mountain of Ingleborough in the background.

The original specification was fulfilled to the letter. There was not a single speed restriction between Settle and Carlisle, and the Midland express trains of 70 years ago went uphill at 65 kph (40 mph), crossed the central tableland at 95–105 kph (60–65 mph) and went downhill on one occasion at a maximum of 155 kph (96 mph) in the early days of the Midland compound 4-4-0 engines. The first of these, now numbered 1000, is one of the treasured exhibits in the National Railway Museum at York. The design was especially prepared to provide ample power for the long uphill stretches of the Settle and Carlisle line; and in those days when each engine had its own crew, and no other, the first engine, then numbered 2631, was stationed at Carlisle and the second one at Leeds. They were exclusive to this route. The line has always been a challenge, and when the LMS was formed in 1923 competitive testing of engines from the former individual companies took place between Carlisle and Leeds. In the mountain country of North Ribblesdale; in climbing to Ais Ghyll; or in racing across that high-level stretch overlooking Garsdale, Dentdale and across the great viaducts and beside the snow fences, locomotive reputations were made and broken or, at least, varied.

After the formation of British Railways in 1948 the Settle and Carlisle became more than ever a proving ground. Testing was much more scientific; the engines to be tried were drawn from wider fields, and the climax came when one of the great Stanier 'Pacifics', the *Duchess of Gloucester*, was driven practically to the limit of her boiler. Then, just as the Shap route had, in 1913, witnessed the highest output of power registered in the old days before grouping, so on the 'Long Drag' from Settle Junction up to Blea Moor the *Duchess* sustained the highest rate of continuous evaporation ever recorded in a British locomotive. Whereas normal passenger trains are now of about 400 to 450 tons, on this test a train of 900

Below. The restored Midland Compound 4-4-0 No. 1000, in the form which she took when she was rebuilt in 1914 from the original Johnson compound of 1902.

Right. One of the Stanier 'Jubilee' class three cylinder 4-6-0s of the LMS, No. 5690 *Leander*, restored to its original livery and photographed in York Station in 1975, on the way to Darlington for the 150th anniversary pageant.

tons was taken up to Blea Moor at 48 kph (30 mph).

Nowadays, the loads on this route are about 300 tons, and the diesels make short work of the long 1 in 100 gradients. The climbing speed is not much less than 96 kph (60 mph). But although there is little sound, and no smoke and steam to mark their comings and goings, this remote high-altitude world of trains still has its own magic. Those who have experienced it will tell you there is nothing to equal the thrill of a ride on the second engine of a double header, when the leader was an old Midland 4-4-0 tearing in the teeth of a mountain storm across the high ground from Blea Moor at a good 112 kph (70 mph).

Bearing in mind the countless miles of service that lies behind them it is fascinating to walk round the National Railway Museum and see such a variety of famous steam locomotives grouped around the central turntable. This is no workaday roundhouse improvised for the job, but a complete rebuilding of the old steam running sheds to provide the spaciousness essential to view these magnificent relics to the best advantage. There are more Midland engines at Leicester and some famous Great Westerns, including the *City of Truro*, at Swindon; but York is now the focal point of England's railway history, as is appropriate.

some heroic attacks on this great summit. The climb from the north side is not so severe, and one Sunday in 1939 when a maximum power test was in progress the 'Pacific' engine *Duchess of Abercorn*, hauling a huge load of 610 tons, approached Beattock summit in a blinding snowstorm, yet charged over the top at 101 kph (63 mph) recording a mighty 3,333 horsepower in the process.

Coming up from the south, where steam and diesel trains were allowed 20 minutes to climb that severe 16 km (10 miles), the 25,000-volt electrics are now given only *seven minutes*, which means that instead of grinding uphill at 48 kph (30 mph) they now have to average 137 kph (85 mph). In earlier days motorists on the adjacent highway could leave the trains standing: in fact an enthusiastic photographer could 'shoot' the 'Royal Scot' somewhere near Auchencastle, jump into his car, and have plenty of time to photograph it again as it pounded laboriously up the last miles to the summit. Not so nowadays as the electrics flash past up the glen. But even with all the modern sophistication they can still be hindered by the weather on the Beattock

Below. A general-utility 'Black Five' 4-6-0 of the LMS on an eastbound goods train between Alloa and Bogside in Scotland.

Below left. Southbound across the Tay Bridge: a double-headed diesel-hauled express from Aberdeen to Edinburgh approaches the Fife shore, with a fine panorama of Dundee in the background.

Above. The two restored Caledonian Railway coaches forming a special train leaving Princes Street station Edinburgh hauled by a British Railways standard Class '2' 2-6-0 No. 78046.
Below. Winter in the West Highlands: a diesel hauled train from Fort William to Glasgow is pictured crossing one of the viaducts between Tyndrum Upper and Crianlarich, Perthshire.
Above right. The Bluebell Line: a beautiful example of the later Brighton engine livery on the 'R4' class 0-6-2 tank engine *Birch Grove*, near Waterworks.
Below right. The preserved LNER 'V2' class 2-6-2 No. 4771 *Green Arrow* on a special eastbound from Carnforth to Leeds, passing Wennington.

bank. On one occasion the 'Royal Scot' electric locomotive was storming up the gradient at 142 kph (88 mph). Then there was a shower of rain. The wheels slipped at once, and in seconds we were down to 121 kph (75 mph). This was still, in fact, a very impressive and exciting speed to climb such a gradient, but it was a dramatic instance of what the weather can still do.

Preserved steam Today, although no regularly scheduled steam operation on British Railways exists, a venture launched more than a quarter of a century ago by a band of enthusiasts with skill, railway know-how, and sound financial backing, has proved the catalyst for a whole series of projects for preservation, providing in working order, not only individual locomotives but whole sections of railway. How the little narrow-gauge Talyllyn Railway in Central Wales, only 11 km (6¾ miles) long, was saved from extinction was an epic in itself. It was of course an entirely self-contained unit; but its success led to others, like the resuscitation of the derelict Festiniog Railway, which was literally rusting away. Its track was over-grown with weeds and saplings, its loco-motives and rolling stock were rotting away amid derelict sheds and workshops and becoming more and more exposed to the weather as roofs and walls collapsed. It was originally built to transport slates, and speed was of no consequence. Now its present locomotives are beautifully maintained and very popular with all enthusiasts. But then there came the great modernization plan for British Railways, that included the whole-sale closing down of many unremunerative branch lines, and the eventual complete supersession of steam traction; and with the examples of the Talyllyn and the Festiniog before them a whole crop of preservation schemes was mooted, not of narrow gauge, but of standard gauge lines, to be operated by time-experienced locomotives and rolling stock. Not all the schemes propounded have yet come to fruition, but then as the time came for famous locomotives to be with-drawn and sold for scrap a collateral move-ment for preservation developed. From these two sources, quite apart from the establishment of the National Railway Museum at York, a number of beautiful and highly colourful enterprises have been firmly established.

That many of the private enterprise preservation schemes for working sections of railway lie in districts away from the areas of intense traffic, which would in other circumstances have compelled the closing down of the lines altogether, has been most fortunate from the scenic point of view. One could not, for example, find a more picturesque West Country branch line than that of the former Great Western Railway, from Paignton to Kingswear, climbing first onto the cliffs overlooking Torbay, and then after breasting the ridge making a sinuous course down the hillside above the

river Dart to the water's edge at Kingswear. The Severn Valley line between Kidder-minster and Bridgnorth runs through con-tinuously lovely scenery, while the North Yorkshire Moors Railway is keeping alive one of the most picturesque parts of the former North Eastern Railway route from Pickering to Whitby. In all these areas locomotives saved from the scrap-heap have been restored by enthusiasts with full technical experience and ability and are going about their new duties lovingly polished and maintained, providing scenes definitely more colourful than in the days when they were struggling forlorn on lines officially discredited up to the time of impending closure.

Then there are the 'steam centres', based on certain running sheds that were no longer required under the general moderniz-ation of the British Railways motive power fleet. These have been taken over by various societies, and provide areas where preserved locomotives may be steamed without en-croaching upon the ordinary running lines.

They also provide bases for the housing and maintenance of those locomotives which on particular occasions are allowed to work special trains along routes over which steam haulage is still permitted. There is the large Didcot depot of the Great Western Society, where a considerable variety of historic coaching stock is also maintained and, in some cases, restored from a condition of serious decay. When these depots stage an open day the colourful world of trains is manifested in the most delightful way. Then again at Tyseley, near Birmingham, formerly an important Great Western steam shed, it is not merely a case of preservation. Machinery has been installed for the under-taking of quite heavy repair work, and with considerable space in the yard an open-day at Tyseley, with locomotives of other railways beside those of the Great Western in steam, is something to remember.

One of the most famous of all British steam locomotives, the *King George V* of the Great Western, was scheduled for presentation as a museum piece and for a

long time was stored in a remote corner of the old stock shed at Swindon. But a group of enthusiasts in the West Midlands, with the enthusiastic backing of H P Bulmer Ltd, the cider manufacturers, formed the '6000 Association', and the engine was restored to full working order; it is now based on a special siding and shed in Bulmer's works. The great engine is now seen on occasions working special trains on the permitted routes, though because of its Great Western ancestry these are less extensive than those permitted to some other notable locomotives. The former GWR inherited from broad gauge days of Brunel a somewhat more liberal loading gauge than those of most other railways, and the 'King' class locomotives

were built to take advantage of this.

One of the most remarkable steam concentration points in Great Britain is the junction of Carnforth, on the west coast main line about six miles north of Lancaster in the north-east corner of Morecambe Bay. In pre-grouping days Carnforth was a triple junction, where the cross-country line of the Midland from Skipton and the cities of the West Riding crossed the London and North Western main line about half a mile north of the station and then came round on an exceedingly sharp curve to join the Furness Railway and come into the station from the west. 'Steamtown' is now on the site of the old Furness running sheds. At first it was intended to be a kind of north country

Tyseley with plans to include one or two unusual locomotives, but since the line from Leeds became available for steam running Steamtown has become an active base of operations for a great variety of trips. The ever-famous Gresley 'Pacific' *Flying Scotsman* has found its home there, together with the companion mixed-traffic 2-6-2 *Green Arrow*, while in addition to certain LMS engines, there is the notable addition of a French 'Pacific' of the Paris, Lyons and Mediterranean type.

Steamtown, Carnforth, has played a very important part in the celebrations of the 150th anniversary of the opening of the Stockton and Darlington Railway in 1975 and those of the centenary of passenger

traffic on the far-famed Settle and Carlisle line of the Midland Railway in 1976.

When the historic LNWR 2-4-0 *Hardwicke* was put into working order once again so that she could take part in the anniversary pageant in September 1975 running under her own steam, she was taken for a trial run down the Furness line as far north as Sellafield. She revisited Carnforth at the time of the Settle and Carlisle centenary celebrations in May 1976 and seeing her there, the thoughts of many may well have turned in imagination to the night of August 22, 1895 when at a time recorded as 11.39¾ pm she hurtled through on the Aberdeen racing train in the course of her record 108.15 kph (67.2 mph) run from Crewe to Carlisle.

The preserved Midland compound No. 1000 has also been a familiar object at Carnforth in 1976. In company with *Hardwicke* she came across from the National Railway Museum to participate in the Settle and Carlisle festivities and in partnership with one of the celebrated Stanier 'Black Five' 4-6-0s, was to have headed some of the special trains run on that occasion. Unfortunately they both failed on the shed and their places were taken by the *Hardwicke* and the *Flying Scotsman*. The Midland ran an excursion over the Furness Line from Carnforth to Sellafield and back. This is one of the many enterprising projects of the '6000 Association'.

Left. On the Wemyss Private Railway, Fife: an 0-6-0 tank engine No. 20 moving coal in Methil Yards.
Above. On the Keighley and Worth Valley Railway, in the Brontë Country, the last of all steam locomotives built for British Railways, the '9F' 2-10-0 No. 92220 *Evening Star* is seen here near Oakworth, on the climb from Keighley to Oxenhope in April 1974. This engine is now in the National Railway Museum at York.
Below. Forlorn last days of steam: two 2-6-4 tank engines, and a 'Britannia' class Pacific No. 70027 with nameplate removed at Manningham shed, Bradford.

Europe

Spain

Above. On the Miranda to Zaragoza line, Spain, one of the numerous and efficient 141 F class 2-8-2s of which construction continued down to the year 1960, seen here in spectacular country near San Felices.

Below right. Amid grandly impressive mountain scenery one of the giant '242F' 4-8-4 locomotives of RENFE heads an express from Miranda to Zaragoza. These engines are the only ones on the Spanish National Railways to have the green livery.

Above right. Along the Ponferrada–Villablino line a local train is running placidly along hauled by a tender-tank locomotive No. 31, built by Maffei, of Munich, in 1913.

Spain by tradition is one of the most colourful countries of Europe and until the protracted Civil War of 1936–9, the individual railway companies provided a picturesque if not very profitable echo of national characteristics. Reputedly influenced by Brunel's advocacy of a wider gauge than the standard 4 ft 8½ in or 1.435 m adopted over the rest of Western Europe, Spain and inevitably Portugal, too, decided upon 1.676 m (5ft 6in), with consequent difficulties for traffic exchange at the international frontiers that have remained ever since, and which are now being no more than partially removed by the ingenious wheel-changing arrangements at Hendaye and Cerbère. The enthusiast travelling upon the Spanish railways will delight in the individualism in locomotive practice of the former independent railway companies evidenced by the many surviving units of the Northern, Western, Andalusian Central of Aragon, and the MZA (Madrid, Zaragoza and Alicante) organizations. Now, however, few steam locomotives remain in regular service on the national system.

It was in 1941, two years after the end of the Civil War, that RENFE was formed – *Red Nacional de los Ferrocarriles Españoles* – and a coordinated national policy for reconstruction and development was formulated. Something was certainly needed after the devastation left in certain areas by the Civil War, but the year 1941 was hardly a propitious time to put plans into execution, with nearly all the most likely sources of materials and rolling stock involved in vastly greater conflict than Spain had ever known. Fortunately much of the locomotive stock of the old railway companies was of sound design. The 4-8-0 had been a favourite type in Spain and impressive examples were to be seen on all the old lines. One of the most interesting and widely used was one introduced on the Andalusian railway in 1935. It was adopted soon after the end of the Civil War by both the Western and the MZA railways, and immediately accepted in 1941 as a RENFE standard. Construction continued down to the year 1953, by which time 247 engines of this class were at work.

The heavy gradients and difficult operating conditions in Spain that make things so exciting and colourful for the photographer have led to the designing of still larger engines than the popular 4-8-0s, and as early as 1925 the Northern introduced a class of 4-8-2s—65 of them in all—which at that time must have ranked among the heaviest and most powerful locomotives in Europe. Certainly the Northern, with its heavily graded lines running from Madrid to Gijón and Santander on the Atlantic coast, had a tough job, and these great locomotives worked passenger and freight trains alike. Most locomotives of the RENFE are plain black, albeit very smartly turned out; but this 240/4001 class was honoured by being lined in yellow.

Europe
Portugal

In Portugal the nationalized railway system was formed in 1947 with the combination of the virtually independent lines lying north and south of the Tagus estuary. The southern group, which was much the smaller, provided the service to the coast at Faro, while the north group included the principal internal main line between Lisbon and Oporto, and the lines carrying the international express trains, via Vilar Formoso, for the north and connections to Paris, via Marvão, to Madrid and Barcelona, and via Elvas, to Seville. But the enthusiast seeking the truly colourful side of Portuguese railroading will travel to the valley of the Douro in the north, and seek out the various narrow-gauge branches that strike off northwards from the Oporto–Barca d'Alva main line where steam is still supreme.

To say that this area is a paradise for the railway enthusiast would be an understatement. There is the happy combination of beautiful country and narrow-gauge steam-operated branch lines. More than this, although this is now becoming a European outpost of steam, there is no evidence of the decay and dereliction that all too often has set in when the time was approaching for the inevitable change in motive power. The black steam locomotives with their polished copper tops to their shapely chimneys are kept in superb condition and provide ample evidence of how splendid a black locomotive can look if it is well cared for. Among individual locomotive types, the Mallet compound tanks are the most interesting. They were all built by Henschel of Kassel, Germany, but are uniformly of a very 'British' appearance. The older ones, dating from 1905, are of the 0-4-4-0 type but in 1911 the much larger variety was introduced having the rather extraordinary wheel arrangement 2-4-6-0. The first batch consisted of four only; but these proved very successful. Two more were purchased in 1913, and in 1923 a large repeat order for twelve more was placed with Henschel. It is worth going to the Douro Valley, if only to see these engines at work.

Right. Amid the rugged scenery of the Douro Valley, a 4-6-0 No. 284 leaves a short tunnel near Tua, working an eastbound train.

Above. Compound 4-6-0 No. 238 with a mixed
load between Panserat and Vesuvio.
Above right. The morning mixed train to
Pochino, crossing the mouth of the river Tua,
where it enters the Douro. The train is hauled by a
2-8-4 tank engine.

Below right. On the 1.676 m (5ft 6in) gauge main line up the Valley of the Douro, North Portugal, an inside cylinder 4-6-0 No. 285 makes a vigorous start out of Pinhao with an early morning freight to Barca D'Alva, on the Spanish frontier.

Left. Two of the Mallet 2-4-6-0 compound tank engines at Sernada-de-Vluga: No. 182 leaving on a train to Viseu; No. 215 shunting.

Below. The morning train from Oporto to Fafe leaves Lousado, behind engine No. 166. An equally resplendent 102 is on the shed.

Bottom. On shed at Nine, Portugal, a Henschel built 2-6-4 tank locomotive, No. 87 of 1929 vintage.

Top. Massed locomotive power in a round-house provides an impressive and colourful sight, especially when the locomotives on shed are so splendidly clean as here, at Contumil shed, Oporto, Portugal.

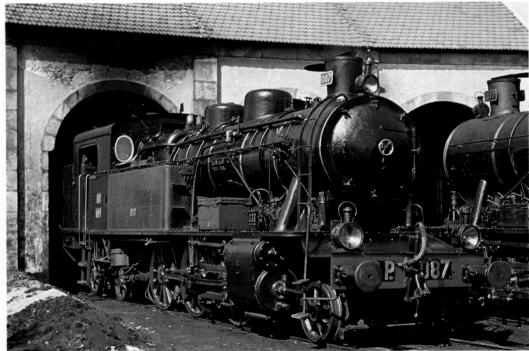

Wheel Notation Systems

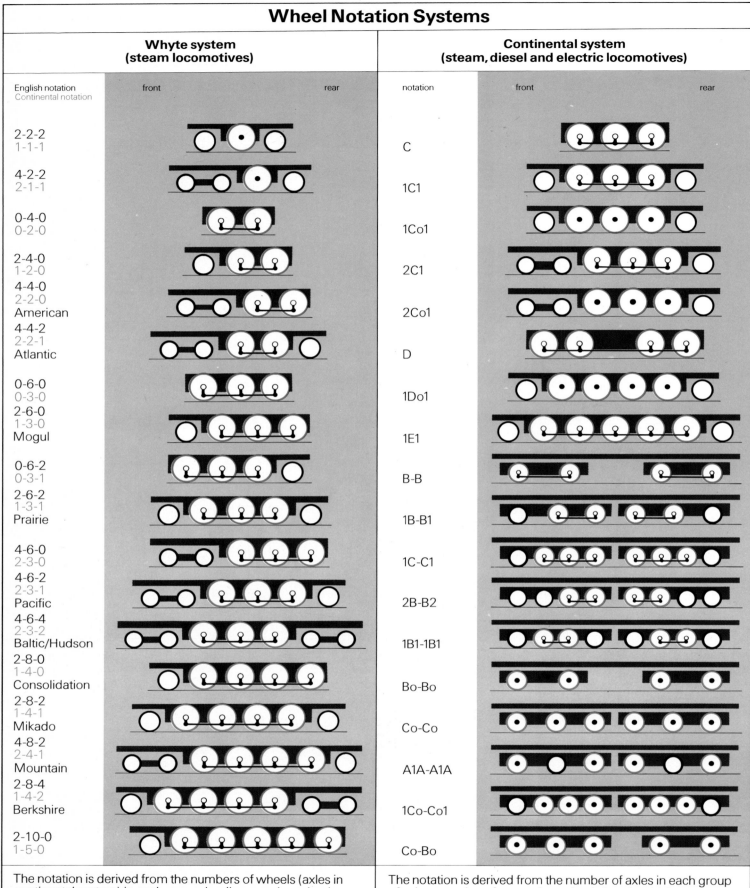

Whyte system (steam locomotives)	Continental system (steam, diesel and electric locomotives)

Whyte system (steam locomotives)

English notation / Continental notation | front ... rear

- 2-2-2 / 1-1-1
- 4-2-2 / 2-1-1
- 0-4-0 / 0-2-0
- 2-4-0 / 1-2-0
- 4-4-0 / 2-2-0 / American
- 4-4-2 / 2-2-1 / Atlantic
- 0-6-0 / 0-3-0
- 2-6-0 / 1-3-0 / Mogul
- 0-6-2 / 0-3-1
- 2-6-2 / 1-3-1 / Prairie
- 4-6-0 / 2-3-0
- 4-6-2 / 2-3-1 / Pacific
- 4-6-4 / 2-3-2 / Baltic/Hudson
- 2-8-0 / 1-4-0 / Consolidation
- 2-8-2 / 1-4-1 / Mikado
- 4-8-2 / 2-4-1 / Mountain
- 2-8-4 / 1-4-2 / Berkshire
- 2-10-0 / 1-5-0

Continental system (steam, diesel and electric locomotives)

notation | front ... rear

- C
- 1C1
- 1Co1
- 2C1
- 2Co1
- D
- 1Do1
- 1E1
- B-B
- 1B-B1
- 1C-C1
- 2B-B2
- 1B1-1B1
- Bo-Bo
- Co-Co
- A1A-A1A
- 1Co-Co1
- Co-Bo

The notation is derived from the numbers of wheels (axles in continental system) in each group: leading carrying wheels, driving wheels, trailing carrying wheels. A suffix 'T' is added to the notation to denote a tank engine e.g. 0-6-2T.

The notation is derived from the number of axles in each group of axles:- numbers for carrying axles, letters for driving axles: A=1, B=2, C=3 etc. Axles individually driven are suffixed 'o'.

⭕ Carrying (non-driving) wheels   Coupled driving wheel   ⦿ Individually driven wheel

The Golden Age 1876-1914

Economic and social effects of railways By 1870 the main lines of the European networks were almost complete, although secondary lines were still being built. In Europe, Britain had the greatest mileage, 24,500 km (15,250 miles), but Germany was catching up fast with 19,500 km (12,100 miles). France and Russia had about 17,000 km (10,500 miles) each, followed by Spain and Italy with about 6,000 km (3,700 miles) each. Belgium had 3,000 km (1,850 miles) and Holland and Switzerland 1,400 km (870 miles) each. Belgium was the country best served by railways, its 3,000 km being spread over a small area. Thanks to its early and rational plan of construction, it had also been the first to reap massive economic benefits. Because of the railways, its exports of cast iron rose by 800 per cent between 1836 and 1845, while coal production doubled. Other countries could show similar results later; not only did the railways cheapen transport, but by widening the market for the goods they carried they stimulated greater production. At first passenger traffic developed faster than freight; the railways were so much faster, cheaper and safer than the road coaches that they not only took all the highway passengers but also carried people who otherwise would not have travelled. With freight traffic, it took time to persuade shippers to change their mode of transport, and because canals still gave a good service the railways never grasped the entire freight market.

The benefit brought by railways was especially dramatic in Switzerland, because transport costs previously had been so high. There, the price of wheat in the cities fell by one third after the railways came. Coal prices fell by a half, and coal consumption increased by more than one hundred times. The tourist trade grew spectacularly. New high-quality industries were established to serve a European-wide market, and the resulting increase in urban wages persuaded many country dwellers to move to the cities. Europe was beginning to function as a single economic unit; the Pyrenees had been crossed at each end, and the Alps had been penetrated through the Mont Cenis Tunnel and over the Brenner Pass. Work started on a third transalpine route, the St Gotthard Tunnel, in 1872, and German exporters were already looking towards northern Italy as a great potential market for rail-borne coal. Only two countries seemed to be lagging behind in western Europe. In Spain the railways passed through a land that was still not capable of originating much traffic, and in Italy railway construction had been bedevilled by political considerations; it seemed that only the French could build successful railways in Italy, and as soon as the Italian nationalist politicians discovered this, they took measures to drive them out.

In the USA there had been a burst of railroad building, in the decade preceding the Civil War, that had almost quintupled the mileage, and further increases brought it to 84,000 km (53,000 miles) by 1870. Apart from easing and cheapening transport in the eastern states, this brought into the American economic system the new lands of the Middle West. Illinois, Indiana and Wisconsin became the leading wheat-growing states after the railroad had opened these virgin territories to settlers, and given their crops access to eastern USA and European markets. Later, as the rails continued west, the same process would open up new lands all the way to California. At the same time, the railroads had become the major market for many industries. It was on the basis of demand for rail that the US iron, and then steel, industry turned over to mass production. By widening the market for manufactured goods, the railways enabled other industries to turn over to mass-production methods, thereby initiating the era of large-scale production and consumption.

In America and Europe the social effects of cheap fast passenger transport were felt as people began to move around, both for business and pleasure. In so doing they became conscious of belonging to a nation, rather than to a state, province, or township. By 1875 a New Yorker could take a job in Boston or Chicago knowing that he would be only eight hours or thirty hours distant from his family. A Scotsman could seek his fortune in London, knowing that if he failed a train could take him back to Edinburgh in $9\frac{1}{2}$ hours; and in any case he could write home every day, taking advantage of the 'Penny Post' which the railways had made feasible.

Scandal and fraud Despite Federal and state assistance, nine-tenths of US railroad construction was financed by the private investor. Never before had so much money sought investment, and many profited from this fact. Some of these profiteers made their own contribution to growth, but others simply milked the railroads and the investors. In the first category comes the New York Stock Exchange, which rose to preeminence among financial institutions because it became the main market place for railway shares at a time when such shares were dominating the market. Also, perhaps, on the creditable side were speculators like Vanderbilt and Hill who, unscrupulous profiteers though they were, had the vision to build up big railway systems that would serve the country well. Vanderbilt, by astute stock manipulation, created the New York Central System from a multiplicity of shorter lines, while the Canadian James Hill before the end of the century succeeded in organizing the two northern trans-continentals, the Northern Pacific and the Great Northern, and in providing them with a big feeder system by adding the Chicago, Burlington & Quincy

Railroad to his empire. Other men, men such as Jay Gould and Jim Fiske, simply grabbed and stole and left nothing worthwhile behind them. Among Gould's exploits were stock manipulations which enabled him several times to buy Erie Railroad shares cheap and sell them dear. He used his profits to buy control of the Union Pacific, and contrived that the UP should pay dividends far higher than its revenues warranted. This raised the market price of UP shares, and he thereupon sold his shareholding at a great profit, using the money to buy the insolvent Kansas Pacific and Denver Pacific railroads. Having done this, he went through the motions of getting the Kansas Pacific to extend its line westwards, threatening massive competition for the UP. To protect itself, the UP had to buy up the Kansas Pacific at an inflated price. The many-times-enriched Gould then left to start a new game elsewhere. Gould was only one outstanding example of a whole tribe of parasites whose activities eventually aroused the farming and industrial interests, the interests most badly damaged by the side effects of these proceedings. Government intervention became more frequent and effective, resulting in the railroads as a whole being burdened with so many state and Federal regulations that their competitive strength in the next century was seriously damaged.

Among the earlier scandals that had aroused public concern was the Crédit Mobilier affair. This was really only a single example of a widespread practice, in which financiers and speculators would form a construction company to build a particular railway. Some of the participants would be directors of the railroad and would arrange a contract whereby the construction company would start building the line in exchange for an immediate payment made in the form of that railway's shares. They then used these shares as collateral to raise the money needed for the construction. At the same time, the shares gave them a controlling interest in the railway, so they could progressively raise the price paid to the construction company until the railway went bankrupt. The Crédit Mobilier was deeply involved in the first transcontinental line, and its insalubrious dealings, which included this kind of fraud, were revealed only in 1872, after it had been found distributing some of its shares as bribes to Congressmen. In general, it was genuine shareholders, and local interests which had supported particular railways, that were the losers in these transactions. The speculators and promoters usually died rich.

Europe was not without its scandals, but they never seemed quite so blatant and large-scale as in the USA. Jay Gould's blackmailing of an established company by means of a threat to build a competing line had several parallels in the old world. Thomas Brassey was the most successful and publicly respected of the British contractors (he built 11,200 km, or 7,000 miles, of railway, including the British Grand Junction, the French Paris–Rouen, and the Canadian Grand Trunk), but he did not consider it dishonest to inspire and build the 'Direct Portsmouth' line in England, and then successively offer it to the three companies already struggling for the Portsmouth traffic, each of which dreaded the possibility of its competitors acquiring a shorter route. Brassey, of course, had not broken the law, and in this he was unlike George Hudson, the most celebrated of British 'railway kings' (for some reason such men

were called 'railway kings' in Britain, but 'robber barons' in America). Hudson, a York draper who had been enabled by a legacy to buy his first railway shares, rose by astuteness and lack of scruple in the years of the British 'Railway Mania', in the early 1840s, when both speculators and confused private investors were recklessly buying railway shares. By exploiting quarrels between competing railways, by judicious share purchases and sales, and by a certain degree of manipulation both of people and of share prices, Hudson bought himself control of railways in the north and centre of Britain. He enriched himself, and ruined many better men, but at least he created one of the greatest of the big British companies, the Midland Railway. He was eventually brought down when he opposed interests more powerful and no more scrupulous than his own, and in the aftermath it was discovered that he had been manipulating share prices by, among other things, paying good dividends on the most impecunious of his companies at the expense of their capital.

Hudson's great enemy, the Great Northern Railway, was damaged in 1857 when it was revealed that the company's registrar had robbed it of almost a quarter of a million pounds. Such frauds were not uncommon. The railways were the world's first big business, and ways to supervise employees and executives were not easy to find; never before had so much money been placed in the hands of so many persons under such little immediate supervision. A similar scandal rocked Italy in 1861, when the vice-president, a banker, of the Roman Railway Company was arrested for fraud.

Continental contractors had no more scruples than their Anglo-Saxon brothers, as Portuguese experience demonstrated. Portugal had been rather slow to build railways, partly because there were several interests zealously squashing any projects other than their own. The French, in particular, wanted to link Portugal with Spain and thus with France, thereby breaking Britain's trading monopoly; in this endeavour Spain was not cooperative, and its adoption of the 1.68 m (5 ft 6 in) gauge, imitated by Portugal, was a blow to the French government. Nevertheless, the first railway in Portugal was a French company. It ran from Lisbon to Cintra, and it was inaugurated by the King of Portugal in 1856; unfortunately the ceremonial train broke down and the king and his entourage did most of their inaugurating on foot. The biggest of the railway companies was the Royal Portuguese Railway Company, which in 1859 had secured a concession to build from Lisbon to the Spanish frontier, with a second line to Oporto. Its promoter was a Spanish contractor, José de Salamanca. Salamanca contracted through a second company to complete and operate the line within three years, and received a government subsidy on the strength of this. He pocketed this subsidy, and kept up the railway share prices by paying dividends out of capital. Construction was still unfinished in 1865, by which year Salamanca and his friends had unloaded their shares in the French Bourse; where they steadily fell to a low of 145 francs per 500 franc share. The cost of the line built by Salamanca the contractor was double the price originally agreed by Salamanca the promoter, but even so the quality was poor. The promised bridge over the Douro was not delivered, so inhabitants of Oporto until 1878 had to cross the river and go out of the city in order to reach the terminus. Still, thanks to Salamanca, Lisbon was in circuitous and expensive rail communication with the rest of Europe by 1866.

As time passed, the activities of the various railway swindlers diminished. Partly this was because railway construction slackened, but mainly it was because investors and governments became less easy to defraud, having learned by hard experience. Closer government supervision, though it led to railway speculators seeking ways to influence government and judges by bribery, was important. Also important were house-cleaning measures by financial and business circles seeking to restore respectability to private enterprise. In the USA the investment banker J. Pierpoint Morgan was the most prominent of several bankers who plainly put their investor-clients first. Morgan refused to invest the funds entrusted to him in doubtful railway enterprises. Moreover, when the fierce railway competition of the 1870s and 1880s brought many railroads to bankruptcy, it was Morgan who was often asked to reorganize them. Thus began the era of railroad consolidation, as men like Morgan, powerful because they were honest, forcibly joined smaller lines to the larger systems. In 1885 Morgan visited Europe and discovered that British investors, who had placed much money in American railroads, resented the expensive competition between trunk lines; at that time the so-called Nickel Plate Railroad was being built solely for the purpose of blackmailing the New York Central, while another was being built eastwards from Pittsburgh with the sole object of blackmailing the Pennsylvania Railroad. Inviting the builders of these and other lines to his yacht, Morgan would apply a mixture of threats and promises to force them to agree on sensible settlements. In helping other ailing companies, including the Baltimore & Ohio, and the Philadelphia & Reading, Morgan established syndicates to provide capital, while insisting on the appointment of competent and honest management. Another important work of Morgan was the creation in 1894 of the Southern Railway. He had a strong and beneficient influence in New England and in the two northern transcontinentals, the Great Northern and the Northern Pacific. His closest imitator in railroad reorganization was Edward H. Harriman. In 1897 he reorganized the weak Union Pacific, restoring branch lines it had lost, paying off its debts, and buying a line to give it access to Southern California. He relaid its main line with heavier rail, eased its curves, and relocated a section so as to save 40 miles; in 1900 the UP once more paid a dividend. He then proceeded quietly to buy the shares of the Southern Pacific, which owned the line to San Francisco from the UP's western terminal at Ogden. Having gained control, he reconstructed its main lines, and the two great systems, which were naturally complementary, were then linked both by ownership and by technical standards. But the nineteenth-century behaviour of big monopolies like the railroads had by that time created a hostile attitude among the public, the legislators, and the courts; in 1913 the UP and SP combination was broken up, having been adjudged contrary to the recent anti-trust laws.

In general during the last quarter of the nineteenth century, the private railways in America and Europe became more stable and service-conscious. Facing little real competition except that of their own making, they settled down to make profits from providing useful services at a fair price. Conscious that their public image had suffered during the years when anarchic competition in some areas had co-existed with grasping monopoly in others, they sought to impress the public by new fast trains that would symbolize speed, safety and luxury. In this aim they were helped by the continuing improvement of the railway track and its structures.

The permanent way The coming of the steam locomotive had coincided with the replacement of the old brittle cast-iron rails with the more durable rolled rails. Further resilience had soon been obtained, both in America and Europe, by the substitution of wooden cross-ties (sleepers) for the old stone blocks on which early rails were laid. In the 1830s two schools of rail design emerged; the British civil engineer Joseph Locke, the brain behind several main lines, perfected the double-headed form of rail, which had a cross-section resembling the figure 8. This rested in chairs fixed to the cross-ties and was secured with wooden wedges. The intention had been to reverse the rail after the top surface was worn, bringing the lower head to the top. This was not successful because after a few months the bottom surface was indented by the chairs. However, Locke's rail had many virtues, and became the 'bullhead' type favoured in Britain and many other parts of the world. In the USA the flat-bottom rail, of inverted T section, became standard. This seems to have been invented by Colonel Stevens during a visit to Britain. Not liking the complication of chaired bullhead rail, Stevens devised a rail that could be held in place by a simple spike driven in by a hammer. The bullhead rail maintained its popularity in Britain until the mid-twentieth century, but eventually even the British decided that flat-bottomed rail was less complicated and therefore cheaper.

Contemporary prints of the early British railways show gaily painted toylike trains passing over massive engineering structures. This adoption of structures many times bigger and stronger than what was needed, of earthworks and tunnels designed to keep gradients moderate, and of curves with a radius as large as one mile, was a characteristic of British railways rarely found elsewhere, except in that second British railway network constructed in India. In the beginning it was probably uncertainty over safety margins and over the future amount of traffic, plus professional pride on the part of the engineers, that set this pattern of construction. One of its consequences was that British railways were heavily capitalized; in 1850 it was estimated that, on average, British railways had cost £35,000 per mile, as against £11,000 in Germany. But another result was that after nearly one and a half centuries Robert Stephenson's bridges and viaducts were still in use, carrying locomotives six times heavier and three times faster than those of 1840. In America the approach was entirely different. Tracks were laid as cheaply and as quickly as possible. The intention was for a railway to pay dividends without delay; only when traffic reached a volume which the line could no longer handle would there be money for upgrading, for strengthening bridges, laying heavier rails, improving drainage, replacing grade crossings by bridges, replacing timber viaducts by masonry or steel, realigning difficult sections to ease the gradients and curves. This was the favoured approach, too, of many colonial railways. In Europe, there was a mixture of British and American practice. The early German railways followed the US model, but those of France approached British standards. Indeed, the Paris–Rouen–Havre line, one of the first, was engineered by Locke and built by Brassey with all the features of a British main line, including tall viaducts made of local materials. This line was to some extent imitated by other French railways, although it was not long before a definite French style of building began to emerge. In Russia, as in many other countries where there was alternation of state-built and privately-built railways, and where the available capital fluctuated, there was a corresponding alternation of engineering standards. The early St Petersburg–Moscow Railway, though supervised by an American railway engineer, was very British in its standards; it was double-track, easily graded, dead straight for most of its length, and very expensive. The subsequent Trans-Siberian, on the other hand, was built as a frankly 'pioneer' line, its upgrading to mainline standards being postponed to subsequent decades.

The most important advance in track standards came with the introduction of steel rails, which spread over most of the world's main lines in the last quarter of the century. Large-scale production of

mild steel first became possible in 1855, and as early as 1857 the Midland Railway in Britain relaid a short section of track at Derby, where exceptionally heavy traffic had meant the replacement of rails several times each year; after relaying with steel rail, no replacement was needed for 15 years. In Britain, by the late 1860s, steel rail was being introduced as fast as it could be afforded. It not only saved expense in the long run, but it also contributed to safety, for breakages of iron rails were quite common. Elsewhere in the world steel rails came later. Some US lines had always been somewhat conservative in this matter, probably fearing that investment in new types of rail would cut into immediate dividends. The old strap rail, lethal when the iron strip became detached under a passing train, was used as late as 1848 by the Galena & Chicago Union. The first Bessemer steel rails were rolled in the USA in 1865, but in 1880 less than a third of the country's trackage used them. However, by the turn of the century the iron rail had virtually disappeared. In Europe progress was usually faster than in the USA. Even in Russia generous hidden subsidies were paid after 1875 to domestic rail producers who changed over to steel. The use of mild steel for bridges came concurrently. Here Britain lagged behind, largely because her bridge inspectors regarded the new material with great caution. Steel made it easier to pass hitherto uncrossed water barriers. The great Forth Bridge, with its two 520 m (1,710 ft) spans

The Indian gauge situation is graphically demonstrated in this diagram published by a British railway journal in 1924. It shows 4-6-2 locomotives supplied by Britain to the Indian railways, with the 5 ft 6 in gauge type in the background, the metre-gauge type next to it, and the 2 ft 6 in and 2 ft gauge types in the foreground.

connecting Edinburgh with north-eastern Scotland, was opened in 1890. A year earlier a more modest but nevertheless important structure at Hawkesbury had at last provided a direct rail link between Sydney and the north of New South Wales. In the USA the first use of steel in a railway bridge was at St Louis in 1874; this crossed the Mississippi and gave St Louis direct access to the eastern states. The first bridge with an all-steel structure came in 1879, crossing the Missouri at Glasgow. The era of the steel railway bridge would continue into the twentieth century, with such structures as the 1932 Sydney Harbour Bridge, used by a new electric commuter railway; the 7 km (4½ mile) Huey Long Bridge, opened in 1935 and carrying the tracks of three railroad companies into New Orleans; the 1935 Little Belt Bridge on the main line from Esbjerg to Copenhagen; and a more recent Baltic bridge over the Fehmarn Sound in Germany, opened in 1963.

The gauge problem A seemingly imperishable question, the gauge problem, entered a new phase in the late nineteenth century. George Stephenson, whose railways and locomotives had such an initial influence on railways throughout the world, had chosen a distance of 1.422 m (4 ft 8 in) between the rails, and most of the early railways had copied this. However, this was not so much a conscious choice by Stephenson as an absence of choice; he merely stayed with the existing gauge of his colliery line. Some later engineers questioned the wisdom of this, and made claims for other dimensions. A broad gauge was claimed to give extra stability and to accommodate more powerful locomotives, while a narrower gauge line was much cheaper to build and could be laid on sharper curves, making it suitable for mountainous terrain. It later emerged that broader gauges, if they carried bigger freight vehicles, also produced lower costs per ton-mile. In the early decades of railway construction there were divergences from the 'standard' of 1.435 m (4 ft 8½ in; Stephenson on second thoughts had added half an inch to his original specification). Such divergences were towards a broader, rather than a narrower gauge. Especially notable was the 2.14 m (7 ft 0¼ in) of Britain's Great Western Railway.

It soon became evident that 4 ft 8½ in was not the ideal gauge, if such an ideal gauge existed. Most engineers, if given a choice, would have preferred a wider gauge. However, as railways grew it became clear that standardization of gauge was more important than choosing the theoretically ideal gauge. Through running of trains was impossible where adjoining railways had a different width between the rails. This soon became evident in England, where there needed to be an inconvenient and expensive transhipment of passengers and freight at the break-of-gauge stations where the Great Western Railway (GWR) connected with other lines. Public outcry was orchestrated by the GWR's rivals, who wished to inflict a grave blow on that company, and resulted in Parliamentary intervention in the 1840s. The Gauge Commission, which Parliament established, staged trials which did show that the broad gauge was technically superior. But because the standard gauge was already preponderant the Commission recommended that no more broad-gauge mileage be built, except in Ireland, where 1.60 m (5 ft 3 in) would remain the standard. So for the next decades the Great Western comprised old broad-gauge and new standard-gauge lines, with the former gradually becoming mixed gauge until finally, in 1892, the GWR became an entirely standard-gauge railway. Other countries faced similar problems, but usually dealt with them earlier. In Holland the 1.94 m (6 ft 4⅜ in) gauge of the first railways became 4 ft 8½ in. In southern Germany there was a similar early abandonment of broad gauge. In Spain a Royal Order of 1844 established six Castillian feet as the standard (this was 1.672 metres, a little less than the 1.676 metres of the 5 ft 6 in gauge chosen by British engineers for India and elsewhere). Although this did not prevent Spain's second railway, a mineral line, adopting 4 ft 8½ in, the Spanish main lines, as well as those of Portugal, were built to the 5 ft 6 in standard. In Russia the first railway was 1.814 m (6 ft), but the second, from Warsaw to the Austrian frontier, was 4 ft 8½ in so that it could connect with an Austrian railway. For the third line, the standard-setting St Petersburg to Moscow Railway, Tsar Nicholas I was persuaded by his American adviser Whistler that 5 ft would be enough, and 5 ft (1,524 m) thereby became the Russian standard. The Canadian government withdrew its approval of the 5 ft 6 in gauge in 1870. In the USA there was a great diversity of gauge in the early years, as there was little coordination, or expected coordination, between the railways of different states. Because the South Carolina Railroad was of 5 ft gauge, this became the standard of most lines in the South until 1886. The Camden & Amboy chose 1.473 m (4 ft 10 in) and this for decades was the standard for New Jersey and for Ohio; some railroads built freight cars with wide wheel treads, the so-called compromise cars, which could run on both standard and 4 ft 10 in tracks. The world's first international railway, from Portland, Maine, to Montreal, Canada, chose 5 ft 6 in, and the Erie Railroad opted for 6 ft. From 1865 to 1871 the 6 ft gauge of the Erie formed part of a group of lines offering carriage from New York to St Louis by what they proudly advertised as 'The Great Broad Gauge Route'. In 1871 there were 23 different gauges in the USA (the twenty-fourth and widest appeared on an Oregon lumber railroad in the 1880s; this was 2.44 m, or 8 ft). The first transcontinental line was intended to be 5 ft, but the final bill that authorized its construction specified 4 ft 8½ in. This bill was something of a milestone towards eventual gauge standardization, a goal seen to be increasingly urgent as the different states were tied into one great economic system. By 1887 all the important broad-gauge lines had changed to standard gauge.

It might have been expected that the British, having had such early experience of different gauges and their problems, would have avoided similar difficulties in their later railway building. To some extent they did, because narrow-gauge lines never took a great hold in Britain; the Light Railways Act of 1896 allowed local railways to economize not by choosing a narrower gauge, but by adopting lower technical standards in conjunction with a low speed limit and other regulations. However, when the British built railways overseas they usually became entangled in gauge difficulties. For example, they built the first railway in South Africa to 4 ft 8½ in gauge but, when this reached the mountains, their engineers decided that 762 mm (2 ft 6 in) would be better; from the resulting political and technical debate emerged the compromise 1.067 m (3 ft 6 in) which became the standard in British Africa. In South America, the railways built by the British in the Argentine were marked by a diversity of gauges which still persists. In Australia they made a great effort to standardize the gauges when Victoria, New South Wales, and South Australia began to build railways at about the same time. But owing to an unfortunate difference of opinion involving an Irishman, a Scotsman, and an Englishman, these good intentions came to naught, and subsequent generations of Australians found that to travel from Brisbane to Perth involved travel by 3 ft 6 in gauge trains in Queensland and Western Australia, by 5 ft 3 in in Victoria and South Australia, and by 4 ft 8½ in in New South Wales and across the desert.

When the first Indian railways were planned the governor-general was Lord Dalhousie, who earlier had played a prominent part, with Gladstone, in regulating the British railways of the 1840s. Dalhousie emphatically forbade the existence of more than one gauge in India, and 5 ft 6 in was chosen. But in the last decades of the century, long after Dalhousie had left, new Indian gauges appeared. Because so many areas needed railways, especially for averting local famines, and because such areas were too poor to warrant broad-gauge lines, it was decided to establish a secondary network of cheaper metre-gauge lines. At first it was not intended that these should be other than short lines, but soon metre-gauge main lines appeared. By the time the British left in 1947 there was as much metre-gauge mileage as broad-gauge. Not only this, but the success of the metre gauge had opened the way for even smaller gauges of 610 mm (2 ft) and 762 mm (2 ft 6 in).

What happened in India was really only a repetition of what was happening elsewhere. In the second half of the nineteenth century those countries which had more than one gauge were either acting, or discussing how to act, in order to establish a single uniform gauge. But in those parts of the world that had hitherto been blessed with a single gauge, various interests were promoting the introduction of a second gauge which, in one way or another, was claimed to be more suitable for certain purposes. The success of the 600 mm (1 ft 11½ in) gauge Festiniog Railway in Wales after it introduced steam traction in 1863 was an inspiration for proponents of narrower gauges. Many foreign officials visited it, among them a delegation from Russia which on its return recommended the adoption of a second, narrower, standard gauge. Russian narrow-gauge lines duly appeared in the 1870s; at first they were 3 ft 6 in, but eventually 750 mm (2 ft 5½ in) predominated. By 1913 there were 2,900 km (1,800 miles) of them. They had been built to narrow gauge mainly to economize, and when a few of them developed a heavy traffic there was not always enough money to convert them entirely to 5 ft gauge. Thus the narrow-gauge line to Archangel, only six years after its completion in 1899, was being converted to mixed gauge in order that its narrow-gauge locomotives might haul broad-gauge trains.

A similar process took place in western Europe. Local metre-gauge lines, independent of the big companies, were encouraged by the French government. Portugal built metre-gauge lines, especially up rural valleys but including some heavy-traffic lines

around Oporto. In Germany narrow-gauge railways were largely of 750 mm and metre gauge. By 1909 there were 2,200 km (1,340 miles) of such lines in a total network of 60,000 km (36,500 miles). Both in Germany and France such lines had little pretence to main-line status, although some networks were quite extensive. In Belgium, a separate state company was set up, the National Company for Local Railways (SNCV), whose shareholders were largely the central and local governments. This company built and operated an extensive and continuous network of metre-gauge light railways, built very often along the roads and totalling 3,200 km (1,950 miles) by 1908. In Switzerland a multitude of metre-gauge railways were built, usually promoted or financed by towns or cantons requiring services that the main-line companies would not provide. These lines varied from rack railways climbing to mountain tops for the tourist trade, to quite sizeable systems like the Rhaetian Railway; this line, beginning as an 8-mile railway initiated by the town of Davos, grew to a 410 km (250 mile) electrified system serving the winter resorts of eastern Switzerland.

State and private railways After a referendum, the main Swiss railways were nationalized in 1902. The new Swiss Federal Railways, however, did not embrace all the Swiss railways. Others were absorbed later while many, like the Rhaetian Railway, still remain outside the state system. The question of state versus private ownership of railways had been raised in almost every railway-building country at one stage or another, and in the half-century preceding World War I it became a hot issue in many countries. There were a number of good arguments for taking a vital public service into public ownership and control, but in this period Britain and the USA remained staunchly on the side of private enterprise, even though one of America's greatest railroads, the Pennsylvania, had its origins in a line built by the State of Pennsylvania. But in continental Europe many governments at an early stage had been obliged to build, or to take over, railways when the task of constructing them had proved to be beyond the means of private companies.

In France the railway companies after 1870 were held in low esteem. The war against Prussia had been lost partly because the Prussian army made better use of railways, and this misfortune was laid at the door of the railways rather than of the French army. Railway rates were a constant source of complaint by constituents to deputies of the parliament. When the Paris–Orléans Railway asked for a government guarantee of interest if it took over the running of some unprofitable secondary lines in the southwest, the chambers refused, and the state itself took over 2,600 km (1,580 miles) of lines in the west and south-west. This Etat railway became a system lying in the Bordeaux–Nantes–Tours triangle, with access to Paris by running powers over the Paris–Orléans and Ouest companies. Meanwhile the chambers had enthusiastically voted for 8,800 km (5,350 miles) of new line to be added to the 1870 network, and most of the new lines became the responsibility of the state, since few companies were willing to risk their capital on them. This was a crippling burden on state finances, and in 1883 there was an agreement by which the companies took over most of the state secondary lines, with the companies retaining the right to receive government money in years in which revenue was insufficient to cover dividends. By 1905 only the Ouest was still making use of that government guarantee, and it was bought up by the state and incorporated into an enlarged Etat system. Thus when the war came the French mainline railways were divided into the Est, Nord, Paris–Lyons–Méditerranée, Paris–Orléans, and Midi private companies, and the Etat state-owned company.

In Belgium there had been much French capital invested in private railways, and the threat to the country's neutrality during the Franco-Prussian War raised doubts in Belgian minds about the wisdom of having so many railways in foreign hands (a similar argument would be used in Japan after the war of 1904–5, culminating in the nationalization of Japanese Railways). Belgium thereupon began a gradual process of buying out the companies, and adding their mileage to the State Railways. The latter began to show the kind of commercial enterprise that many did not expect to see from a state corporation. In particular, its rewarding experiments with cheap passenger fares were studied by other railway administrations, and sometimes copied.

Bismarck would have preferred to nationalize the railways of the new German Empire, but in that Empire there were powerful states apart from Prussia. Bavaria, especially, wished to preserve its independent railway system. However, the Prussian State Railway grew with the incorporation of Hanover, Hesse, and Nassau, and with the acquisition by conquest of the Alsace–Lorraine Railways. Its head office in Berlin was almost next door to the new Imperial Railway Office, which had been established to coordinate the railways of the Empire. In Prussia, moreover, Bismarck was able to take over most of the remaining private lines. By 1914 the Prussian State Railway owned about two-thirds of the Empire's network, and could usually get its preferred policies adopted by the remaining one-third. Of the other imperial railway systems, that of Russia veered between state and private ownership according to the availability of capital; at one point the government even sold Alaska and its St Petersburg to Moscow Railway in order to raise money for more state lines. By 1914 most of the Russian private railways had been taken over by the state. In Austria, the great reorganization would take place after the war. In the meantime the Austrian State Railway, privately owned by mainly French interests, continued to dominate, except in Hungary, where its lines were nationalized. In Italy, as in Hungary, railway nationalization was largely a nationalistic gesture and brought no real benefits. It began in the 1860s and continued sporadically into the late 1880s. But since the state railways were so obviously inefficient they were handed back to new companies (for operation, not for ownership) before being renationalized in 1905; it was in that year that the Italian State Railway (FS) was established.

Transcontinental travel The successful completion of America's first transcontinental railway soon inspired other projects. Several more lines would span America within a few decades. Among them were the Northern Pacific and the Great Northern to Seattle, the Southern Pacific's line from New Orleans to Los Angeles and, a latecomer, the Chicago, St Paul and Milwaukee's 2,300 km (1,385 mile) extension to Seattle. The latter line was undertaken simply for competitive reasons; the Milwaukee Railroad felt it was in danger of being squeezed out of business by the James Hill combination of the GN and NP, which naturally routed their western traffic over the Milwaukee's rival the Burlington Railroad (also a Hill line). Thanks to modern construction methods, the new line was completed in three years, and opened in 1909. By 1916 710 km (438 miles) of it had been electrified. But this line never paid; there were too many lines between the Midwest and Seattle, and the opening of the Milwaukee route coincided too closely with the opening of the Panama Canal, which took freight traffic from all the transcontinentals.

Perhaps the most ambitious transcontinental project was that for the Canadian Pacific Railway. Even more than the first US transcontinental, this line had major political objectives. At the time it was by no means certain that British Columbia would remain in the British Empire; it was isolated from the rest of Canada and close, geographically and commercially, to the north-western states of the USA. The confederation of the Canadian colonies was seen as a way to retain British Columbia, and a railway from the older colonies of Ontario and Quebec to the Pacific was part of the price which British Columbia exacted for joining the new federation. It was a very difficult line to build, for not only were the Rockies an obstacle but there was also the swamp and muskeg territory around Lake Superior to be conquered. The project nearly failed through crises of confidence and of finance, but it had strong political support in London and Canada, financial backing from the rich Hudson's Bay Company, and the dauntless American contractor, Van Horne. The line was completed in November 1885 and the first through train to the Pacific left Montreal in July 1886 and arrived 139 hours later.

Two decades later another Dominion-binding transcontinental was opened; this was the Trans-Australian Railway, begun in 1913 and finished in 1917. Built largely across featureless and waterless terrain this 1,700 km (1,051 mile) standard-gauge line linked the railways of the isolated state of Western Australia with those of the eastern states.

The Canadian Pacific inspired the Russian government to build its Trans-Siberian line. This aimed to develop the economy of Siberia, to support a Russian fleet on the Pacific, and to extend Russian commercial and political influence in China. Part of it, the Chinese Eastern Railway, passed over Chinese territory, where it soon sprouted a branch line to Port Arthur, the South Manchurian Railway, whose purpose was frankly military and expansionist. It is hardly surprising that the completion of the Trans-Siberian route coincided with the Russo-Japanese War, which resulted in Russia losing the South Manchurian Railway. The Chinese Eastern Railway was by no means the only new line with expansionist motives. The never-to-be-completed Cape to Cairo project was to provide an all-British route from top to bottom of Africa; and the German-financed Baghdad Railway from Turkey to the Persian Gulf was regarded as a threat to British influence in that sensitive region.

The new transcontinentals regaled their wealthiest passengers with trains of great luxury, at the same time providing trains of great austerity but tempting cheapness for immigrants. The Trans-Siberian Express, though slow, had a lounge car complete with piano, and a bathroom with a marble-tiled shower. In the 1920s the thrice-weekly Trans-Australian train between Port Augusta and Kalgoorlie also provided a piano, even though the journey took only 37½ hours compared to the nine days of the Moscow-Vladivostok journey. The US transcontinental lines relied on Pullman to provide fitting accommodation for sleeping, dining, and lounging passengers, and were not disappointed.

In Europe Pullman was emulated by a Belgian, Nagelmaekers, who on a visit to the USA had been impressed by Pullman cars and in 1869 endeavoured to start a similar service in Europe. Although Belgian railways were sympathetic, most of the other Continental systems at first were not. After a number of false starts and failures he eventually scored a great success with his Paris–Vienna service, and this was the real beginning for his *Compagnie Internationale de Wagons-Lits*. He not only provided in his cars luxurious sitting, sleeping, and dining accommodation, but also arranged for the traditionally tedious frontier document and baggage examinations to be carried out on board the moving train. Like Pullman, he provided the cars and expected the railway companies to haul them; the railways received the first-class fares while Nagelmaekers' Wagons-Lits received the passengers' supplementary fares. In 1883, after lengthy negotiations between Nagelmaekers and seven railway companies, the first of 'The Great International Trains' began to run; this was the Orient Express, providing a service between Paris, central Europe, and Turkey. It captured the public imagination, brought in profits at least for the Wagons-Lits company, and was followed by many other similar trains, including the Trans-Siberian Express. In the meantime, all over the developed world, railways were operating faster and more comfortable trains. In America, competition for the New York–Chicago traffic resulted in the Pennsylvania and the New York Central railroads introducing amid great publicity a series of fast luxury trains, culminating in the Broadway Limited and the Twentieth Century Limited; in 1914 these covered the distance in 20 hours, requiring an average speed of 77 km/h (48 mph) from the Twentieth Century Limited. In Britain the 'Races to the North' of 1888 and 1895, in which two rival associations of railways, making up respectively the West Coast and the East Coast routes to Scotland, tried to outpace each other, gave way to a more sedate competition. But in 1914 the Great Western Railway could offer two 95 km/h (59 mph) services from London to Bath (174 km, or 107 miles), and the North Eastern had a train covering 71 km (44 miles) in 43 minutes.

Locomotive development Although by 1860 the layout of the classic Stephensonian steam locomotive was already established, this did not mean that locomotive technology remained static. Apart from the introduction of larger and more powerful machines, there was a qualitative improvement, as well as a growing divergence between the locomotive styles of different countries. As a rough generalization, the period from 1875 to 1914 was marked in America by a quest for ever more haulage capacity whereas in western Europe it was the question of improved thermal efficiency that was uppermost.

The steam locomotive gave back in the form of useful work only five to seven per cent of the potential energy of the fuel it consumed. One cause of this inefficiency was premature condensation of the steam in the cylinders, and inventive designers tackled this problem in two ways. Some tried to find a workable compound system, while others tried to find a way to increase the temperature of the steam (that is, to superheat it) so that even with heat losses in the cylinder it would still be too hot to condense. With compounding, the steam was first led into one, or two, high-pressure cylinders and then, having expanded to work the high-pressure pistons, was passed to one, or two, low-pressure cylinders where its remaining pressure was utilized to drive another set of pistons. Expanding the steam in these two stages reduced the temperature drop in each cylinder and greatly reduced the total amount of condensation. In the two-cylinder compound system, developed largely by the Prussian engineer von Borries, there was one large cylinder for the low-pressure steam and one smaller one for the high-pressure. A system developed in France by du Bousquet of the Nord Railway and de Glehn of the Alsacienne Works comprised two high-pressure cylinders outside the frames and two larger low-pressure cylinders between them. This was probably one of the most successful systems, although the three-cylinder layout, with a central high-pressure cylinder and two low-pressure cylinders outside, also had its champions; Sauvage of the Nord Railway and Smith of the North Eastern Railway were the men most responsible for developing this. Compounding did seem to bring the benefits of improved efficiency, perhaps adding one or two per cent to the steam locomotive's overall thermal efficiency. On the other hand it was a complex system, which added to the capital and maintenance costs of the locomotive, and which ideally required highly trained locomotive men. Possibly because of the latter factor, it was France which made the greatest success of compounding.

Superheating, which had been attempted by several engineers, became a real success after the German Wilhelm Schmidt ('Hot-Steam Willy' to his friends) had devised his firetube superheater. In this, steam from the boiler, instead of going direct to the cylinders, was taken through small pipes inside tubes carrying some of the hot gases from the firebox to the chimney. In this way it received a final input of heat, raising it to a very high temperature. Superheating, because of its simplicity and genuine benefit, was soon applied to almost all of the larger locomotives. In a sense it was a cheap substitute for compounding, although experiments showed that the most efficient use of steam was achieved in locomotives that used compounding as well as superheating.

One of the pioneers of compounding had been the Swiss engineer Mallet. In order to make the compound idea attractive he designed what would later be known as the Mallet locomotive. This was an articulated machine in which there were two cylinder-and-driving-wheel units. The leading unit, under the front of the boiler, was pivoted and could accommodate itself to curves independently of the rear unit, which supported the rear of the engine. This arrangement permitted the use of very long, heavy, and powerful locomotives; that is, it was just what many American railroads had been looking for. It was not long before the Mallet locomotive,

By most parameters the biggest steam locomotives ever built were the American 'Big Boy', Mallet units built for the Union Pacific Railroad, which used them for fast heavy freight haulage in the foothills of the Rockies.

either compound or non-compound, became the favourite American type for the heaviest freight haulage.

An alternative to the Mallet was devised by the British engineer Herbert Garratt. Garratt worked on railways in various parts of the world before returning to Britain with his idea for a new type of locomotive. This had the boiler supported at each of its extremities by two pivoting engine-and-wheel units, making a very long and flexible locomotive which spread its weight over a sizable length of track, and it could run at good speed over curves. It was ideal for cheaply built lines with a heavy traffic, and became a great favourite of railways in the British Commonwealth, especially in Africa. It was manufactured mainly by the firm of Beyer, Peacock and therefore became known as the Beyer-Garratt type.

Some influential locomotives were designed for the Great Western Railway in Britain by George Churchward, who skilfully combined features of Continental and American practice into designs which really did represent the best of both worlds. From America he took the tapered boiler, more efficient although marginally more expensive, and the casting of one outside cylinder and one half of the smokebox saddle in one piece, so arranged that the cylinders could be removed without first removing the boiler. From the Continent he took the Belgian Belpaire boiler (already used by some British designers) but improved it with wider water spaces and strong well-rounded corners, and from France he took the bogie design and the cylinder layout favoured by the French team of de Glehn and du Bousquet. Most important of all, Churchward provided wide steam passages, and significantly reduced energy losses by so doing.

After Churchward, probably the most individualistic designer was Gölsdorf of the Austrian State Railways. He was an adherent of compounding, but his engines were also remarkable for their gaunt appearance and for the way in which their designer solved the problems of providing powerful engines for mountainous main lines with difficult curves and axle-weight restrictions as low as 14 tons. He used very thin frames to save weight and to give a certain flexibility, and preferred to use rolled steel plates, often perforated, for purposes which in other countries would be served by cast steel. He avoided four-wheel trucks at the front because they added too much weight, but was often forced to use these constructions at the rear, to support large fireboxes intended to burn low-grade coal. His death in 1916 closely coincided with the end of the Austrian Empire, and his influence therefore lived on not only in Austria, but in Czechoslovakia, Hungary, Romania, and to some extent in Poland.

Braking systems Although the increasing comfort of passenger vehicles was perhaps the most noticeable improvement in rolling-stock design in the half century before 1914, the more fundamental changes concerned safety in operation. In particular, the period was marked by the advent of reliable braking systems and of safer couplings. The USA led the world in both these fields, possibly because the USA had the most alarming accident rate. On average, in America in the 1850s, the railways killed one passenger in every 200,000, compared to one in 1,700,000 in France and one in 6,680,000 in Britain. What railways the world over needed above all was a brake that could be operated from the locomotive yet act all down the length of a train (that is, a 'continuous' brake), and that would apply itself automatically in case of failure, especially after a train had split in two. There were a number of brake systems in existence but none of these quite met the need for an automatic and continuous brake, and in any case they were only applied to passenger trains. Freight trains had hand brakes; in the USA these were applied by brakemen running along the roofs of the cars and screwing down the brake handles. In Britain and elsewhere there were brake levers operated from ground level; before descending a steep gradient a train had to be halted for its brakes to be pinned down. For stopping a freight train in motion there were only the locomotive brakes and the brakes operated by the train's guard in the rear brakevan. Naturally enough, with such inadequate brake power fatal runaways were common. The American George Westinghouse produced his automatic brake in 1872. This used compressed air supplied by a steam pump on the locomotive. All the vehicles had compressed-air reservoirs which applied pressure in the brake cylinders to keep the brakes off. Brake applications were made by releasing this pressure, which meant that in the case of a train breakage the broken air pipe would allow pressure to drop and thereby stop both halves of the train. By 1885 nearly all American passenger trains used this brake, but with long freight trains the brakes at the rear tended to come on much later than those near the locomotive. However, in 1887 Westinghouse had alleviated this latter defect.

Train couplings on most US railroads were of the link-and-pin type, in which a man had to stand between the two vehicles as they met and drop the pin in the coupling at precisely the right moment. Many fingers, arms, and lives were lost in this process until in 1863 Ezra Miller invented the Miller Hook, which enabled cars to couple automatically by engaging movable coupling hooks. However, this device was only suitable for passenger cars. But in 1868 Major Janney invented the Janney coupler, the forerunner of most automatic coupling systems, which was a central movable-jaw coupler robust enough to take both the tractive pull and also the buffing stresses. This 'buckeye' coupler was followed by a marginally improved version, the Willison coupler, in which instead of the movable jaws of the Janney an arrangement of fixed jaws with movable locking jaws was used. It has been calculated that in the 1880s there were almost 40 different types of coupler used in the USA, and a large number of braking systems. The existence of good systems did not guarantee that all companies would use them, especially in view of the high cost of installation. It was only in 1893 that the American railways agreed to standardize the Westinghouse brake and buckeye coupler, and then only because the federal Interstate Commerce Commission, which was already closely supervising railroad behaviour, secured the passage of the Railroad Safety Appliance Act which enforced this standardization. In Europe, Westinghouse brakes (or in some countries, especially Britain, the new automatic vacuum brake) were introduced in due course, but not always full-heartedly. The British railways were especially casual in their approach, and for their freight cars continued both with archaic chain couplings and hand brakes. Even with passenger vehicles, some British lines showed scant regard for safety. The aggressive management of the London & North Western Railway was particularly nefarious in this regard. The chief mechanical engineer of this company was drawing good patent royalties from the somewhat mediocre brake designs he had devised for his vehicles, and was accordingly reluctant to introduce the Westinghouse system. Only when the British government compelled them did some British companies fit continuous automatic brakes to their passenger stock. However, British lines did adopt the buckeye coupler for certain of their passenger trains, and because it was strong it often held a train together in derailments. In western Europe automatic couplers for freight work were not fitted, partly because the existing screw coupler, though time-consuming, was otherwise very satisfactory, and partly because, with vehicles being constantly interchanged over frontiers, it would have been necessary to obtain the agreement of all the western European railways to make the change at the same time. The Willison coupler, however, was adopted by a few of the world's railways, including those of the USSR.

Freight cars everywhere became larger during this period. The standard American vehicle was the eight-wheel box-car destined to be built right up to the present in steadily increasing sizes, and used for traffic that in Europe would often have been carried in specialized cars. However, in one specialized field America did lead the way. This was the use of refrigerator cars. Although milk had been carried into New York in primitive ice-packed cars as early as the 1840s, it was really the Chicago meat-packer Swift who developed this technique. Sending cattle to the eastern markets on the hoof resulted in loss of weight, so the concept of slaughtering animals in Chicago and packing the meat in refrigerator cars had obvious attractions. The success of this venture soon led to imitation by the fruit growers of California and elsewhere, and it was not long before trains of refrigerator cars (owned not by the railroads but by specialized companies) were plying over US railroads. In later years a feature of these trains was that they left the fruit-growing areas with no fixed destination; only as they approached the eastern cities did their operators specify a destination in accord with the current pattern of demand for fruit. Outside the USA a somewhat similar fruit-hauling operation was soon organized to take Spanish fruit to northern destinations; in due course these refrigerator trains were fitted with vehicles whose gauge could be changed en route from the Spanish 5 ft 6 in to the standard European gauge.

Safety Many railways did not appear to place safety at the top of their priorities. From time to time important advances in signalling were devised, applied by some companies, but ignored by others until a bad accident or government intervention (and often the one followed by the other) caused them to change their mind. In the last decades of the nineteenth century railway safety improvement generally took the form of widespread application of advances first made in earlier decades.

The first serious railway accident occurred just six weeks after the Battle of Waterloo; this was a boiler explosion in Britain, a type of mishap quite frequent during the early decades of the steam locomotive, even after most governments had established their own boiler inspectorate. However, the most frequent serious accident was collision, and in time a complex system of devices was brought into use for the control of train movements. On the first railways train movements were regulated by 'policemen', who would require a time interval between successive trains, using sand-glasses to measure the interval and hand signals to instruct locomotive crews. But this did not prevent rear-end collisions if, for some reason, a train broke down en route; what was needed was a space interval, not a time interval. Such a space interval became possible with the telegraph, first used by Britain's Great Western Railway in 1839. With this it was possible to report back down the line when a train had cleared the intervening section of track. This was the origin of the block system, later applied almost universally on double-track routes, whose principle was that no train could enter a given section between two control points (usually stations or signal cabins) until the previous train had cleared it. British companies often seemed somewhat reluctant to introduce the telegraph for this purpose, but changed their minds when they discovered that they could make good money by offering a public telegraph service at the same time. Meanwhile the railway policeman had been replaced by various types of mechanical signal operated from the control points. In Britain and many other countries the semaphore signal became popular, thanks to its good visibility and simplicity. France was one of a number of countries that favoured discs and boards in addition. There developed a divergence between countries like Britain and Germany, whose signals were so arranged as to indicate at junctions the route for which points and switches had been set, and countries like France

where, instead, the signals gave an indication of the maximum speed limit, corresponding to the route that had been set up.

In America, long double-track sections were infrequent, and before the telegraph came traffic moved according to strict schedules which stated where opposing trains would cross. But if one train was late the crew of the opposing train sometimes decided to push on to the next crossing station; indeed they had no way of knowing whether their opposite number was merely delayed, or completely broken down and cancelled. In these conditions horrifying head-on collisions, known popularly as 'cornfield meets', did happen. Only after Samuel Morse had devised his version of the telegraph could the American lines reorganize their train control. Dispatchers, equipped with telegraph machines, were housed in offices at passing stations and could hand written orders to the crews of trains whose original instructions needed to be changed.

It was often a bad accident that persuaded companies that new procedures were needed. In France, an 1842 collision on the Paris to Versailles line at Meudon, which was followed by a fire and the incineration of many passengers including the famous Admiral Dumont d'Urville, persuaded the French railways that locking passengers into their compartments between stations, a practice regarded as a safety measure, was not so very safe after all. The introduction of the block system to America came in 1865 after a very lethal rear-end collision of two troop trains in New Jersey. In 1874 a fatal collision of two British trains at Norwich made it clear that the telegraph alone was not a foolproof safeguard on single track, and four years later Tyer introduced

An early diesel-electric locomotive design. Six of these 450 hp units were built for the Royal Thailand State Railway by Sulzer of Switzerland in 1931. Of metre gauge, these machines worked well for many years in a country which, being without coal, was one of the first to try diesel traction in mainline service.

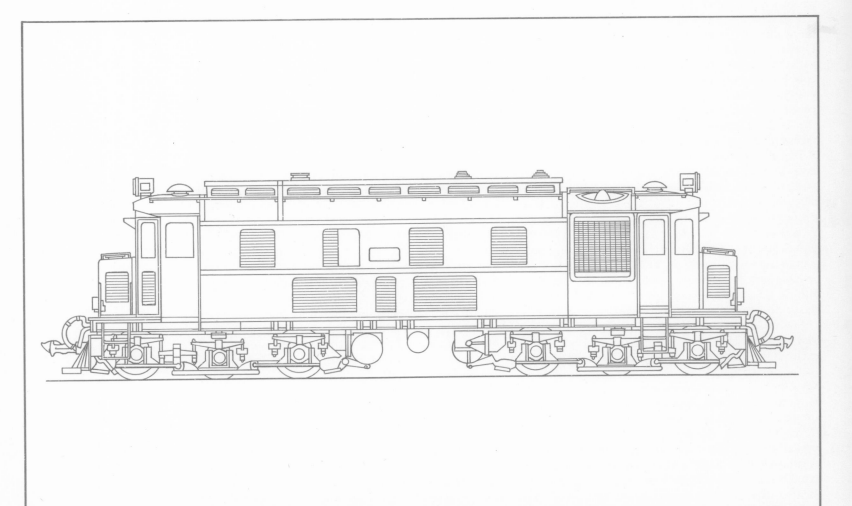

his electric token machines. Tokens were a locoman's authority to proceed on a single-track section, and Tyer's machine ensured that only one token could be in use at any given time. A frequent cause of accident, the setting of signals to give clearance to two conflicting trains at the same time, as well as the setting of signals in conflict with the setting of points and switches, began to be eliminated by mechanical interlocking machines. These prevented signals being cleared until conflicting signals and switches were set in agreement. The first such interlocking gear seems to have been that at Bricklayer's Arms, near London, in 1856. This was designed by Saxby, who became one of the world's best-known names in train signalling apparatus. In 1889 the Regulation of Railways Act made interlocking compulsory on British main lines. An advance made in America was the use of compressed air in interlocked signal and switch control. This first appeared in 1890, and similar pneumatic interlocking was soon adopted in Britain after a delegation from the London & South Western Railway had made a visit to the USA and been impressed by this apparatus. Electric track circuiting, which indicates the presence of a train in a given block section, was also in use on a few lines by the end of the century. With power signalling (pneumatic was followed by electric operation) and track circuiting, it was a short step to automatic forms of train control, notably automatic signals and automatic train control ('cab signalling'). Automatic train control, as it emerged from the experimental stage in America and Europe, applied a train's brakes automatically when the signals were set against it, if its driver had neglected to do so, and gave an indication in the locomotive cab of the signal's aspect. This was not only intended to eliminate the very occasional but sometimes very lethal accidents caused by the misreading of signals, but also to permit near-normal speeds in foggy weather. Perhaps this was why the Great Western Railway in Britain was one of the most advanced in this technique. Automatic signalling, in which the trains themselves actuate the signals, was also available at the end of the century; one of the first lines to use it was the Budapest underground railway opened in 1896.

Different countries were individualistic in their signalling arrangements. Semaphore signals could be of various shapes, positions, and colours, and many railways, as in France, liked to use rotating discs, diamonds, checkerboards and other indicators. Many countries continued to use white as the all-clear light long after Britain and other countries had changed to green. In central Europe, signals were more rarely encountered; the custodian of the clock telegraph at a station would stand on the platform as an indication to a passing train that all was well, a practice that has still not quite disappeared. But despite individualism in choice of indicators, good ideas spread fast. Taking one country as an example, Italy installed its first Saxby interlocking frame in 1874, and this was quickly followed by others. But Italian railways seem to have been first to use yellow as a colour indicating caution, and also made early use of the telegraph and telephone. The first use of the latter in signalling was probably the 1882 connection between the Turin stationmaster and a nearby Saxby signal cabin.

One of two diesel-electric locomotives built in England by Armstrong-Whitworth for the North Western Railway of India in 1935. Each unit weighed 113 tons and could develop 1,300 hp. They were designed to haul 600 tons at 96 kph (60 mph) on the level, their anticipated duty being the haulage of the daily mail train across the Sind Desert.

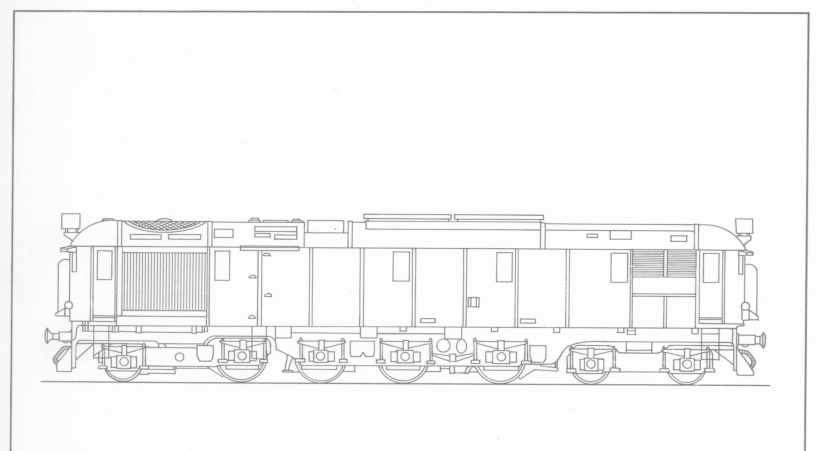

Diesel traction

Diesel traction It was in the inter-war years that diesel traction, which had been tried tentatively before 1914, was developed so successfully that it promised to displace the steam locomotive entirely. Development took place in several directions and for two motives, the wish to economize on working expenses, and the quest for more traffic. The need to attract traffic was, it seemed, possible of satisfaction in the passenger field by providing eye-catching streamlined diesel trains over main lines and by substituting diesel railcar services for conventional steam trains on secondary services. Railcars were also cheaper to operate and for this reason were often used by impecunious short lines and light railways. In freight haulage the diesel was slower to win adherents, except in yard work, where it began to appear in the early 1920s. In general, adoption of diesel traction was slow, and was further retarded by the outbreak of World War II. It was not suffi-cient to show that the diesel was merely a little better than the steam locomotive; railway companies were short of capital and in any case disinclined to make radical changes. They realized that to operate both diesel and steam locomotive fleets simultaneously would be wasteful, and could see that the benefits of dieselization were not so overwhelming as to warrant a wholesale abandonment of steam traction. The diesel locomotive, especially in its early stages, faced serious technical difficulties, the most important being the never entirely satisfactory conversion of the engines' high-speed revolutions to the range of relatively low rotation speeds required from the wheels.

The first successful diesel locomotive was probably that built by the British firm of Hornsby & Company in 1896. This firm, as Ruston & Hornsby, subsequently made a great success of small diesel locomotives. Its 1896 design, using an engine that

Soviet Railways pioneered the use of mainline diesel traction, and in the 1920s several Russian-designed prototypes were built in Germany for the USSR, using German components. This freight locomotive was built in 1926 by Hohenzollern, incorporating a MAN diesel and Krupp gearing. Transmission was mechanical, through gearing and jackshaft, and 1,200 hp was the designed power output.

was not quite the same as that developed by Dr Diesel, had a mechanical transmission. Soon afterwards a number of manufacturers began to apply petrol engines ('gas engines' in the USA). The gas-engined railcar supplied by the McKeen Company was bought by many railroads in the USA, seeking cheaper means than the conventional steam-hauled trains for serving lightly loaded lines. However, the McKeen railcar, as well as General Electric's railcar, which also appeared before World War I, lacked a good transmission system. The General Electric design, it is true, was advanced in that it was a petrol-electric, thereby anticipating the later diesel-electric, but like the McKeen car its transmission was unreliable. General Electric also built, in 1913, four petrol-electric locomotives for the Dan Patch Lines; these were of 350 hp and ran on four-wheel trucks. In France at about the same time there were built some Westinghouse petrol-electric railcars which were used, with mixed results, by a few minor railways. The petrol-mechanical railcars supplied by a British firm to India had a new type of gearbox and were relatively successful. Most promising of all were some railcars and small locomotives built in Sweden. In particular, a small railcar using a diesel engine and electric transmission, supplied to Swedish State Railways in 1912, gave good results. However, it should be noted that the relatively superior results obtained from the European designs do not necessarily mean that the American designs were inferior; American steam locomotives had always received rougher treatment and poorer maintenance, and this was a tradition that had its effect both on the early results and the subsequent design of US diesel equipment.

The Swedish locomotive, like diesel locomotives subsequently, was assembled by the builder from components which to a large extent were made elsewhere; in this particular case the Swedish ASEA firm supplied the electrical equipment (generator and motor) and the German firm of Atlas supplied the diesel engine which drove the generator. With subsequent diesel-electric locomotives, wherever they were built, it was typically a combination of three firms that was involved: the locomotive manufacturer, who made the chassis and body, an electrical-engineering enterprise, and a diesel engine manufacturer.

During World War I there was a requirement for narrow-gauge trench railway locomotives which would not give away their position by smoke. The result was that a number of manufacturers began to build gasoline-engine locomotives and after the war the experience so gained was applied to the construction of small internal-combustion locomotives, generally for industrial use. These were little more than four-wheel trucks carrying a motor that drove the axles either through gears or chains. Some designs also included a cab. A number of US builders offered small switch (shunting) engines that used components from motor trucks. In continental Europe very small yard engines were made by several builders; slow and not very powerful, they were cheap enough to induce some railways to 'issue' a unit to intermediate stations where there was any switching to be done. This practice, which speeds up operations, is still widespread; in the Netherlands, for example, the tiny four-wheel locomotives built by Werkspoor for this service

before the war have been succeeded by locomotives for the same duties that are only marginally more powerful. Generally, such locomotives were of from 50 hp to 100 hp.

Diesel yard locomotives, in which transmission problems were eased by the limited range of speed required, were an obvious line of development. Steam locomotives were never efficient for this work, given the long periods spent idling; the diesel, moreover, could work 23 hours each day and almost seven days a week, having few of the fuelling and servicing requirements of the steam locomotive. A landmark was the production in 1924 of a 60-ton 300 hp yard engine by the American Locomotive Company (Alco), using components supplied by Ingersoll-Rand and General Electric. This type, which externally seemed little more than a box mounted on two four-wheel trucks and with a cab at each end, is regarded as the first full-size diesel locomotive to be commercially successful. The Baltimore & Ohio and the Jersey Central railroads were among those that bought these units, which had a long life. In the early 1930s Alco created the present-day shape of US yard engines, with a cab at one end and a long hood covering the engine compartment. Meanwhile, builders in Britain, France, and Germany were evolving their own versions of the yard locomotive.

In France, however, more attention was accorded the diesel railcar. This was because not only the main-line railways, but also the numerous independent secondary lines, badly needed a cheap-to-operate passenger train for lines where traffic was light. Starting from units which were simply conventional buses mounted on steel flanged wheels, a large variety of types were built, and used with great success. Steam railcars were also tried, but the internal-combustion engine proved to be far superior for this purpose. In Britain, diesel railcars were not widely used, partly because few light railways survived beyond the 1920s. Only the Great Western Railway acquired a fleet of semi-streamlined diesel railcars, which it found very useful. The London & North Eastern Railway preferred to buy a fleet of that British speciality, supplied also to colonial lines, the Sentinel railcar; this used a small high-pressure steam engine and chain drive. However, several British firms exported diesel railcars, particularly to South America and to colonial lines. Other railways, notably the Reichsbahn, also used railcars in secondary service.

Up to the end of the 1920s diesel locomotives for line service were limited to a few semi-experimental units supplied to enterprising railways. These were of the so-called 'box-cab' type, resembling the box-like switching locomotives already in service but possessing more powerful engines and capable of higher speeds. Among them was a fairly successful unit built by Alco and Ingersoll-Rand for the Canadian National Railways in 1927. This was of 1,330 hp, and could do good work despite a variety of teething troubles which revealed themselves in service. The British firm of Armstrong Whitworth built several diesel-electric units for India and the Argentine. The latter's railways were one of the most receptive markets for diesel railway equipment. In addition to the diesel locomotives they also acquired from Britain a pair of high-speed railcars built of steel, aluminium and plywood, and carrying only 20 extra-fare passengers. One Argentinian railway in the 1930s was using in its dense suburban service out of Buenos Aires a fleet of two- and three-unit railcars built by Ganz of Hungary, one of the most successful exporters of this type of equipment. Another, perhaps unexpected, early user of diesel locomotives were the Thailand Royal State Railways, which imported several units from Denmark and Switzerland from 1931 onwards. In Russia, an ambitious dieselization programme was adopted in the 1930s, based on promising experience with German-built diesel locomotives. However, this scheme was premature and virtually abandoned after a few years.

run from Denver to Chicago (1,640 km or 1,015 miles) the *Zephyr* averaged 120 km/h (77.6 mph), an unprecedented speed over such a long distance. This run, and the publicity surrounding it, assured a promising future for the high-speed diesel train. Meanwhile the Union Pacific's M-10000 had entered service. This was like the *Zephyr*, although the external styling was different and the engine burned distillate rather than diesel oil. The UP soon ordered a bigger version, the M-10001, with a diesel engine and consisting of six rather than three articulated cars. This was put on the transcontinental service from Chicago to Portland, reducing the schedule to less than 40 hours, compared to the 60 hours

But it was the advent of the 'streamline era' that gave diesel traction its big chance. Anxious both to improve their public image and to maintain their long-distance passenger business against competing forms of transport, the railways were not slow to introduce streamlined trains as soon as one or two enterprising companies had shown the way. These companies were the Union Pacific and the Burlington railroads, which both ordered streamlined high-speed trains for delivery in 1934. First to be ordered was the *Zephyr* of the Burlington Railroad, a streamlined train of three articulated stainless-steel cars, powered by a 600 hp diesel engine driving, through a generator, electric motors mounted on the trucks. The advent of this train coincided with the Chicago Exhibition, and on a demonstration

of conventional trains; this reduction was due to high running speeds and to that great attraction of the diesel, its ability to run great distances without stops for water or engine-changing. Within months of these Burlington and UP trains coming into service, other US lines decided to obtain their own streamliners. Some of these were like the original pair, others had non-articulated construction so that an entire train need not be put out of action because of a defect in one part of it. A number of railways, too, took an unadventurous path, introducing trains of conventional but vaguely streamlined rolling stock hauled by standard steam locomotives covered in a streamlined cowl. These presumably satisfied the demands of public-relations departments, without actually costing very much.

Aesthetically they varied; some railways employed commercial designers to style their streamliners, others applied their own ideas. A New York Central streamlined steam locomotive was said to resemble an upturned bathtub, and it is unlikely that the streamlining had any appreciable effect in producing more speed from the same power output.

Abroad, the American fashion was soon imitated. The two largest British railway companies introduced streamlined steam locomotives, and so, after exhaustive air-tunnel tests, did the Canadian National Railways. Most of the continental European railways experimented with one or two standard locomotives streamlined in various forms, and all found that except at the very highest speeds streamlining had little benefit and was merely an extra maintenance problem. Nevertheless, in faraway Manchuria the Japanese introduced a streamlined 4-4-4 tank locomotive which no doubt impressed their Manchurian subjects but did little to advance locomotive technology.

However, though streamlined steam locomotives eventually disappeared, the diesel-electric passenger train had come to stay. Its success in America signalled the entry of a new giant firm into the railroad equipment business, for the two streamliners were products of the Electro-Motive Division of General Motors. The Electro-Motive Corporation had originated in 1922 when H. Hamilton started a company to produce passenger railcars which would combine the good features of the old McKeen and General Electric vehicles with a recently improved gasoline engine and lightweight body construction. He was immediately successful, even though he had to subcontract most of the construction work, and by the end of the 1920s he had sold about 500 units to American railroads. His corporation then became part of General Motors, which not only had a new diesel engine with a good power/weight ratio but also the money and experience to make a real commercial success of the new possibilities of diesel traction.

In 1935 General Motors built what was regarded as the first successful single-unit passenger diesel-electric locomotive, which was put into service on the Baltimore & Ohio's *Royal Blue*. The following year General Motors moved its Electro-Motive Division to a new plant at La Grange, Chicago, and soon afterwards brought out a new passenger locomotive of 2,000 hp; the so-called 'A' unit, with a driving cab at one end, supplemented by a 'B' unit, without a cab, so that a 4,000 hp or 6,000 hp locomotive could be created by using two or three units. This multiple-unit facility, the possibility of using any number of units controlled from a single driving position, was one of the great attractions of the new generation of diesel locomotives.

But the big market was for freight locomotives, and American railway managements were reluctant to change from their well-tried and powerful steam locomotives. General Motors, however, with its enormous financial strength, could embark on a demonstration involving its new four-unit 5,400 hp locomotive, running in ordinary service on the large railroads. This locomotive was similar to the passenger locomotive, except that it was shorter (freight locomotives did not need a steam generator for train heating), and ran on four-wheel instead of six-wheel trucks (being geared for lower speeds,

two-axle truck provided sufficient stability). It was an immediate success, giving high outputs at low speeds and thereby dispensing with the use of helper locomotives on steep grades. In 1941 the Santa Fe Railroad bought the first of the General Motors production-line freight diesels and thereby began the process of completely eliminating the steam locomotive on US railroads.

In 1941 Alco, anxious to regain its lead in diesel traction (an aim in which it never quite succeeded), introduced the first road-switcher, a truly general-purpose locomotive of 1,100 hp, unstreamlined aspect, and with a cab near one end suitable for running in either direction. However, this promising idea could not be fully exploited because during World War II Alco was required to concentrate on steam locomotives while General Motors continued to build diesels.

In continental Europe, progress was slower than in America. However, the railcar idea was developed, especially in France and Germany. In France there was some experimentation with rubber-tyred railcars, and the Bugatti high-speed streamlined railcars attracted much attention (the streamlining of the Bugatti cars was imitated in a class of streamlined steam locomotives built in Britain by the London & North Eastern Railway). By early 1938 the SNCF had over 650 railcars at work, accounting for almost one quarter of non-electric passenger-train miles. Some cars had Renault engines of as much as 500 hp, and the speed limit for fast railcars had been raised to 120 km/h (87 mph) following a demonstration run from Paris to Le Mans by a Bugatti railcar during which 195 km/h (120 mph) was attained. At off-peak times fast railcars plied over several main lines, leaving conventional trains to handle the heavy-traffic period of the day. Their use over the transverse lines, not passing through Paris, revolutionized some of the hitherto inconvenient inter-city passenger connections. The Danish State Railways, which had introduced railcars in 1925, had 88 in service at the beginning of 1939, plus eight streamlined diesel-electric trains. The latter, the *Lyntog* ('Lightning trains'), had won great popularity when they were introduced in 1935, and were being multiplied so that passengers could be offered an extra-fast, supplementary-fare, service on all the main routes. In Germany, the birthplace of Dr Diesel, diesel traction had been more developed for naval than for rail use. But there was the *Flying Hamburger*, which broke several world speed records. This was a twin-unit streamlined passenger train equipped with high-speed engines designed by the firm of Maybach and driving the axles through a hydraulic transmission, a mechanism that was to achieve great popularity in Germany. The *Flying Hamburger* was introduced on the Berlin–Hamburg run in 1933, and frequently attained 160 km/h (100 mph) or more. It offered 102 seats, and weighed 77 tons ($\frac{3}{4}$ ton per seat, compared to 2 tons per seat of a conventional train). Its schedule of 138 minutes to cover the 287 km (179 miles) implies an average of 125 km/h (78 mph); the early services over this line, in 1845, had been scheduled at $8\frac{1}{2}$ hours. In Switzerland, where electric traction seemed likely to dominate, the firm of Sulzer continued to develop its range of diesel engines which, built under license, would power many of the diesel locomotives introduced after the war by European builders.

Europe

The Low Countries

Above. A TEE train *(Trans European Express)* soon after leaving Amsterdam.
Overleaf. Electric locomotives in use on Dutch Railways in 1965 lined up in Amsterdam.

The railways of Belgium and Holland, in their inception, subsequent development and physical characteristics are in some contrast. In Belgium, railways were almost from the outset planned as a single state owned national network and grew to such an extent as to become one of the densest systems in the world, reckoned in terms of mileage per square mile of territory served. The State Railways had an interesting history of engineering progress, and two men whose names are household words among steam locomotive men, Egide Walschaerts of radial valve gear fame, and Jules Belpaire, originator of the square topped firebox, were both Belgians. Unlike those of Holland, Belgian railways had some very heavily-graded routes, particularly that running south from Namur into Luxembourg. These conditions bred a race of very large and powerful steam locomotives, while the need to provide rapid commercial service between the packet port of Ostend and Bruxelles made equally severe demands.

Today all the principal main lines are electrified at 3,000 volts dc and Belgium is in the strange position of having on its international frontiers *three* other traction systems, in the 1,500 volts dc of Holland, the 15,000 volts ac of West Germany, and the 25,000 volts ac of France. So far as through working is concerned the transition at the frontiers can, if necessary, be made without stopping, using multi-current loco-

motives as introduced in France. There are now in service Belgian quadri-current electric locomotives of similar design and power capacity to the original French units. On the main line from Antwerp to the north locomotives are changed from Belgian to Dutch or vice-versa at Roosendaal, while the TEE services crossing Belgium from France to Germany are nowadays mostly of the diesel multiple-unit type, with power units at each end.

The Luxembourg line is in a class by itself in the severity of its gradients, and recently some very powerful electric locomotives of the C-C wheel arrangement have been introduced. These are designed for operation only on 3,000 volts dc. They weigh 110 tons, and are of 7,000 horsepower. The Luxembourg is of necessity not a high-speed route but these new locomotives have a maximum authorised speed of 217 kph (135 mph). This relates to their own machinery rather than the possibilities of the route. They are of striking appearance. finished in the standard green livery relieved by longitudinal white bands. With the pointed shape at each end these bands have the effect of accentuating the great length of these locomotives—actually 23.5 m (77 ft) over buffers.

In the level, often waterlogged country of Holland a number of independent, yet closely interlinked railway companies grew up, each with its own marked individual characteristics of locomotive and coach

liveries, and proud traditions. The nature of the land set some great problems for the civil engineers, in carrying their lines on soft and often unstable ground, and crossing the many canals. Most of these were crossed at low level, and bridges with lifting or opening spans had to be devised, so that when opened there was clearance for the masts of ships. Most of the nineteenth century locomotives were of British build, and the gay colours reflected British railway traditions at that time. One saw grass green locomotives on the State Railway, embellished with much brass and copper work; red brown, on the Dutch Rhenish; dark

blue on the North Brabant, and yellow on the Netherlands Central. It was only on the Holland Railway that a rather dull and unattractive dark green style was used for the locomotives.

In contrast to all this variety which prevailed into the early years of the present century, the fast and efficient trains of today are all of the multiple-unit type, at any rate so far as internal services are concerned. A notable feature of the timetable organization is the system of close interconnecting trains for all the directions possible at such nodal junctions as Rotterdam, Utrecht, Arnhem, Haarlem, Deventer, and so on. There are no such things as favoured main lines in Holland. All the cross-connections are served by fast trains, and the waiting time at junction points is minimal. Such a closely dovetailed network requires a very high standard of punctuality, because one train running no more than 15 minutes late could set up chain reactions in many different directions.

If there is a uniformity about the bright yellow multiple-unit trains that one sees throughout the electrified network, it does not need much imagination to realize that there is a master organizational control over train movements throughout the country. It is natural therefore that running of the international express trains, originating in France, North Germany or as far away as Switzerland can introduce a degree of uncertainty. It is fortunate therefore that international connections with the steamer sailings at the Hook of Holland are inward at about breakfast time and outward in the late evening, when the intensity of the internal electric service is not at its height. Because of the level nature of the country Netherlands Railways do not require electric locomotives of exceptional power. The Bo-Bo type is capable of hauling a 630 ton passenger train at 112 kph (70 mph) on level track, or a freight train of 1,250 tons at 80 kph (50 mph). This capacity is generally well in advance of everyday requirements.

A Belgian Class 210 diesel electric Bo-Bo heads the Antwerp—Lille Train (1968).

Europe
Scandinavia

At the Hook of Holland, after the arrival of the overnight packet boat from England, two famous international express trains leave; one is the TEE 'Rheingold' for South Germany and Switzerland, and the other is the 'Holland–Scandinavia Express' with through carriages to Copenhagen, and connecting there with a through sleeping car express to Stockholm. But a glance at the map shows that some considerable waterways have to be crossed; indeed the Kingdom of Denmark, through which this fascinating journey leads, has a railway system in which the running of trains on land is closely integrated with their transport by ferry across the intervening channels.

The 'Holland–Scandinavia Express' travels through North Germany, via Osnabruck, Bremen and Hamburg, and thence via Lubeck to the Baltic port of Puttgarden. The ferry service to Rodby is operated jointly by Germany and Denmark, and takes an hour. But another two hours elapse before one finally arrives in Copenhagen. Internal services in Denmark are provided mostly by diesel-electric railcar sets, including a number of 'Lyntog', or 'lightning' high-speed trains.

Swedish State Railways constitute a thoroughly modernised and efficient net-

A Danish M2 locomotive hauling a freight train.

Right and bottom. The Finnish State Railways operate under extremely severe weather conditions in winter. Certain freight trains, as these between Kemi and Kemi Harbour, are run only when the Baltic Sea is frozen over and extra traffic has to be taken by rail. In both these photographs the locomotive is TR3 2-8-0 No. 1153, a wood-burner, with the special spark arresting chimney.
Below. A Swedish 2-6-4 tank No. 1306 running a special train from Ludvika to Fagersta, amid beautiful and characteristic lake country.

work, more than two-thirds of which is electrified. The traction system is 15,000 volts ac, as in Germany, and the passenger services include some really fast running. The 'Goteborgen' express, for example, covers the 456 km (286 miles) between Stockholm and Gothenburg non-stop in 238 minutes, an average of 115.9 kph (72 mph). Another fast route is that providing the through communication between Stockholm and Copenhagen over the Helsingborg–Helsingor ferry. The distance between the two capital cities is just 647 km (400 miles), and the time is $7\frac{1}{2}$ to 8 hours by the best trains. Non-stop runs are made over

the 330 km (205 miles) from Stockholm to Nassjo in a little over 3 hours, and the trains themselves are lavishly equipped with attractive restaurant car facilities. The connection with the 'Holland–Scandinavia Express' from the Hook of Holland leaves Copenhagen at 21.19 and arrives at Stockholm at 07.44 next morning. It makes a considerable number of intermediate stops and carries sleeping cars.

The fame of Swedish engineers in the design of electric locomotives is world-wide, and in recent years they have been called in as consultants on several new electrification projects of outstanding importance. They are of course expert in providing against extremes of winter weather, but the 'Rc2' type passenger locomotives of Swedish State Railways are designed for running up to a maximum of 160 kph (100 mph). Their horsepower rating of 4,900 is exceptional for a unit weighing no more than $68\frac{1}{2}$ tons. The latest technique in power control has been embodied in their design, exercising the required variations in a continuous and entirely smooth process, instead of the older method of cutting out resistances step by step. This method, notably developed by the Swedish firm of ASEA, is one of the most effective means yet devised of combating the tendency of a locomotive to slip on a bad rail. These, of course, are part of the ordinary conditions of running in the Scandinavian countries.

Swedish State Railways are of course not solely concerned with fast passenger services, important though these are. The line to the north from Stockholm carries a heavy traffic in iron ore from the sub-Arctic cross-country line operated jointly with the Norwegian Railways from Lulea, on the Baltic, to Narvik. On this line are used some of the most powerful single locomotives in the world. They consist of a triple-articulated unit, each section of which has eight coupled wheels. The six traction motors, which between them have a shaft horsepower of 9,780, drive in pairs on to lay shafts situated midway between the groups of coupled wheels on the three articulated sections. Each complete locomotive weighs 267 tons. There are 19 of them and they work iron ore trains of 5,000 tons over the steep gradients between Kiruna and Narvik, where this line crosses the great mountain chain that forms the frontier between Norway and Sweden.

In Norway itself Oslo is the grand junction of the State Railway system, with lines radiating to Stavanger, Bergen, Trondheim, eastwards to the Swedish frontier and Stockholm, and south-eastwards to Troll-hattan, and thence into Sweden for Gothenburg and the ferry ports opposite Copenhagen. There is another important cross-country line eastwards from Trondheim to connect with Swedish State Railways at Storlien, and freight traffic on this is dealt with in the large Swedish mechanised marshalling yard at Ange. But from Trondheim an entirely new line, the Nordland Railway, was opened in 1962, running for 756 km (450 miles) inland from this fiord-indented coastline to Bodo. The main lines

Above. A Norwegian electric locomotive number 14,2176 stands at Voss station with the Oslo Express.
Right. A Danish express passenger train speeds through the countryside, headed by locomotive number 1153.
Above right. A Swedish three-carriage electric passenger train passes over a river.

from Oslo to Bergen, and to Trondheim run through exceedingly mountainous country in which elaborate provision is made by extensive snowsheds against the extremes of winter weather.

Locomotive power is entirely electric, or diesel. The latest passenger units are of the Co-Co type, and significantly carry small snow ploughs in front of each leading wheel as a permanent feature of the equipment. They are smartly finished in a russet shade of red, distinguishable from the orange red of the latest Swedish passenger locomotives. In the far north, on the Narvik line, Norwegian State Railways have their own counterpart to the triple articulated giants of Sweden, in some very powerful Co-Co units having a horsepower rating of 7,350. But a single one of these is not enough to cope with the tremendous gradients on the Norwegian side of the mountains, and they are normally used in pairs.

Europe
Italy

The railways of Italy share with those of Belgium the reputation of having produced some of the most curiously shaped steam locomotives ever to run. The days of Signor Plancher's cab-in-front type of 4-6-0 have long passed. In some ways these were the forerunners of the gigantic cab-in-front articulated engines on the Southern Pacific in the USA; but the Italians being coal burners required the coal to be near at hand, and it was stacked in narrow and inconveniently shaped bunkers on either side of the footplate. Between the disappearance of Plancher's 'masterpieces' and the present time, rapid strides have been made towards the building up of a complete electric railway network; and as in France, all the earlier electric locomotives were dull to look at.

In the 'autumn' of steam working in Italy the vogue of the curious shape reappeared, not as a created style with the idea of attracting attention, but in the never-ending quest for improved thermal efficiency. An Italian engineer, Attilio Franco had begun experiments to produce more efficient boilers in 1914; but the times were not propitious and it was not until 1932 that any result emerged, from a Belgian works at Nivelles. Then, in 1937, a Franco boiler was put on to one of the Plancher cab-in-front 4-6-0s, with good results. It was nevertheless something of a 'box-of-tricks', and the first truly practical exposition of the Franco boiler principles came from Piero Crosti. There were two subsidiary boilers slung pannier-wise along each side of the main boiler, and the steam and exhaust gas circuit was such that the chimney was not in its usual place but duplicated one half each at the near end of the subsidiary boilers. To the casual onlooker it seemed that engines with the Franco–Crosti boiler had no chimney at all. They were a great success and the Italians had many of them. Oddly enough Venice was one of their principal haunts, at a large depot by the station at the end of the causeway, from which one's taxi into the city is a gondola.

One of the numerous '640' class 2-6-0s which were unusual in having inside cylinders but outside Walschaerts valve gear. In this picture taken at Aosta engine No. 640.071 is specially turned out, with national flags for a special train working in 1972.

Never were beauty and mis-shapedness so violently contrasted as by the watercraft of Venice and the locomotives with the Franco–Crosti boiler!

One of the most interesting and distinctive among Italian steam locomotives in recent years were the 2-6-0s of 'Group 640'. These were express passenger engines for use on secondary routes that were laid with light rails, but were distinctive in having inside cylinders, though with the valve gear and the piston valves outside – an inversion of the normal order. They were fast and very sweet running machines, travelling in almost complete silence. Some of them were later rebuilt with the rotary cam type of valve gear invented by Arturo Caprotti, a mechanism that won considerable acceptance outside Italy and was used on a number of British and Indian locomotives.

Right. A Locomotive with the Franco-Crosti boiler
Above left. 2-6-0 No. 625.042 on a special from Salerno, in June 1974, pictured here at Lagonegro.
Below left. The GRAF special of June 1974 preparing to leave Salerno. It has the same 2-6-0, No. 625.042 as shown at Lagonegro, but is here assisted by a 2-8-0 No. 744.015.
Below. On the Sardinian Railways: a 2-6-2 narrow gauge tank engine No. 400, on a special train from Arbatax to Mandas at the station for Villanova Tulo.

Europe
Turkey

In no country of the world, perhaps, has political and economic development had such an effect upon railways as in Turkey. The old Ottoman Empire straddled the Bosphorus, and to most travellers of international experience Turkey meant no more than the easternmost sections of the long run of the 'Orient Express', from Paris to Constantinople, as it was then. But the Balkan War of 1913 left Turkey with no more than a foothold in Europe, and it is with the Turkish railways in Asia Minor that we are here concerned. At the outbreak of World War I there were in that territory about 4,000 km (2,500 miles) of route in operation, mostly independent and unconnected and serving only the most fertile and prosperous areas. There had been a major though somewhat disjointed project, started in 1903, to build a through, standard-gauge line connecting Constantinople with Baghdad, and under strong German influence and finance this was pushed through to completion in 1918; but during the war the Turkish railways generally, starved of essential supplies and denuded of key labour, fell into a sorry state, and after the surrender a few old Great Western Railway 0-6-0 goods engines that had been used on the Salonica Front were transferred to help the system to keep going.

The emergence of the distinguished military commander Mustapha Kemal, afterwards so well known as Ataturk, as a strong and far-seeing national leader, and the subsequent proclamation of the Turkish Republic in October 1923, changed everything. The capital city and the seat of government was moved from Constantinople to the wholly Turkish but hitherto remote Ankara, then served by no more than a branch from Eskisehir, on the Baghdad railway, that made a meandering course towards the Mediterranean coast through Konya. A balanced system of railways was essential for the economic development of the country as a whole, and in 1927 the General Management of the Railways and

Through passenger train from Kurtalan to Istanbul in rugged country between Ergani and Maden. The locomotive is one of the standard oil fired 2-10-0s of the TCDD, built between 1937 and 1949 by Henschel, in Germany, the Vulcan Foundry, Great Britain, and Skoda, in Czechoslovakia.

Harbours of the Republic of Turkey (TCDD) was set up. Since then the railway mileage has been almost doubled in building up an integral national system. Ankara, of course, was placed on the principal main lines leading to the Iraqi and Soviet Russian frontiers, though the route of the celebrated 'Taurus Express', from Istanbul to Baghdad, did not become any less important a line for that.

The countryside is everywhere extremely mountainous and, unless an altogether disproportionate expense had been incurred in colossal earthworks and long tunnels, the new lines had to be built following the winding river valleys and high mountain passes. The gradients in many places are very severe and this, together with the spectacular scenery, has provided the attraction for railway photographers and a challenge to their skills. The sight of a heavy train being hauled up a 1 in 40 gradient by two large 2-10-0 locomotives and pushed in rear by a third is naturally irresistible. Since the formation of TCDD most of the steam locomotives have been of German origin and manufacture, the earliest being direct developments of earlier standard Prussian State designs. In 1937, however, the famous firm of Henschel of Kassel delivered the first of a class of 2-10-0 mixed traffic locomotives that was destined to be international in its construction. Although the first 79 of a very successful design were built by Henschel, a further 37 were built in England after the war and delivered in 1948. A further 50 were supplied by Skoda, of Czechoslovakia, in 1949.

The period of World War II, and its aftermath, saw many locomotives of foreign origin drafted to the TCDD. Among these were the German 'Kriegslok' 2-10-0, which proved very useful on some of the Turkish secondary lines where axle loads were limited. Then there were British 2-8-0s of the Stanier LMS '8F' class, and American 2-8-0s and 2-8-2s. Among locomotives built specially for service in Turkey some of the most spectacular are the enormous three-cylinder 2-10-2 tanks, for rear-end banking on the ten-mile long incline between Bilecik and Karakoy, on that part of the original main line from Istanbul to the Iraqi frontier that still remains the main route, after the later diversion of the section further east to pass through Ankara instead of through Konya. Four of these enormous engines were delivered from West Germany in 1951-2.

Below left. One of the American-built 2-10-0s making a spectacular start from Cankiri on a mixed train from Zonguldak to Irmak. The locomotives are mechanically stoked and the fireman was evidently making full use of his equipment when this photograph was taken.
Above left. One of the American-built Vulcan 2-10-0s in wild mountain country near Tuney on a freight from Zonguldak to Irmak.

Indian summer 1914-1945

Railways in World War I However much the course of World War I may have confounded the military prophets, in at least one respect it did come up to expectations: this was very much a railway war. The gradually increasing role of railway transport in nineteenth-century conflicts had not been unnoticed by the general staffs of the military powers, and by 1914 they were not only well prepared, but had actually based their strategies on the potentialities of railways to shift and to maintain armies of a size never before seen. It was the Germans who were best prepared. In their wars against Denmark (1864) and Austria (1866) the Prussians had gained much experience which they put to good use in the subsequent Franco-Prussian War (1870-1). In the American Civil War (1861-5) a successful general, who relied greatly on rail transport, had spoken some immortal words about the importance of 'getting there firstest with the mostest'. In accordance with this advice, it had been a Prussian priority to build as many railways as possible to the frontiers, so that in the event of war it would be Prussian troops who would be in position first. This policy brought dramatic benefits in the victorious war against France.

The Prussians had also trained several railway operating battalions. In this they were not alone, but they were exceptionally thorough in their training; they had even built a railway that was operated by railway troops in peacetime, handling mainly civilian traffic. In this war the importance of rail communication was emphasized by the French *franc-tireurs*, who attacked Prussian trains in the occupied zones; the Prussians showed that they agreed that their trains were important by executing as many *franc-tireurs* as they could capture, for which they were duly accused of barbarism. After the war Bismarck, largely for military reasons, wanted to nationalize the German railways, but never quite succeeded. However, the German, and especially Prussian, railways already had a certain military aspect. A German historian described the railway and postal services as 'merely the civil sections of the army' containing 'three-quarters of a million men who stood stiffly at attention when their superiors spoke to them'. Railway directors were often generals, and strict military-style discipline was enforced. All this, apart from its military significance, helped to give German railways a fine reputation for smart railway operating, and also stifled the emergence of any strong trade unionism.

After the Franco-Prussian war, it was clear to the staffs of the European powers that in the next war it would be fatal to lag behind the enemy in mobilizing and deploying the troops. Year by year new mobilization plans were drawn up in accordance with the latest changes in army strength and availability of railways. Moving massive reserves in a couple of weeks to the frontiers was a complex operation, for those men (and their horses) had also to be fed. Thus mobilization plans were weighty documents composed by special mobilization staffs. Individual army units and railway stations would be issued only with those sections of the plan that concerned them. These were secret documents, and stationmasters were usually provided with a safe in which to lock them up until mobilization was declared, when they were to unseal them and discover what they were required to do.

Those powers fortunate enough to be surrounded by water barriers took matters a little less seriously, but for the Continental powers there was constant worry and agitation about the sufficiency of existing railways in an emergency. New lines began to be built for purely military reasons. Germany, facing the prospect of war on two fronts, built an exceptionally dense network of lines, and this alarmed France and Russia, which to a certain extent tried to keep pace. A railway race was part of the arms race. Russian railway building was badly distorted by military requirements. Around the end of the nineteenth century Russia had been feverishly building railways in the west and south-west, in anticipation of war against Austria or Germany. But when war came in 1904 it was against Japan, and the Russian army had to be served by the rickety single track of the hardly finished Trans-Siberian Railway. After this unsuccessful war Russia began to strengthen her railways in the east, in the expectation of another conflict with Japan. And when the next war came, it was against Austria and Germany.

When mobilization was declared, the railways of Germany, France, Russia and Austria cancelled most civilian trains in order to free resources for military movements. All countries deployed their troops according to plan and usually a day or two ahead of schedule (probably because railway officials, being railway officials, had left themselves hidden reserves, 'recovery margins', when they informed pre-war military planners of their lines' capacities). In Russia, where despite double-tracking of strategic lines there was still a lack of line capacity in certain frontier areas, military trains moved so smoothly that civilian freight, hastily dumped at the lineside when the crisis began, was picked up and dispatched even before the fifteen days of initial mobilization were completed.

In France mobilization also went well, but the early retreat to the Marne put a strain on transport from which the French railways never really recovered. Much rolling stock was lost (British railway companies made good part of this loss by sending spare locomotives to the Western Front), and plans were disrupted by the unexpected change of traffic flows caused by the redeployment of masses of troops to positions in what was once regarded as the rear. One handicap borne by the French railways was a lack of standardization, making it difficult to shift equipment from one railway to another that was more hard-pressed. Prussia and Russia had long ago solved that problem by standardizing locomotives and equipment. Thus in Russia there was a standard 'government' 0-8-0 locomotive numbering more than 8,000 units and used by most of the different companies. It was this engine that was most frequently transferred from one railway to another (even the initial two weeks of the Russian mobilization plan had envisaged the transfer of 1,360 locomotives from the rear railways to those closest to the frontiers).

As the war developed, the demands on rail transport grew. In 1914, on average, the Anglo-French Western Front required 80 military trains each day but in the final hectic months, from March to November 1918, there was an average daily requirement of 74 trains for shifting reserves, and 217 for moving supplies. At the peak of operations 198 trains in one day were run to move troops, and 424 to transport supplies.

Most of the belligerents divided their railways into war and civilian zones, with military control dominant in the war areas and often in the rear areas too. Coordination of military demands and railway operating requirements was difficult, and was never achieved perfectly. Possibly the Germans did best in this; there was strict military control over all railways, but the civilian railwaymen were quite happy to work under military dictation. The Russians were the least successful in solving this problem. Indeed they got themselves into the same kind of situation that Abraham Lincoln had encountered in the American Civil War: a peremptory and uncomprehending attitude towards railway operating men on the part of army officers entrusted with transport arrangements. The Russian railways were divided into those serving the frontiers ('the railways of the military zone') and those which were far in the rear. Cooperation was lacking and this showed itself most damagingly when the military authorities began to hoard rolling stock 'in case of need'. The civilian railway authorities were unable to get these valuable freight cars released, with the result that vital materials (as well as bread for angry citizens) became unavailable where they were needed. One crisis led to another; coal mines closed, crowds rioted, and 1917 arrived. At one stage a desperate government halted passenger trains on the key St Petersburg to Moscow route for a week so that grain could be taken to the capital.

Railway-operating battalions, which had existed in most of the big armies since the nineteenth century, had to be rapidly expanded during the war. This expansion was largely achieved by allocating former railwaymen to them, but in all armies there were examples of skilled railwaymen being drafted as cooks, officers' orderlies, or infantrymen. Some belligerents, notably Britain and Russia, had to recall railwaymen back to civilian life when labour shortages developed on the home railways. One important task was the operation of narrow-gauge trench railways, which plied between the main line railheads and the front line. Here again Germany was perhaps the best equipped, but it was France that had done most to develop this technique; Paul Decauville in 1876 had introduced his 'portable railway' mainly for agricultural use, but then found that among his best customers were the war departments of several military powers. The British government, presumably anticipating yet another war on India's North-West Frontier, had even ordered a Decauville kit with a locomotive divisible into two sections suitable for transport by elephant.

Another task of the railway battalions was the restoration of lines damaged by a retreating enemy. When the Germans advanced into Russia they had the additional task of converting the Russian 5 ft gauge to the European standard. Up to the middle of 1916 they had so treated over 7,500 km (4,700 miles), mainly in Russian Poland. The method was to shift one rail by 80 mm ($3\frac{1}{2}$ inches), which was not difficult with wooden cross-ties. In favourable conditions a railway troop detachment (two NCOs and about 34 men) could convert 1,200 metres in one day's work, but this fell drastically when there was snow on the line. The Russians also damaged the track by, typically, blowing up every second rail joint. Later they developed the technique (imitated by the Germans in World War I) of dragging a heavy hook behind a locomotive to break the cross-ties and distort the rails.

Physical damage to the railways was much less than in World War II. The worst war damage was caused by scorched-earth tactics; hence the areas most affected were north-eastern France, Poland, and Belgium. In the last-named it was only in 1930 that the last of the temporary bridges erected by the British army's Railway Operating Division was replaced by a permanent structure. Damage by shellfire was noticeable in certain hard-fought areas, Verdun being an obvious example and northern Italy another. Damage from bombs was slight; bombing did sometimes disturb supply depots and transhipment points close to the front, but material damage was slight. However, London's Waterloo Station was one victim, receiving a bomb on an empty passenger car. Venice Mestre station was also badly damaged by bombing. German railways and stations, however, escaped fairly lightly, since little actual fighting took place inside the country's frontiers.

In Britain and America the war situation was different as there were no frontiers to be fought over. At the outbreak of war the British railway companies were taken over by the government's Railway Executive, composed of leading railway managers. These handled the task of carrying changed traffic flows so well that their work did much to prepare public opinion for the elimination of the old railway companies, which when contrasted with the work of the Railway Executive seemed hopelessly uncoordinated and wasteful. In fact, the Railway Executive had an easy job, but this was not realized at the time; it could enforce much-needed intercompany coordination, and the government ensured that it was not troubled by profit-and-loss considerations.

When the USA entered the war in 1917 there was an immediate build-up of traffic, which the railways soon seemed incapable of handling. Much of the trouble was in the dock areas, where loaded freight cars were held for weeks awaiting a suitable berth. But part of the problem was caused by the persistence of old habits. Notable among these was the practice of sending freight by roundabout routes so that it would

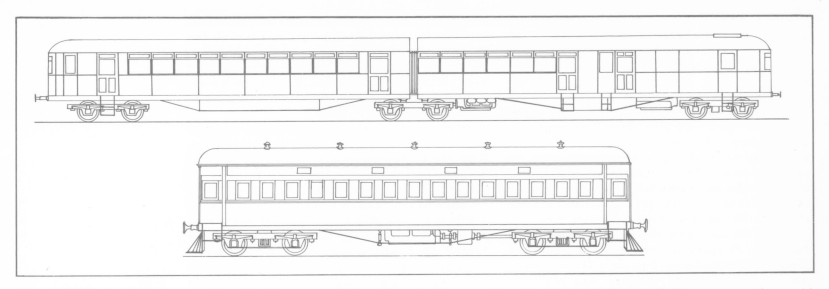

Above: A British steam railcar built for the London and North Eastern Railway in 1930. Named *Phenomena*, it was an articulated 2-car unit for secondary services. Its boiler had a pressure of 300 p.s.i. (21 kgs/cm²) and it was built on the 'Sentinel – Cammell' system, like several other British steam railcars.
Below: An early railcar built for low-traffic lines in Australia. Devised in 1923 by the New South Wales Government Railways, it is an ordinary American-type suburban passenger car modified to accommodate a petrol engine.

register the biggest possible mileage (and revenue) on the originating railway. At the end of 1917 President Wilson took control of the railways under his emergency powers, paying each company a rent for its services. This control, exercised through the United States Railroad Administration, succeeded in transferring much traffic to shorter routes, avoided routing traffic through congested terminals, cut out other wasteful manifestations of competition, and reduced passenger train-mileage by about one-sixth. It also introduced standard 'USRA' designs for locomotives and rolling stock, and many of these items were produced for various railroads. Apart from the changes brought by the USRA, the war did not affect American railroading to the same extent as in continental Europe. Exports of US-built locomotives did take a different pattern, however. To France, America sent narrow-gauge trench-railway locomotives and also, later, some main-line freight engines to meet urgent French requirements. To help beleaguered Russia obtain supplies from the west via Siberia, many hundred units of a 2-10-0 locomotive, jointly designed by a Russian railway mission and US locomotive builders, were exported. Because of the Russian Revolution some of these locomotives remained in America, and most of those that reached Russia arrived too late to help the Allied cause in World War I, even though they lasted long enough to serve the same purpose in World War II.

Many of the world's railways not directly involved in the war nevertheless suffered from the unavailability of new equipment traditionally bought from one other of the belligerents. Most of the railways of the British Empire additionally endured deferred maintenance, and some of them had sent some of their railway equipment overseas: Indian railways sent metre-gauge locomotives and track to supply British troops fighting the Turks in Iraq, and some double-track lines in Western Canada were singled in order to obtain rails for France.

Post war reorganization Thus for one reason or another, the immediate post-war years were difficult for most of the world's railways. But these were temporary difficulties; only the far-sighted visualized the more permanent problem which would arise during the 1920s and 1930s, namely the competition of the internal-combustion engine. In the meantime many countries were reviewing the ways in which their railways were organized, and in particular they were asking themselves if privately owned railways were really necessary.

In 1918 the railways of different countries could be divided into those that were wholly state-owned, those that were privately owned, and those in which some were private and some state-owned. The last category was the largest. It included most countries of western Europe, in which the state at an early stage, in order to speed up construction of railways, had taken a share in building and running them. Sweden is a good example, for her first private railway and her first state railway were opened in the same year of 1856. The western European countries already envisaged the eventual takeover by the state of all lines, and this was often written in the charters of the private companies. Thus in 1938 the French state took over the French private main-line companies and joined them to the state-owned lines to form the French National Railways (SNCF). In Belgium and Italy a similar process had been virtually complete before 1914. In some countries, including Sweden and Switzerland, the process of nationalization has not yet been completed, although the state railways of both these countries have a greater share of the mileage. A feature of Swedish policy has been the steady nationalization of the narrow-gauge lines, followed by their conversion to standard gauge. In Holland the coexistence of a large private system with an equally large national system ended only in 1938, when the Holland Railway Company and the State Railway Company were amalgamated to form the Netherlands Railway Company (NS), in which all shares were held by the state. But before that, in 1919, the two companies had at last come together to make a working agreement to standardize their practices. One big difference had been that the State Railway had located its signals on the left side of the track, even though it had right-hand running; this was because it had bought its locomotives from England, where a left-hand driving position was normal.

In three west European countries, Britain, Spain and Germany, the situation was exceptional. In Spain, the private railways continued, but in 1924 the Spanish government introduced a statute by which it shared in the financing, management and profits of the railways. However, this arrangement was overtaken by the Spanish Civil War and in 1941 the war-ravaged railways were nationalized to form the Spanish National Railways (RENFE). In Britain, government control ended only in 1921. In the meantime there had been a big railway strike in 1919, even though a few months previously the government had

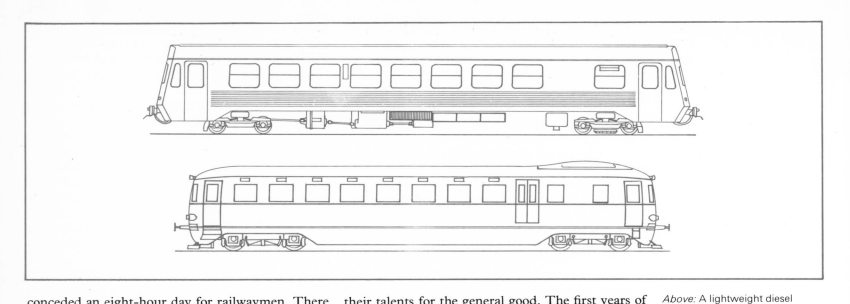

conceded an eight-hour day for railwaymen. There had also been much discussion of how the railways should be organized, as there was a general reluctance to return to what was regarded as the wasteful and over-competitive multiplicity of private companies. Many expressed a preference for nationalization, on the familiar grounds that railways were too important a national service to be left in the control of dividend-seeking companies. The government, however, rejected nationalization. In 1920 it published very advanced proposals which suggested the amalgamation of the old undertakings into six new big companies, each with a territorial monopoly and including separate companies for Scotland and for London. It also proposed that manual workers should have a place on the boards of the new companies. However, combined opposition from those who wanted outright nationalization, with scant regard for the shareholders, and those who rejected any form of government intervention at all, encouraged the government to abandon these proposals. Instead, the Railways Act of 1921 compelled the 123 companies to form four new large enterprises, each with a territorial monopoly. Of the old companies only the Great Western survived, absorbing sundry Welsh companies to cover the western part of England, with Wales. The three new companies were the Southern, the London Midland & Scottish (covering the Midlands, the north-west, and part of Scotland) and the London & North Eastern (covering eastern England and part of Scotland). There was no worker participation in this new organization, but the railways were compelled to negotiate with the unions on wages and conditions; for that period, this was a quite radical imposition.

In Germany, the break-up of the old Empire necessitated a reorganization of the railways; with the end of Bismarck's imperial dream came, paradoxically, the realization of Bismarck's unfulfilled hope for a completely unified railway system. The Reichsbahn (DR) was set up as a national railway company, incorporating all the main-line systems of the individual states. It naturally had its headquarters in Berlin and was really the old Prussian State Railway writ large. As would happen when British railways were finally nationalized in 1948, the biggest of the former companies became dominant and imposed itself, with results good and bad, on the new enlarged organization. One of the bad results was that many good administrators outside the Prussian system lost the chance to employ

their talents for the general good. The first years of the Reichsbahn were exceptionally difficult; although war damage was small, the reparations demanded by the victorious Western powers had included the handing over of 5,000 locomotives and 150,000 freight and passenger vehicles. Moreover, when in 1923 it became obvious that Germany could not pay the crushing reparations indemnity, the 'Dawes Plan' included a provision that the railways were to be independent of the German government and for five years the Reichsbahn had to include foreign specialists in its management.

The US railroads were released from wartime government control in 1920, after several years of debate as to their future. However, the feeling against the old company structure was not as strong as in Britain, and the companies resisted government intervention more actively than did the British companies. In the end President Wilson's Transportation Act of 1920, which returned the railways to company control, merely strengthened the power of the Interstate Commerce Commission; in particular, the Commission could henceforth set minimum as well as maximum rates, in order to prevent the kind of ruinous rate-cutting wars that had so damaged the railroads and their clients before the war. The ICC did try to persuade the railroads to merge into larger units, but without success.

In Canada, however, the railways were in a state that made any return to the old ways highly unwelcome, if not impossible. When the very successful Canadian Pacific transcontinental line was finished in 1885, Canada possessed, apart from this private company, the Intercolonial Railway, and the private Grand Trunk Railway. The former had been built largely to persuade the Maritime Provinces to join the Canadian Federation. With a main line from Riviere du Loup to Halifax, this well-built line was finished in 1876, two years after it had been decided to entrust it to the Department of Public Works of the Canadian government. The Grand Trunk included the earliest public Canadian railway, which connected Montreal with Portland in the USA; the lines of the former Great Western Railway, which connected Toronto with the US railways via Windsor and Sarnia; and the Grand Trunk proper, whose main line from Montreal to Toronto was built by British capital to British constructional standards. The Grand Trunk also ran eastwards as far as Riviere du Loup to connect with the Intercolonial.

Above: A lightweight diesel railcar prototype, designed to replace railbuses on the German Federal Railways during the late 1970s. New construction techniques enabled a light axle-load (11.5 tonnes) to be achieved without the use of expensive lightweight metals. 64 seats are provided, transmission is hydraulic, and a maximum speed of 120 kph (75 mph) is permitted.
Below: An example of the European inter-war railcar. This is a diesel-electric single-unit car built by Skoda for the Czechoslovak State Railways in 1920. Of 400 hp, this vehicle could accommodate 56 passengers and reach a speed of 110 kph (70 mph).

Government influence on Canadian railway-building in Canada has usually been more enthusiastic than rational, with the result that at almost any given time every railway management has been either anticipating, or participating in, or recovering from a Royal Commission of enquiry into the railways. It was a Royal Commission that in 1851 recommended that all new lines receiving financial assistance should be of 5 ft 6 in gauge, and this provision for three decades did much to hinder the interchange of traffic with the US lines. In the years before World War I, for reasons that are even harder to justify, or even discern, the government approved the building, simultaneously, of not one, but two, new transcontinentals. One was the private Canadian Northern Railway, which from small beginnings in Manitoba expanded by 1918 to a coast-to-coast route, constructed very cheaply and with one exception to low engineering standards, but adequate for the underdeveloped territory through which it mainly passed. The exception was a substantial tunnel under Mount Royal at Montreal, which did much for the development of the northern suburbs. The third transcontinental was a combination of the private Grand Trunk Pacific and a government-built line from Moncton in New Brunswick, through Quebec City and on through the wilds to Winnipeg. The latter was the National Transcontinental Railway, built to exceptionally high engineering standards with moderate gradients and curves; British-style in engineering, it was also mainly British-financed. At Winnipeg it joined the new Grand Trunk Pacific. This company, sponsored by the Grand Trunk, was also to be responsible for the operation of the National Transcontinental Railway. That is, it was to operate the whole route which, measuring 5,700 km (3,543 miles) from Moncton to its terminus at Prince Rupert on the Pacific, was finished in 1914. The Canadian Northern's line to the Pacific at Vancouver was finished the following year. Both these new and hostile lines used the Yellowstone Pass through the Rockies, where their single-track lines were so close that most casual observers thought that this was one double-track railway.

Such blatant duplication of lines was evident elsewhere in Canada. The Canadian Pacific had also been expanding. It provided a second route from Montreal to the Atlantic, and also duplicated the Grand Trunk's line from Montreal to Toronto with its own single track, which for miles ran side by side with the Grand Trunk's double track. These obvious deficiencies of the existing company structure were made intolerable by the financial difficulties in which the railways found themselves. The Canadian Pacific was generally profitable, but the rest were not, and were heavily over-capitalized. The Grand Trunk, managed in London, was not administered well, partly because its board was more interested in dividends than in maintaining its property.

In 1919 the Grand Trunk directors warned the Canadian government that they would have to default on bond interest payments, but the government refused to help. The directors then refused to continue to operate the Grand Trunk Pacific, whereupon the government put the company into receivership and then bought it up. One of the final acts of the British board was to vote itself five years' salary, and a year's salary to its top officials, the funds coming from the Company's fire-insurance fund. Eventually in 1923 a new government-owned company came into being, Canadian National Railways.

Canadian National Railways, the biggest and uniquely state-owned North American railroad, included not only the Grand Trunk, but also the Canadian Northern, Intercolonial, and other lines in financial trouble; it was virtually all the main Canadian companies except the Canadian Pacific. Thus Canada found itself with two railway companies of approximately equal size, one profitable and self-confident, and the other an amalgamation of 149 demoralized and mainly unprofitable enterprises. But so intelligent and energetic was the CNR's first president, Henry Thornton, that by the end of the 1920s the CNR had become a coherent enterprise, capable of making an operating profit, and already outpacing the Canadian Pacific in quality of service. This spectacle of a state company threatening to excel over a private company was not pleasing to many, and after Thornton retired in 1932, no man of similar calibre was ever appointed as president. Quite the contrary, in fact.

In another British dominion, Australia, the question of railway nationalization was still premature, as the different state governments would refuse on principle to transfer to the Federal capital their authority over the state railways. It would not be until the 1970s that some Australian states, unwilling to bear any longer the financial burden of their ill-managed railways, would forget earlier principles and hand over their railway systems to Canberra. In the meantime, however, the nucleus of a state railway organization already existed in the Commonwealth Railways, organized to run the new Transcontinental line, the line from Port Augusta to Alice Springs, and also the hopelessly unprofitable and isolated line to Darwin. The Transcontinental could also be regarded as the first step in Australian gauge standardization, for it was a 4 ft 8½ in gauge line, implying that if there was to be any conversion, it would be to, and not from, the standard gauge of New South Wales. The next gauge move, though not really a conversion, came when the New South Wales Railway was connected by a new line to South Brisbane in Queensland, bringing standard gauge into that state. In 1962 a similar standard-gauge extension in Victoria would at last make it possible to travel from Sydney to Melbourne without the need to change trains at Albury, where the NSWGR and the Victorian Railways joined.

In New Zealand, where the 1870s had been the great railway-building years, the 5 ft 3 in gauge had not long survived the government's decision to standardize 3 ft 6 in. The choice of this narrower gauge was in keeping with the 'American' style of New Zealand railway construction: the building of the greatest mileage for the least capital, upgrading the lines only when increasing traffic should justify the expense. As for nationalization, most of the railways were government-built, and the few large private lines had been absorbed into the New Zealand Railways before World War I.

A feature of World War I had been the great use which the belligerents made of motor transport, and of the aeroplane. The development of these two technologies was thereby accelerated, bringing closer the day when their civilian application would present a damaging, perhaps mortal, threat to railway transport. To a certain extent the railways had already suffered from one kind of competition before the war, that of the electric streetcar. But except in America, where the streetcar's enlargement into the interurban electric car had robbed the main-line railways of some useful traffic, the electric vehicle had only taken away traffic that because of cheap fares and short distances had never been really profitable.

The growth of motor transport When the war ended, many soldiers had been taught to drive motor trucks, and many motor trucks were sold by the various armies to the public at giveaway prices. The subsequent transformation of demobilized soldiers into one-man motor-haulage businesses was hardly surprising, and some of these enterprises survived to grow into serious transport undertakings. In few countries was motor transport regulated by the government, and road hauliers were free to set their own prices for each operation (unlike the railways in most countries) and to take or reject traffic offered to them according to its likely profitability (again unlike the railways, which were common carriers, bound to take all traffic that was offered and, in many countries, to charge each client the same price). Moreover, road transport used 'permanent way' that was paid for, maintained, and policed by public authorities, whereas the rates charged by the railways had to cover the cost of their tracks and installations. These 'unfair' advantages of the motor truck were backed by some real technical benefits. A shipper might find that he could get faster service from a motor truck; whereas a freight car would wait around until enough cars had been assembled to form a train, the truck could leave as soon as it was loaded. Also, for all except large enterprises, which might have their own private railway siding, the motor truck eliminated transhipment; goods did not need to be taken down to the railway freight station and transhipped into a railway car, with a reverse process, time-consuming and costly, at the other end. Thus many shippers, who could enjoy the 'unfair' advantages of the cheap rates that could be offered by the motor transport firm, and faster door-to-door transit too, were inclined to abandon the railways in favour of the roads. In addition, there was another and rarely mentioned reason why shippers might prefer the road haulier; from a small and insecure haulage company they received personal and helpful attention, whereas from a big and long-established railway they all too often did not.

In most of Europe and America, the share of the railways in total freight traffic began to decline after about 1920, due partly to highway competition (which took away mainly those items of freight for which the railways charged high rates), and to industrial depression (which reduced those low-value, low-rated, bulk traffics for which railways were more suited than road vehicles). Added to these problems were higher wage and fuel costs. In the USA and Britain the wartime government controllers had granted wage increases which, left to themselves, the companies would have been very unwilling to accept. Parallel processes took place in other countries and were especially marked in Germany, where the railwaymen were actually willing to consider strike action after 1918.

In the 1930s, with the Great Depression, the railways' situation worsened. In most countries the railways' reaction was policies designed on the one hand to restrain highway competition, and on the other to make the railways' own services more attractive. Action on the political and publicity level did help to persuade governments to introduce regulations which it was hoped would enforce 'fair' competition on the road operators. These regulations varied from country to country. In the USA the railways received little help in this respect, but in western Europe various licensing restrictions were imposed on road-transport firms. Such regulations were strong in France and Germany, where it was realized that if motor trucks 'skimmed the cream', that is, took the most profitable traffic from the railways, then the railways would no longer be able to perform the vital public service of carrying the less profitable traffic. But the road operators were never required to pay their fair share of highway costs, and because they were such small and numerous businesses, it was impossible to supervise them in the same way that railways were supervised; while railways diligently observed safety regulations, road truckers regularly overloaded their vehicles beyond their rated capacities, and quite often scheduled their services at such speeds that breaches of speed limits were inevitable.

Measures to make railway service more attractive included acceleration of freight trains, and especially the introduction of fast freight trains running on regular timetables at passenger train speeds, guaranteeing a next-morning delivery between cities up to 500 miles apart. In the USA, the first of these services was the Cotton Belt's *Blue Streak*, introduced in 1931. New types of freight cars were designed to suit special traffic which it was considered worthwhile to retain or win back. In order to provide the same door-to-door service offered by motor trucks, the demountable container was used by some European railways. This was virtually a freight car body which could be easily transferred from a railway flat car, used over the long haul, to a flat motor truck for the pick-up and delivery sectors of the trip.

Passenger traffic declined slower than freight in most countries, though there was a deep trough during the Depression. In most countries the railways themselves attempted to exploit the motor bus by acquiring vehicles which they used to operate feeder services to their stations. This was a sensible method of coordinating the 'retail' advantages of the motor vehicle with the long-haul 'wholesale' advantages of the train, but in some countries it was stopped on grounds of so-called monopoly. In Britain the railways, apart from operating motor buses, also organized successful internal air services. In the meantime railway passenger services were greatly improved. The highly-publicized streamline train aroused public enthusiasm, and the passenger train was still considered to be a natural form of long-distance transport, even though motor-car ownership, despite the Depression, was increasing rapidly.

In some countries, especially those that had undergone revolution, different processes took place. In Russia, where war, civil war and revolution had left railway transport in a sad state, the industrialization plans led to great increases of traffic, which the

Above: Electric passenger locomotive ordered in 1927 by the Midi Railway of France for use on its Bordeaux to Irun line. The locomotives of this design were among the first to be designed specifically for high-speed work, with the motors and transmission arranged for minimum oscillation and stress. *Below:* A battery-powered electric shunting locomotive built for Italian State Railways in 1922. It was used for marshalling passenger trains at Milan Central, recharging its batteries during the night. Similar battery locomotives, typically for use on non-electrified sidings joining electrified main lines, have been built in small numbers in many other countries.

government at first attempted to carry without a corresponding capital investment in railways (even though, mistakenly, a disproportionate amount of capital and labour were expended to improve canal and river transport). In the early 1930s it was obvious that the Russian railways could not cope, and recourse to executing railwaymen on charges of 'sabotage' and 'wrecking' did not help. Eventually, realistic resources were allocated to help the railways and there was much construction of new lines, double-tracking, and modest starts in electrification and dieselization. In Turkey and Iran, where new leaders had taken over after revolutions, railway-building was initiated as a kind of nation-building exercise. The Trans-Iranian Railway, from Bandar Shahpur on the Persian Gulf to Teheran and Bandar Shah on the Caspian, was finished in 1938, being the first major railway in Iran. It had been built by American contractors in its northern part, by German contractors in the south, all under the supervision of a Scandinavian planning consortium.

On the whole, railway managements in the twentieth century were conservatives, not innovators. But when railway companies tended to be small and numerous there were usually, apart from the mass of unenterprising railways, one or two that would take the risk of putting new ideas into practice. When railways became larger, often becoming the sole railway in a given country or territory, it was natural that they should settle complacently into old and well-tried routines; indeed, it seems fairly clear that it was only the new difficult conditions that made technical, commercial, and operating changes seem acceptable. In America and western Europe, at least, railway improvements over the last half century have been due not to the inventiveness and energy of service-conscious railway administrators, but rather to the pressures put upon them by competing forms of transport, and by the rising costs of their traditional inputs, coal and labour.

Electric traction

Electric traction Around the end of the nineteenth century several of the world's railways began to use electric traction. There had been much experimentation previously, but the first successful attempt to capture the public imagination was made by von Siemens, who during the 1879 Berlin Trade Exhibition carried 80,000 passengers on a 300-yard electric railway. This demonstration showed that it was technically feasible to power a train by electricity, but not that it would be necessarily advantageous to do so. The electric locomotive did, of course, possess the advantage that it was smokeless, and therefore ideal for long tunnels; the first electric underground line was the City and South London Railway, which

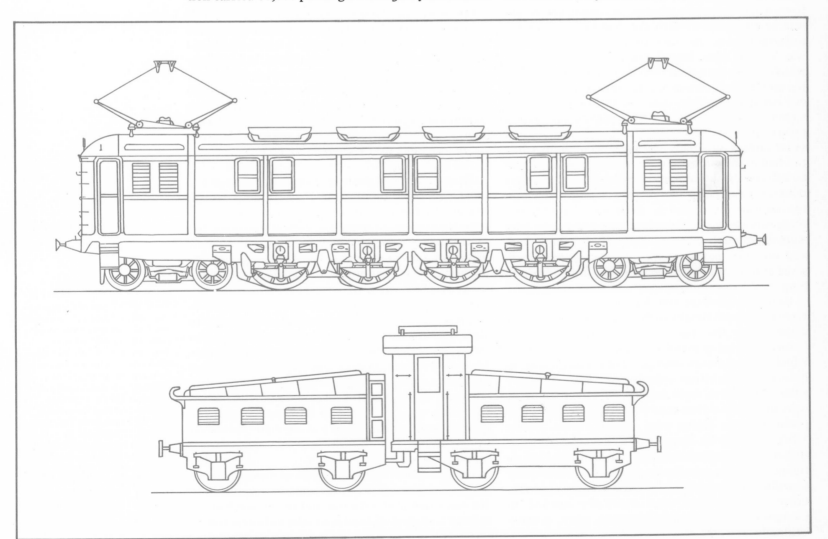

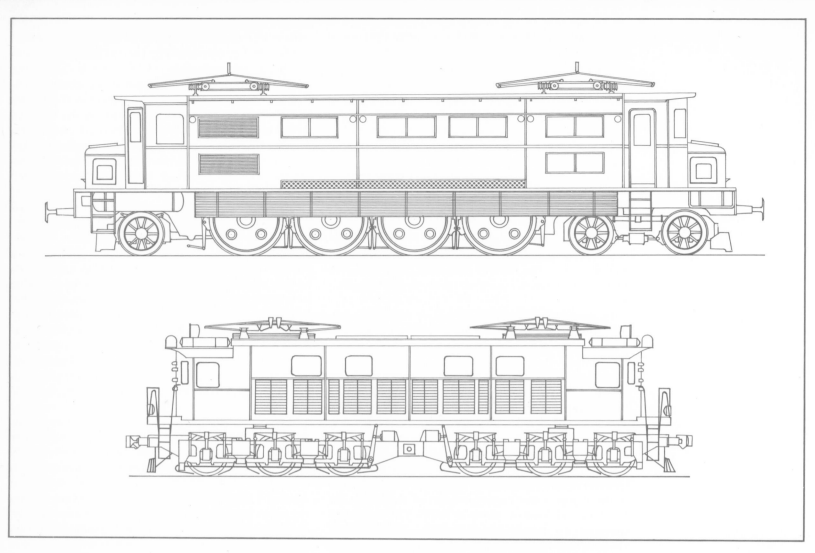

was opened in 1890, using 100 hp locomotives supplied with 500-volt current from a conductor rail laid between the running rails.

The first substantial American electrification occurred in Baltimore in 1895, where the city authorities insisted that the Baltimore & Ohio Railroad should eliminate the smoke nuisance of its line through the city. The General Electric Company executed this scheme, gaining experience which served it well when in 1909 it carried out another project. This was the electrification of the Great Northern Railroad's line over the Cascade Mountains. Although only 10 km (6 miles) long, this section included a 4.2 km (2.6 mile) tunnel. Steep grades and heavy loads meant that the tunnel was filled with dense smoke and steam when conventional locomotives were used, and the suffocation of train crews, and even of passengers, if a locomotive slipped to a halt in the tunnel, was a real possibility. General Electric's solution was a three-phase system of 6,600 volts, for which it supplied locomotives weighing 105 tons and exerting 1,500 hp on hourly rating. In 1914 the Great Northern's competitor, the Milwaukee, electrified 438 miles of mountainous line in Montana and Idaho and later, in 1921, electrified another separate 200-mile section through the Cascades. Meanwhile the New York, New Haven & Hartford Railroad electrified its lines into Grand Central Terminal, New York, in order to eliminate the smoke nuisance; by 1914 this electrification had been extended to New Haven (116 km or 72 miles) and was carrying locomotive-hauled freight and passenger trains as well as trains of self-propelled passenger cars (or multiple units, as they would be later called).

Other railways apart from the New Haven had appreciated that suburban passenger service was another field in which electricity could be superior to steam. With many frequent stops, the ability to accelerate quickly was important, both to maintain high average speeds and to enable as many trains as possible to be handled over a given railroad. The electric multiple unit, in which electric motors were distributed down the length of the train, driving the bogie axles, had this power of acceleration. It could also be driven from either end, which meant that at a busy terminus at rush hour there was no need for trains to be manoeuvred; an incoming train could depart as soon as its driver had changed ends. The New Haven had experimentally electrified a branch line in 1895, and this was followed by the electrification in 1903 of 61 km (38 miles) of the Long Island Railroad, a specialized commuter line out of New York, and in 1905 of the North Western Pacific's line out of San Francisco.

Suburban electrification also interested some of the British railways, each of which tended to differ in its preferred voltage and transmission system: 600-volt dc with two conductor rails was favoured by some of the London suburban lines, but the Liverpool to Southport electrification of 1913 (60 km or 37 miles) and the North Tyneside 51 km (32 mile) scheme of 1904 used a single conductor rail. The 16 km (10 mile) Lancaster to Heysham electrification of 1908 was notable in that it used 6,600-volt single-phase alternating current at 25 cycles. With the high voltages, overhead wire transmission was necessary for the Heysham scheme and for the London, Brighton & South Coast Railway's 6,600-volt zone.

Above: Type AE/7 mixed-traffic electric locomotive of Swiss Federal Railways. Built in 1927 by Brown-Boveri and the Swiss Locomotive Company, these 15,000 volt units were designed for speeds of up to 100 kph (62 mph).
Below: A VL19 class electric locomotive of Soviet Railways. Introduced in 1932 and incorporating features of imported locomotives, this was the first Russian-built class of electric locomotives. Of 2,750 hp, these locomotives weighed 120 tonnes and worked on 3,000-volt electrified lines. Construction was by the Kolomna Works, with the Dynamo Works providing the electrical equipment.

In continental Europe, Switzerland and Hungary pioneered the use of electric traction. In 1899 a 45 km (28 mile) Swiss line was electrified. This was the heavily graded Burgdorf to Thun branch, which was converted by Brown Boveri to 3-phase 750-volt operation, with current being transmitted by tramway-type overhead wires. Electric motor coaches were used in passenger service, and locomotives on freight trains. These made use of current regeneration: the ability on falling gradients to use the electric motors as generators, supplying current to the overhead wire. Following this successful conversion several other Swiss lines experimented with electric traction, while the Hungarian firm of Ganz electrified the Valtellina and Giovi mountain lines in Italy. These were also on the three-phase system, and were eventually extended to and through the Simplon Tunnel.

In contrast to steam-locomotive development, the railways' engineers did little to develop electric traction. It was the electric engineering companies which innovated, and then asked the railways to sample their products. Thus in 1901 Oerlikon electrified at its own expense a 23 km (14 mile) line of the Swiss Federal Railways in order to demonstrate its new single-phase system (which required only one overhead wire, instead of the two of the 3-phase system). But after the line had worked well for over a year, the Swiss Federal Railways asked for the removal of the equipment. Again, in the first years of the century the German firms of Siemens and AEG built two test tracks near Berlin. On these they operated, at 10,000 volts, electric test cars which carried transformers to reduce the voltage supplied to the motors. One of them reached 216 km/h (135 mph), but no railway administration was prepared to invest in the system.

Other countries in which the first electrified lines appeared before 1914 were Austria, Cuba (the Havana suburban line), Hungary (150 km or 94 miles by 1914), the Netherlands (The Hague to Rotterdam), Bolivia (an 8 km or 5 mile line out of La Paz up the side of the volcano crater in which La Paz is situated), Japan (a Tokyo suburban conversion and a short rack railway), Sweden, Norway, France, Spain (the 29 km or 18 mile Nacimiento-Gador line), and Germany. The French schemes included the early conversion of the metre-gauge St-George de Commiers to La Mure line in 1903. This 30 km (19 mile) line with stiff gradients was noteworthy at the time because it used 2,400-volt dc. The Midi Railway electrified two lines, the 54 km (34 mile) metre-gauge branch to Bourg Madame in the Pyrenees and the standard-gauge Perpignan to Villefranche line, both of which used 12,000-volt single-phase $16\frac{2}{3}$ cycles current. On the Perpignan line it tested six different experimental locomotives from six different makers. Meanwhile, the Paris–Orleans in 1900 embarked on a scheme which by 1926 would bring the 130 km (81 mile) Paris to Orléans line under overhead wire carrying 1,500 volts. Other French conversions included the dense-traffic Paris–Versailles r.g. suburban line of 18 km (11 miles), electrified in 1902 at 650 volts with third-rail transmission, and the metre-gauge St-Gervais–Vallorcine line in the Alps. In Germany there were suburban electrifications at Hamburg and Berlin, the beginnings of an extensive system in Bavaria, a 48 km (30 mile) system around Zell using 15,000

volts at 15 cycles, as well as an 18 km (11 mile) line in the Isar Valley electrified in 1909 at 1,000 volts with overhead transmission. Moreover, in 1911 the Prussian State Railway decided to convert the Breslau–Königszelt line at 15,000-volt $16\frac{2}{3}$ cycles ac. This was a heavily-graded line in the Silesian mountains, and work was not finished until 1922. Further extensions were made and it totalled 350 km (217 miles) by 1928. After 1945 the whole system, catenary, locomotives and substations, was removed to the USSR.

This early but fruitful period of railway electrification is noteworthy for its intense experimentation, financed by the big electrical manufacturers. Electric technology at the time was developing fast, and a railway that had heavily invested in one year's system might find that it would have got better value by waiting for tomorrow's developments. At such a time, wait-and-see was the best policy for any railway not facing urgent problems which only electrification could solve. The fate of three-phase electrification emphasizes this. At one early period three-phase seemed to be the best prospect. Electricity was generated and transmitted in this form, and the three-phase electric motor was the simplest and lightest type. But three-phase demanded two conductor wires, and three-phase motors could offer only one running speed, a disadvantage only partly solved by installing more than one motor on each locomotive. When better systems were developed the Swiss and Italian railways electrified on the old system eventually changed over, rather expensively. The Swiss Berne–Lötschberg–Simplon Railway, which at various times made great contributions to electric railway technology, changed to single-phase alternating current in 1930, and those Italian railways on the other side of the Alps that had the same system were all converted by the 1970s. On the eve of World War I the competition was no longer between three-phase and the others, but between low-voltage dc and high-voltage single-phase ac. In general, main-line electrifications used the latter, with overhead wire conductors. Suburban electrifications used conductor-rail dc, the high-voltage ac current received from the electric grid being converted to low voltage (600–750 volts) dc at substations along the line.

In the last half century, improvement and innovation have probably been due to the pressures of competition rather than to inventiveness on the part of administrators; and railway electrification certainly seems to support this view. It was technically possible in the prosperous years before 1914, but it was not until the difficult inter-war years that it became widespread. Managements discovered that electric traction could both decrease their costs and make their services more attractive. By 1945 eight countries had electrified mileages of more than 1,500 km (935 miles). These were, Italy (7,100 km or 4,400 miles), Sweden (5,400 km or 3,350 miles), USA (4,980 km or 3,090 miles), Switzerland (4,760 km or 2,960 miles), France (3,520 km or 2,190 miles), Germany (2,740 km or 1,460 miles), Russia (1,675 km or 1,040 miles) and Britain (1,545 km or 960 miles). Twenty-seven other countries had smaller systems, and these included several colonial railways (India, Java, Morocco and Algeria).

Technical development continued fast during this period, making it difficult for managements to decide whether to electrify on the latest system or to wait a few years in the hope of something better. Of the railways that went ahead confidently with good but obsolescent systems, one of the most successful was Britain's newly constituted Southern Railway. This had inherited a 650-volt dc system with third-rail conduction and enlarged it into a dense outer-suburban network to the south of London, including long routes like that from London

improved services which they brought, attracted greatly increased traffic. Only two suburban electrifications were relative failures, those of Havana in Cuba, which ceased operating electric passenger trains in 1940, and of Batavia in the Dutch East Indies, which was not revived after World War II.

Inter-war main-line electrification was largely divided between a northern and central European system using 15,000 or 16,000 volts 16 2/3 cycles ac

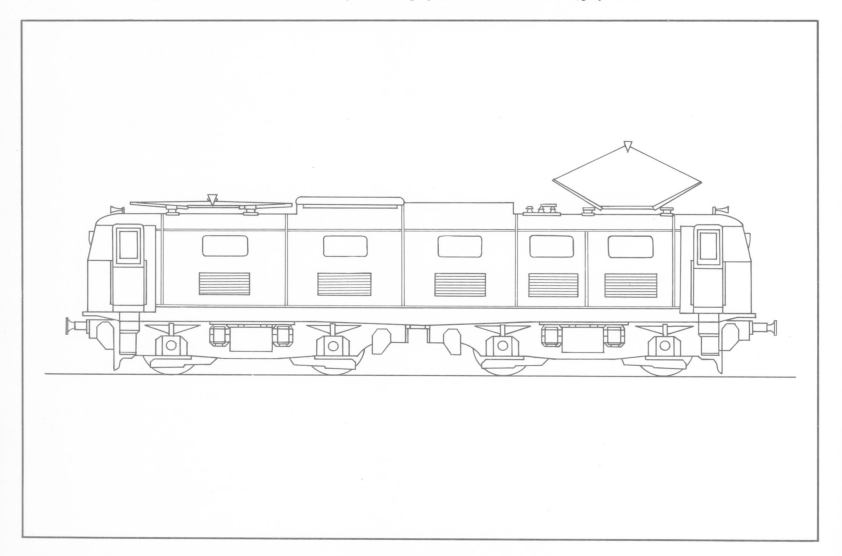

to Portsmouth (119 km or 74 miles): all this despite the greater suitability of higher voltages and overhead transmission for lines longer than about 20 km (12 miles). But the increased traffic resulting from the prompt change to electric traction more than outweighed the economic deficiencies of third-rail electrification. London's suburbs developed rapidly, housebuilders made fortunes, and for a time the Southern Railway was one of the few to make profits from commuter traffic. It was only in winter, when rain sometimes froze on the conductor rails, that the Southern's management asked itself whether, perhaps, a wrong decision had been taken.

Similar urban transformations occurred wherever railways electrified their suburban networks. Quick frequent trains encouraged town dwellers to move first to the suburbs and then to the outer suburbs. Among the big inter-war schemes were those of Sydney, Melbourne, Tokyo, Berlin, Moscow, Budapest, Leningrad and Capetown. Paris suburban lines were electrified as part of mainline schemes, and the same happened in New York, which also benefited from the electrification of the outer-suburban Long Island Railroad. These conversions, because of the

current, a western European system of 1,500 volts dc, and an American system of 11,000 volts 25 cycles ac. Towards the end of the period a 3,000-volt dc system was beginning to supersede the 1,500-volt method. The two basic, and conflicting, factors in choice of system was that electricity was generated and distributed, for good technical and economic reasons, as high-voltage 50 or 60 cycles alternating current, but electric traction motors, if they were to be simple and to function well over a wide range of speeds, were best designed to use low-voltage direct current. In the inter-war period, despite some interesting experimentation, a really good technique was never developed for electrifying railways at 'industrial frequency' (50 cycles, except for the USA and Japan where it was 60 cycles). With the suburban electrifications at 650 or 750 volts, substations had to be located along the track at about 10-km (6-mile) intervals. These converted, with some energy loss, the industrial frequency high-voltage three-phase alternating current to low-voltage direct current. With so low a voltage, conductors of wide cross-section were needed; hence the use of a third rail rather than overhead line. The big advantage of

The Manchester–Sheffield 1,500-volt electrification work in England was suspended during World War 2. This locomotive was the only unit built before this suspension and, hitherto unused, was loaned to the war-ravaged Dutch railways in 1945, where it was named *Tommy*.

this system was that low voltage dc motors were cheap and simple. With higher-voltage dc the sub-stations could be farther apart, and overhead transmission was possible. The Milwaukee Railroad's two electrified sections through the Rockies was an early (1916) example of 3,000-volt dc successfully applied but it was not until the 1920s, when a new (mercury-arc) rectifier made possible the conversion of three-phase ac into direct current with little loss,

Electric locomotives at first included many features of steam-locomotive practice, and this was emphasized by the use of traditional locomotive driving wheels and coupling rods. Axle-mounted motors succeeded this approach, and a landmark came in 1944, when the Swiss Berne–Lötschberg–Simplon Railway acquired its series AE 4/4 locomotives. This was not the first design to be mounted on trucks, with all axles powered, but it was the first

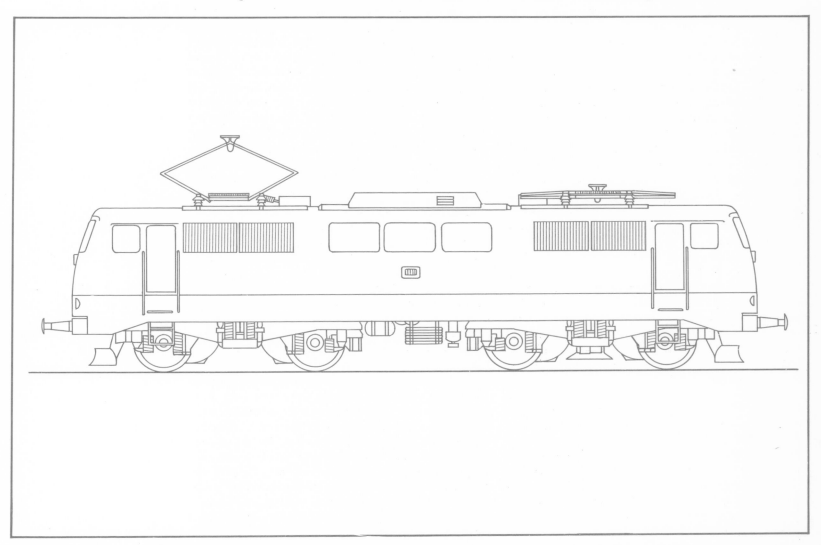

German Federal Railways (DB) Class 111 electric passenger locomotive. Designed for a maximum speed of 150 kph (95 mph), this class was built in 1975 and 1976 by Krauss-Maffei, with electrical equipment by Siemens.

that higher-voltage dc became a real attraction. With 3,000 volts the substations could be as far apart as 40 km (25 miles), with a corresponding saving in capital costs. However, the 1,500-volt system was preferred by a number of railways; although it required more substations, its locomotives were simpler and therefore cheaper.

The $16\frac{2}{3}$ and 25 cycles ac systems, used in northern Europe and America respectively, had their origin in the fact that it was fairly easy both to convert industrial frequency current to these frequencies and to design effective electric motors working up to 25 cycles. With ac, voltages in the overhead wire could be high, thereby enabling thin wires to be used while reducing voltage drop so sharply that substations could be very widely spaced. The use of industrial frequency itself, 50 cycles at 16,000 volts, was achieved in Hungary by the Ganz company as early as 1923, and in the 1930s over a hundred miles of Hungarian main line was equipped with this system. However, after World War II much better systems of using 50 cycles current would be applied, the fruit of experiments being carried out in Germany, France and Russia.

to have a truck design that allowed regular running at high speed. This locomotive may therefore be regarded as the prototype for the post-war electric locomotives, in almost all of which the typical inter-war wheel layout of small carrying wheels and larger, usually rigidly mounted, driving wheels, was abandoned.

Most of the main-line electrifications were of lines with heavy traffic (making the heavy capital cost of electrical installations worthwhile), and usually lines that presented particular difficulty for steam traction. Electric locomotives never ran short of steam, and could exert high tractive force for long periods over heavily graded lines. This was one reason why mountainous areas like Switzerland, Austria, Sweden and Bavaria witnessed large-scale conversion; another reason was that such terrain also tended to be without coal but with good hydro-electric potential. In France, where there was considerable main-line conversion, such factors hardly applied, but the operational and economic advantages of electrification were considered well worth the expense. The same was true of Holland and Belgium. In the latter, electrification was slow, the short

Brussels to Antwerp main line being the biggest conversion, In Holland the Amsterdam–Rotterdam electrification was extended to the Hook of Holland, and the main lines radiating from Utrecht, carrying very heavy traffic, were also electrified. In Holland, as well as in Germany and France (but not in Britain), electrification continued during the war, although at a slower pace.

Among the notable inter-war electrifications was that of the Lapland Railway in Sweden, a heavy-traffic ore carrier. This conversion had its origins as early as 1910, when the first contracts were placed, and the entire 450 km (280 mile) length was finished in 1923. The short continuation of this line across the frontier to Narvik in Norway was electrified also, thereby providing an electrified railway linking the North Atlantic with the Gulf of Bothnia. Meanwhile the Swedish Railways started to convert the main line from Stockholm to Gothenburg, the 460 km (285 miles) being finished in 1925. Many more lines were electrified in the 1930s, including private narrow-gauge lines, the Swedish ASEA company being responsible for the majority of electric locomotives. By 1945 Sweden and Switzerland were leading the world in the proportion of their lines under electric catenary; both had their main lines electrified and both had a large number of electrified private lines (including narrow-gauge railways) under catenary. Both, too, were self-sufficient in the production of electric locomotives and rolling stock. Swiss firms, like Oerlikon and Brown Boveri, had made great contributions to the technology of railway electrification, and the Swedish firm of ASEA would soon do likewise.

In Austria where, like Sweden, Switzerland, and Germany, the $16\frac{2}{3}$ cycles high-voltage system was preferred, a similar process took place, with the west to east main line through Innsbruck and Salzburg being the longest and one of the earliest schemes. In Germany, however, electrification was perhaps slower than might have been expected from the advanced state of German electrical engineering; one reason for this was the availability of good cheap coal, and it was no coincidence that most electrification was achieved in Bavaria, which was most distant from the coalfields. In France the Sud-Ouest region of the SNCF (formerly the Paris–Orléans Railway) achieved the greatest electrified mileage with its two lines from Paris to the Spanish frontier; it had electrified the Paris–Orléans section in the 1920s, and by 1938 two long extensions from Orléans had been completed, via Tours to Bordeaux and the western Pyrenees, and via the Massif Central to Toulouse and the eastern Pyrenees. In addition the Ouest Region (formerly the Etat Railway) electrified from Paris to Le Mans, and there was also considerable electrification in the south. All these schemes used 1,500-volt dc. However, the 730 km (454 mile) electrification carried out by French engineers of the Marakesh main line in Morocco used 3,000 volts.

In the USA electrification was never as popular as in Europe, partly because of relatively low traffic carried by most of the main lines. In fact, it is in America that most of the rare cases of de-electrification have occurred. Thus the Norfolk & Western Railroad electrified a 48 km (30 mile) heavily-graded line passing through the Elkhorn Tunnel in 1915, and in the 1920s extended this to make a 180 km

(112 mile) section. But it was not long before the Elkhorn Tunnel was rebuilt with a bigger cross-section (to speed smoke clearance) and some of the gradients and curves eased, after which steam traction returned. However, a neighbouring coal-carrying line, the Virginian Railroad, retained its 216 km (134 mile) electrification through the mountains down to Roanoke. The most ambitious of the American electrifications was undertaken by the Pennsylvania Railroad, which had already established a progressive reputation in steam motive-power policy. This began as a New York to Washington electrification, which was finished in 1935, and then extended to Harrisburg to make a total of 1,105 km (688 miles). Like other contemporary US mainline conversions, it used 11,000-volt 25 cycles alternating current; it was the most successful of the big US electrifications, and enabled the Pennsylvania Railroad to handle an increasingly dense traffic economically and at higher speeds.

Italy electrified its lines faster than anywhere else. From 1934 until the war the Italian State Railway converted an average of 492 km (275 miles) each year. Partly this speed was due to the nature of the regime, Mussolini having earlier established his reputation as the leader who 'made the trains run on time'. Partly, too, it was for reasons of self-sufficiency; the government in particular and Italians in general did not relish the dependence on foreign coal, especially as hydro-electricity could be obtained from the Alps. Electrification often went hand in hand with the construction or reconstruction of high-speed routes (*the direttissime*); the first major electrification was of the new Bologna–Prato *direttissima* in 1934. By 1941 all the main lines were electrified, and 110 kph (70 mph) schedules were offered by long-distance passenger trains. The old three-phase system still existed in the north, and had indeed been extended, but most of the new electrification was at 3,000-volt dc. Despite the generally unimaginative design of past Italian steam locomotives, Italian designers and manufacturers produced a distinguished and highly standardized range of electric motive power. In particular, a three-unit air-conditioned articulated passenger train appeared just before the war, carrying 100 passengers. The first set, on trial, ran from Florence to Milan at an average of 164 kph (102 mph), and touched 200 kph (125 mph).

Apart from the Southern Railway's extension of its third-rail system, there was little electrification in Britain between the wars. One scheme which was started was for the conversion of the heavily-graded Manchester to Sheffield line at 1,500 volts. This was one of the railway investment schemes which had financial support from the Government, anxious at that time to ease unemployment. It was halted during the war. British electrical engineering companies, lacking a good home market, did undertake substantial projects abroad. These included a 286 km (178 mile) section of the Paulista Railway in Brazil and an 140 km (87 mile) stretch of the Sorocobana Railway. Both these used 3,000-volt dc. In India the first electrified line was that of the Great Indian Peninsula Railway from Bombay up the steeply graded sections to Poona and Igatpuri, electrified in the late 1920s at 1,500 volt dc. A short stretch of the Bombay, Baroda, and Central India Railway's line from Bombay was also converted on

Prototype electric high-speed multiple-unit train of German Federal Railways (DB). This type ET403 set was built in 1974 and is intended for first-class-only services, with a maximum speed of 200 kph (125 mph).

The 'Sprinter' of Dutch Railways. This is a new two-car multiple unit electric suburban set, first delivered in 1974 and expected to replace older sets. 145 seats are provided, and the top speed of 125 kph (80 mph) can be reached in 80 seconds from start.

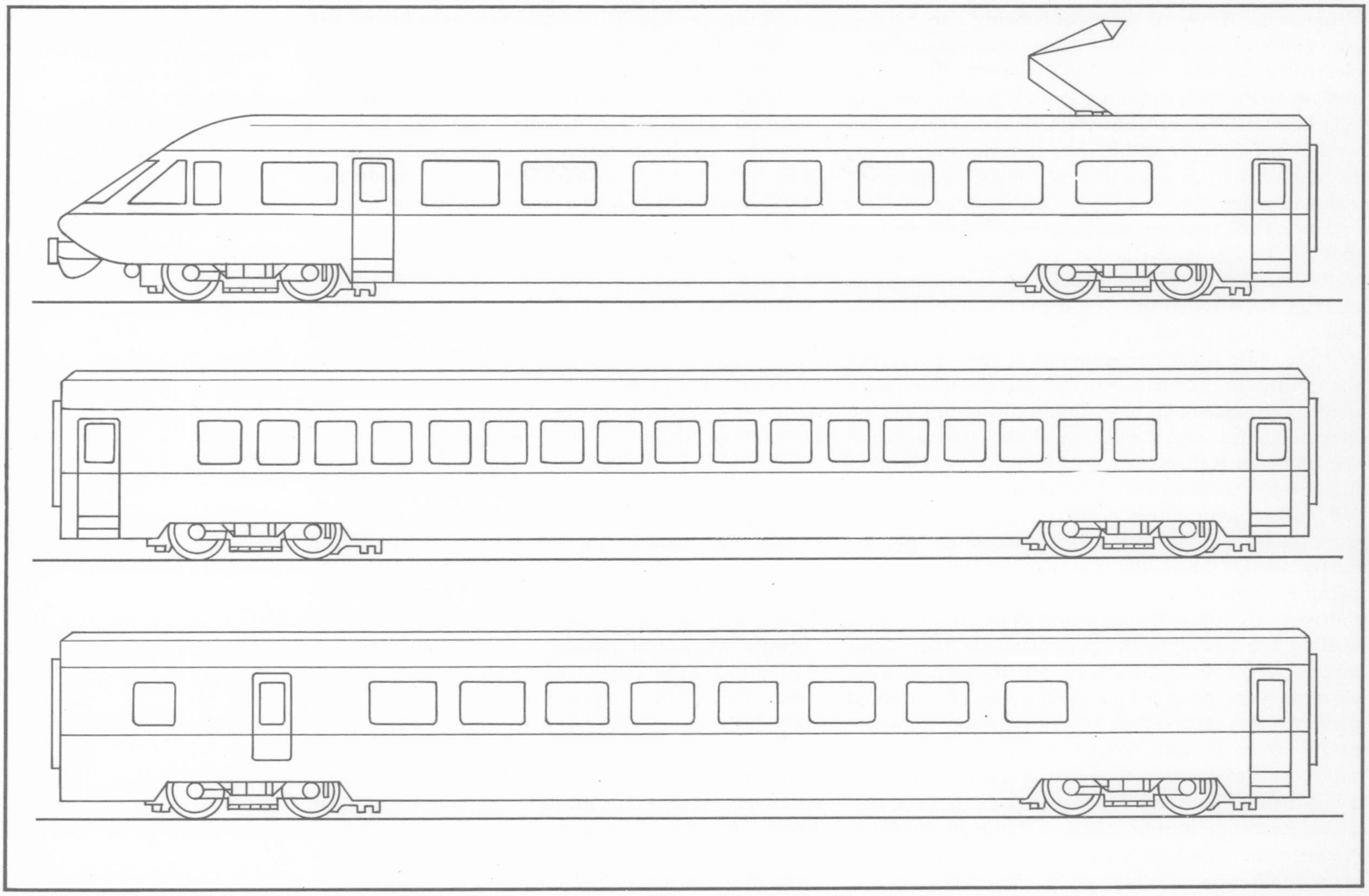

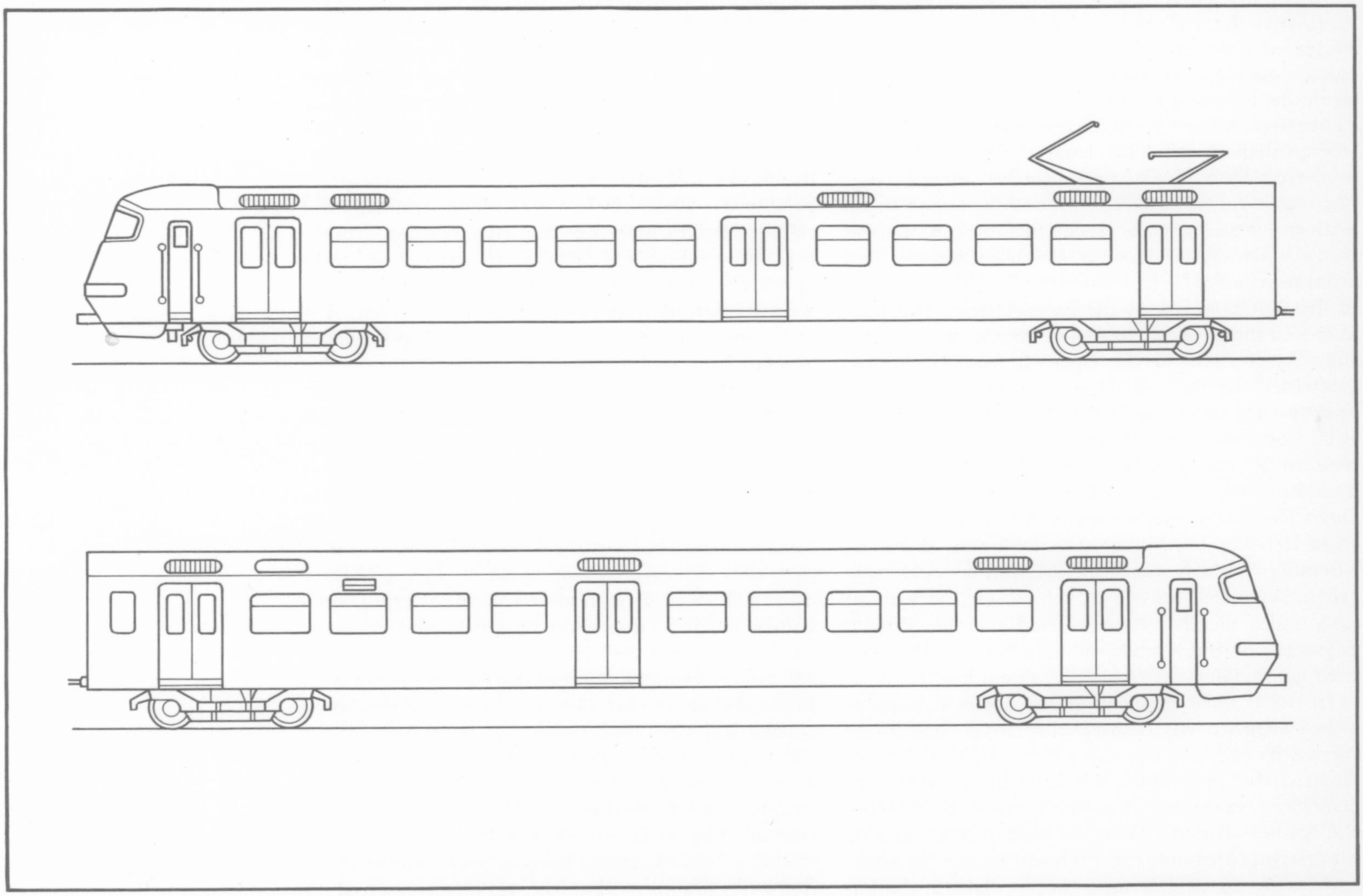

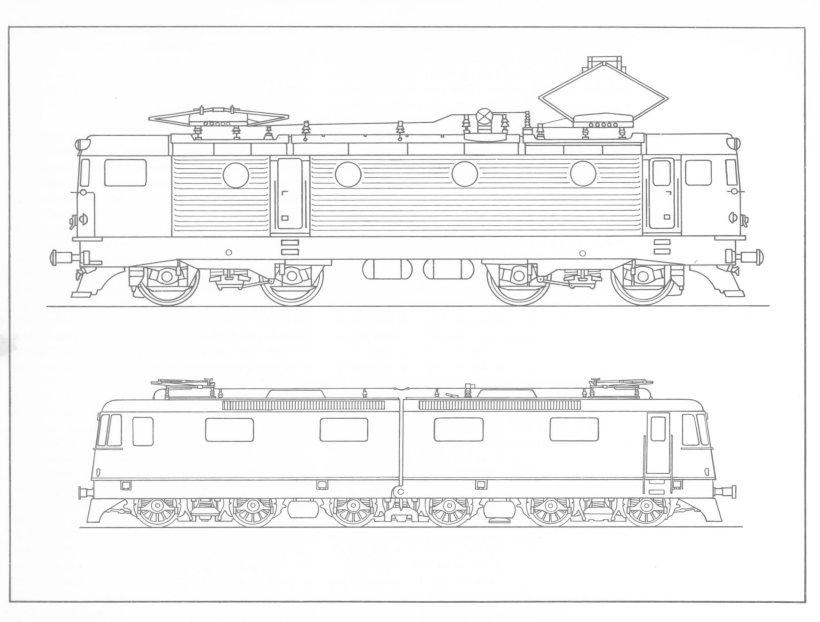

the same system. The metre-gauge line from Madras to Tambaram, carrying a dense passenger traffic, was electrified in 1931. This 29 km (18 mile) line, in addition to multiple-unit passenger trains, was also provided with electric locomotives which had batteries for use on non-electrified sidings. In New Zealand three sections were electrified at 1,500 volts. These were a difficult section through Arthur's Pass, a short section out of Christchurch, and two Wellington suburban lines. In South Africa the heavily-graded and heavily-trafficked line from Durban to Volksrust was electrified at 3,000 volts between 1926 and 1940, the 554 km (344 miles) of this scheme including a substantial suburban electrification around Durban.

In the USSR conditions were rather different from elsewhere, the main preoccupation being the passage of greatly increased traffic without corresponding capital investment. On the one hand, electrification demanded much capital, but on the other the extra carrying capacity of electrified lines meant that electrification could make it unnecessary to double-track a single line. Inter-war Soviet electrification was therefore modest, comprising suburban conversions at Moscow, Leningrad, and Baku (this last being the pioneer electrification scheme and sponsored by the local government rather than the railway), and short main-line conversions where grades and heavy traffic made electrification worthwhile; part of the Trans-

Caucasus line over the Suram Pass, some dense traffic lines in the Donets Basin, the Murmansk line, a 490 km (305 mile) line through the Urals, and a line in the new heavy industrial area of the Kuznetsk Basin. Most of these schemes were at 1,500 volt dc, but the Baku conversion was at 1,200 volts and a 3,000-volt system appeared just before the war. Electric locomotives were built in Russia after some US (General Electric) and Italian (Italian Brown Boveri) units had been first acquired for the Trans-Caucasus scheme.

Later developments in steam traction Despite the advent of diesel and electric traction, steam locomotive technology made notable advances in the inter-war years. The leading designers were now more scientific in their approach, encouraged partly by the publication of academic research into some of the longstanding problems of locomotive design. In a number of countries, stationary locomotive testing plants had been built, in which a locomotive could be tested under standard conditions. As we have seen, this idea was introduced in Russia, where in 1881 the Russian engineer Borodin mounted a locomotive clear of the ground and used its driving axle to drive the belt of the workshop line shaft while he measured its steam consumption. Professor Goss of Purdue University in Illinois took the concept further by mounting on rollers the locomotives under test, with provision for varying the resistance of those rollers. It was as a result of Goss's experi-

Above: Class Rc2 of the Swedish State Railways. This class, built by ASEA in 1967, was the first electric locomotive class to be equipped with thyristor control. Similar locomotives were supplied to the Austrian Federal Railways in 1972.
Below: Class Re 6/6 electric locomotive of the Swiss Federal Railways. Delivered in 1972, these locomotives are designed for high power output (10,600 hp) as they are intended for use on the St Gotthard line, hauling 800-tonne trains at 80 kph (50 mph) over 1 in 37 gradients.

ments that US designers were provided with a formula for determining the most efficient proportions for cylinder and blastpipe. Goss's work was carried further by the Pennsylvania Railroad, which installed its own testing plant and which in many ways surpassed the American locomotive building companies in the quality of the locomotives it built.

In the inter-war years there were three main schools of locomotive design. The American and Russian aim was to design locomotives which, within the limitations imposed by track standards, would pull the maximum weight of train at the maximum average speed; the Americans needed this haulage capacity to provide a faster and more economical service, while the Russians needed it so that a given line could handle increasing traffic. Eventually, after trying a prototype with the unprecedented 4-14-4 wheel arrangement, the Russians chose fairly orthodox American-style locomotives of the 2-10-2 and 2-8-4 wheel arrangements. In the USA, Woodard of the Lima Works introduced his 'super power' concept. He knew that while some railroads were content to enlarge the Mallet type of articulated locomotive this solution was not entirely satisfactory, and that the solution chosen by the rival Alco designers, a change from two-cylinder to three-cylinder propulsion, would raise capital and maintenance costs. He realized that the vital need was to increase steam-raising capacity, for existing locomotives had enough cylinder-power already but could not always make proper use of it. Woodard therefore introduced an enlarged firebox, and to support it provided a four-wheel trailing truck. This implied 2-8-4 and 2-10-4 wheel arrangements. Then, to ensure that the expansive power of the steam was properly utilized, Woodard incorporated a maximum cut-off device that made it impossible for locomotive men to admit steam to the cylinder for more than 60 per cent of the piston stroke. As this measure would inevitably reduce the maximum tractive effort of the locomotive, which was needed at starting, Woodard provided a compensating increase in the steam pressure, in the first instance raising boiler pressure from the usual 13.3 kg/cm² (190 pounds per square inch) to 16.8 (240). Other Woodard features were an articulated connecting rod, which spread the thrust of the piston over two crank pins, and cast-steel cylinders, which were each one ton lighter than iron. Woodard's A-1 of 1925 was a demonstration model 2-8-4 which went

to the Boston & Albany Railroad and immediately showed that it could produce greater horsepower for a smaller fuel consumption. Other railroads quickly ordered similar units from Lima, and in general Woodard's work set the standard for US non-articulated designs right up to the end of steam traction.

This American development had little influence in Europe, although Woodard's split-drive connecting rod was tried in Britain. American conditions, the need for great haulage capacity and ability to endure rough maintenance, made US experience inapplicable, except perhaps in wartime conditions. Another country that pursued interesting design policies without affecting the rest of the world was Britain, with its four new railway companies. The Great Western Railway was content to sit complacently on the laurels of Churchward's great designs of the previous generation, and Churchward principles were applied to Southern Railway and London Midland & Scottish Railway locomotives in the inter-war years. On the LMS they were somewhat improved upon, resulting in some very useful standard types, as well as the streamlined Pacifics which hauled the fastest trains in the 1930s. On the London & North Eastern Railway Nigel Gresley was addicted to the three-cylinder system, using a beautifully engineered valve gear called Gresley's conjugated gear, although it was not Gresley who had invented it. Using this valve gear and, more important, providing big boilers, Gresley built some outstanding locomotives, including the streamlined Pacifics of Class 'A4', one of which, *Mallard*, achieved 212 kph (126 mph). However, the Gresley valve gear, which in one important respect defied theory, was not as good as Gresley believed, and was an early victim of poor wartime maintenance. After Gresley died in 1941 his successor chose to build simpler, more reliable, but less spectacular machines. In the meantime, Gresley's colleague Bulleid had moved to the Southern Railway. Bulleid innovated almost as a matter of principle, and the 'Merchant Navy' class of Pacific which he built during the war was novel in many respects, including a chain-driven valve gear. Bulleid's designs, too, were disliked by his successors even though they had exceptional performances to their credit.

In Germany the Prussian school of locomotive design was applied to the new Reichsbahn by Richard Wagner, who designed a series of standard

Gresley's A4 Pacific, a very successful British class. *Mallard* was the most celebrated example of the type, achieving the world speed record for a steam train of 202.8 kph (126 mph) in 1938.

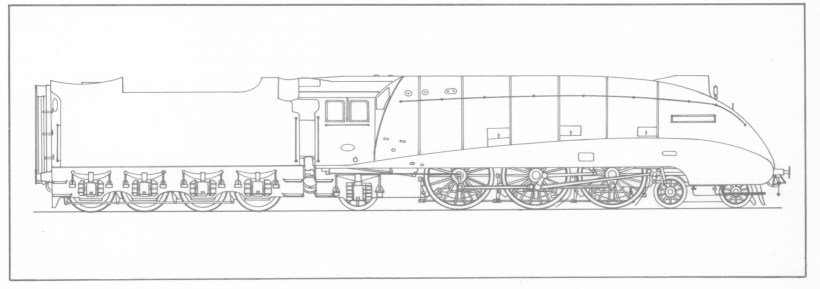

locomotives. The Prussian tradition aimed especially at low maintenance costs and moderate fuel consumption, with little attempt to achieve high horsepowers. (Wagner's design office worked on the principle that outputs greater than 1,000 hp were unnecessary.) Thus there were fairly low boiler pressures (to save boiler maintenance costs), compensated by rather large cylinders, a preference for the simple two-outside-cylinder layout, well-braced bar frames, round-top fireboxes, general simplicity, but careful design of every detail. In the 1930s there were variations from these themes, with a few prototypes of high-speed streamlined locomotives filling the headlines for a few weeks of glory, but in general the Prussian principles persisted and today there are still Wagner locomotives at work in the two Germanies.

The greatest of the inter-war generation of locomotive engineers was probably the Frenchman André Chapelon, whose success in obtaining great increases of power by rebuilding locomotives according to principles that he had worked out from theory attracted the attention of foreign locomotive designers and provided the SNCF with what was probably the most efficient stock of locomotives ever possessed by a railway. Chapelon's rebuilding followed three lines. He improved the draught, without increasing steam back-pressure in the cylinders, by a carefully calculated blastpipe design (the 'Kylchap' chimney); he enlarged and streamlined the internal steam passages even more than du Bougguet and Churchward had done, thereby eliminating the 'throttling' of steam which had hitherto been unnoticed; and he increased the degree of superheat, bringing the steam temperature to the maximum possible without burning up the lubricating oil. Applying these principles to specific locomotives, Chapelon (who had a mathematical background) was guided by theory, and could forecast precisely the results of his modifications. Because in the 1920s he was claiming that he could rebuild modern locomotives so as to produce 50 per cent more power for the same fuel consumption, he was not at first believed. But in 1929 his first conversion for his employer, the Paris–Orléans Railway, did just that, and Chapelon's reputation was made. Subsequent French designs, both for new types and for rebuilds, followed his principles. Just before the war he built an experimental 2-12-0 with many novel features, and after the war a prototype 4-8-4, but these promising machines, which might well have taken steam locomotive technology another long step forward, were early victims of the French National Railways' decision to electrify.

Rolling stock Although there were no spectacular improvements in rolling stock design in the inter-war years, there was steady progress, despite the Depression, in extending improvements first adopted before 1914. In particular, there was an increasing use of steel, not only for the underframes of passenger and freight cars, but for the bodies too. Although steel was heavier than wood, it was more robust in accidents, and it lent itself better to mass-production methods; the old coach-building tradition of hand-made bodies was finally disappearing. In America, where passenger cars had always been much heavier, in response to the public demand for more protection in case of accident, there was an effort to reduce weight by the use of aluminium. Also

to this period belongs the widespread introduction by the Budd Corporation of stainless-steel passenger-car bodies, welded by a patented process. The fluted steel side panels of Budd-built stock, very strong for their light weight, became a familiar feature of US railroads, and after the war they were adopted for certain trains of French National Railways. In inter-war France, weight reduction was achieved by using a 'monocoque' construction in which the body and underframe were designed and built as one unit, with a pronounced tubular cross-section; in effect, this used the former body section as a load-bearing member, thereby adding strength without demanding a corresponding weight increase.

The best trains became more luxurious, especially in the USA. Air conditioning was introduced in America in the late 1920s and was imitated elsewhere, although on a smaller scale; among the first non-American users were the Australian Commonwealth Railways, which applied it to the Trans-Australian service, the Federated Malay States Railway, and certain French colonial railways. The provision of train hostesses, hairdressing salons, public telephones, typists, and radios soon followed on a few trains but most of these innovations had a publicity rather than a practical value and did not last long. On the bulk of long-distance passenger trains, however, there was a steady improvement in basic facilities. The previous competition between electric and gas illumination had been finally won by electricity, and showers appeared on more long-distance trains. Accommodation for the lower-fare passengers improved considerably in the USA; some of the eastern railroads, conscious of highway competition, began to offer luxury all-coach-class trains, including observation saloon cars, hitherto rigidly reserved for the first-class passenger. In Britain there was a longstanding tradition of providing comfortable accommodation for the third-class passenger, but in continental Europe the third-class passenger still rode on uncomfortable wooden seats, and often in four or six-wheel cars; second class, long abolished in Britain, provided an intermediate standard of accommodation, usually inferior to the British third class. The superior comfort of British third-class travel (renamed second class after nationalization) has persisted up to the present day.

Freight cars became bigger, for good economic reasons, and highly specialized vehicles were built. Among the most exceptional of these were a 28-axle cantilevered car built by the London & North Eastern Railway for conveying power-station stators, a Japanese vehicle conveying live fish in tanks, and an ornate Egyptian car for conveying the Holy Carpet. Some progress was made in Europe with automatic brakes, especially when, for competitive reasons, high-speed merchandise services were introduced. However, the rear brake van on British railways, and brakemen sitting in wooden perches on Continental freight cars, were still the rule. The Russian railways opted for a complete change to automatic brakes and a modified Willison automatic coupler, but the process was not finished until the mid-1950s. In Japan, however, where at the time of nationalization in 1906 all except two railways were using screw couplings, a complete change to automatic centre couplings was accomplished in five hectic days in 1925, after seven years of preparation.

India

There is no more interesting day excursion than the one from Delhi to Agra, and none but the keenest and one-track-minded rail buff would go to Agra and not see something of the marvellous array of monuments within easy distance of the city centre. To work the 'Taj Express' is a prestige job for the locomotive department, and the big semi-streamlined Pacific of the 'WP' class is resplendent in black and pale green. The green indicates Central Railway, and is symbolic of the more colourful era now existing on the Indian railways. To appreciate its significance one has to take the history of railways in India back roughly 100 years, when the present network was being built up. Then, although there were a considerable number of apparently independent companies, some with their head offices in London, the prospect of eventual takeover by the State hung over them all. The contracts they held were for a limited number of years only, and by the latter part of the nineteenth century quite a number were wholly State-owned and managed, though retaining names appropriate to the territorial activities.

Long before the Indian Empire gave place to the Dominion of India, and then to the Republic, the majority of the railways had passed into State control, though there remained the former individual features of great lines like the East Indian, the Great Indian Peninsula, and the Bombay, Baroda and Central India, together with their distinctive locomotive and carriage liveries. With the granting of independence in 1947, and the establishment also of the states of West and East Pakistan, some of the former railways, notably the North Western and the Bengal and Assam, found their main routes severed, and drastic revision of their activities became necessary. Of the great and efficient North Western Railway only the lines southeast of Amritsar remained in India, and in due course some

Top right. A 0.760 m (2ft 6in) gauge 0-6-2 tender engine built by Bagnall of Stafford in 1912 in service at Bhavnagar in December 1974.
Centre right. Another Bagnall narrow gauge, a tank engine, of 1926, 0-6-4 'WT' class in service on the Western Railway.
Right. A highly decorated 0.760 m (2ft 6in) gauge 0-6-2 'W' class built 1913, and in service at Nadiad, Western Railway in 1974.

regrouping of administrative areas was necessary, to set up regional territories of approximately equal business extent, though not necessarily of equal mileage, or ownership of rolling stock. Some of the new 'railways' approximated to the older 'companies'. For example, the 'Central' covered most of the area formerly worked by the Great Indian Peninsula; the 'Western' took over the B.B. & C.I, while the South Eastern took that of the Bengal-Nagpur.

While a huge programme of standardization of locomotives, to cover requirements of all India, was set in motion, aiming to have the minimum number of separate classes, distinctive colours were adopted by the different railways, and passenger engines of all vintages, and some freight also, were finished in two-tone colour schemes, with black as the unifying tone. Thus one finds leaf green as the second tone on Central Railway engines; orange for the Southern, red-brown for the Northern, and blue-green for the Eastern – to mention only a few. The bullet-nosed smokebox fronts of the 'WP' Pacifics, as exemplified by the engine of the 'Taj Express', are embellished with ornamental stars, the points sometimes alternating between colour and stainless steel. Then take a look inside the cab of the 'Taj' engine: the various fittings gleam like the contents of a jeweler's shop, and over the firehole door is a beautiful silhouette of the Taj Mahal itself, worked with all the skill of the Indian craftsman in brasswork. Yet to ride to Agra on the footplate is to discover that once it has started and worked up to a steady 96 kph (60 mph), that decorative engine reverted to the commonplace; she rattles and bangs along just like any other hard-worked unit and devours all the coal that two firemen, shovelling in turn, can get through the firedoor.

The Indian railways started before political control of the subcontinent passed to the Crown in 1858, and before it had achieved its later Imperial status, and it was when administration was in the hands of the East India Company that the great Governor-General, the Marquis of Dalhousie, drew up the scheme of main routes which is still the backbone of the Indian railways today. He went to India straight from an important post at the Board of Trade, in England, and had been so involved in all the controversy over railway gauges, following Brunel's adoption of 7 ft or 2.133 m for the Great Western, that he laid down emphatically that in India there must be only one gauge. The starting points of the pioneer Indian railways were originally very far from each other – in Bombay, in Calcutta, and in Madras; but the plan he drew up envisaged a connected and integral network, and a standard rail gauge of 5 ft 6 in or 1.676 m was laid down.

As the master plan took shape, however, it was apparent that to take full advantage of railway transport many feeder lines would be needed. There were times of famine and distress that could be relieved only by effective transport, and yet there was little prospect of major 5ft 6 in gauge lines in such areas paying their way. Thus was conceived the idea of having a subsidiary network of feeder lines built on the metre gauge. Some were entirely new railway systems, like the Southern Mahratta and the Assam–Bengal; there were metre-gauge branches built within existing companies, of which the network west of the Bombay, Baroda and Central India broad-gauge main line was one of the notable examples, and there was an extensive mileage built up in the southernmost part of India. The Burma railways, separated from those of India by the intervening mountain ranges were built entirely on the metre gauge. For the lighter traffic and slower speeds many picturesque locomotives were built specially, and as many of them survive today they are much sought after by photographers, who travel far off the beaten track of tourists in India to find these old locomotives still at work.

At the same time traffic conditions in many parts of India have changed considerably in the 100 years since the Viceroyalty of Lord Mayo, when construction on the metre gauge was first authorized. The changes are nowhere more evident than in the far south, in the populous state of Kerala, and there at least one section of a line built on the metre gauge has been converted to the broad, 5 ft 6 in, gauge, between Ernakulam and Trivandrum. Travelling on this line, seeing the works in progress, and the continuous forests of palm trees that make the countryside look like a vast impenetrable jungle, it was hard to realize that this is the most densely populated part of India. There may be intense concentrations in the great cities of the north, but between them in the valley of the Ganga, for example, the countryside is entirely rural for hundreds of miles. Not so in Kerala, where the villages follow thick and fast, and every country station has its crowd of gaily attired passengers waiting for the train. In recent years new and powerful locomotives have been designed specially for the metre gauge and in their various operating areas they carry the colours of their regions.

The electric suburban trains of Bombay and Calcutta have a colour and character that is unique among commuter services around great cities. It is not so much the trains themselves, although the working observed from one or another of the modern efficiently controlled push-button panel signal boxes is impressive enough, it is the passengers who provide most of the colour. One does not fully appreciate what crowding means on a railway train until going to Howrah, or Sealdah in Calcutta, or to Churchgate, or Victoria Terminus in Bombay. The fast electric suburban trains have sliding doors, but nobody ever attempts

Left. One of the finely embellished 'WP' streamlined 4-6-2s of the Central Railway passing Delhi Junction with an express for the south.
Above right. A passenger train passing Delhi Junction, hauled by a standard 2-8-2 'WG' class, with decorated smokebox.
Right. The Matheran Hill Railway is one of the most accessible of the hill railways of India, starting from Neral, on the main Bombay–Poona line. A little 0-6-0 tank engine of 1905 vintage, built by Orenstein & Koppel, of Berlin, toils up the 1 in 20 gradient.

to close them. During the day they are left open to keep the carriages cool inside, and in the rush-hour peaks the trains are so jam-packed inside that there is a bunch of passengers hanging on around the doors. The trains present an extraordinary sight with these clusters, two to every carriage all along the lengthy trains. Most of these intrepid commuters are clad in white, but at the doors of the 'Ladies Only' carriages there are equally animated clusters, in saris of every colour in the rainbow, with draperies flying in the wind as the trains sweep along at anything up to 50 mph.

To see Indian commuting at its most intense one needs to be at Howrah on the right bank of the Hooghly River, about 10 am, when three of these packed trains come into the terminus simultaneously and together discharge between *nine and ten thousand* people into the station concourse within seconds of each other! The railway operating is as smart and efficient as in any London station. These multiple-unit electric trains are never at the platforms for more than about six or seven minutes. They go out either as empty stock, to await the needs of the outgoing suburban rush, or provide an outward passenger service. There is no time to spare for the platform space is needed for the next inward-bound train, bringing another 3,000 passengers.

A colourful Indian Railway scene at Danapur, with a 'WG' class standard 2-8-2, and passengers, squatters and others disporting themselves on the track.

In complete contrast are the 'hill' railways of India, on the narrow gauge. As British administration developed, from the early days of the East India Company to the Imperial epoch of the latter part of the nineteenth century, the seat of Government was transferred in the hot season from Calcutta to the hill stations of the Himalayas, and two spectacular little railways were built climbing high into the mountains. The first of these mounted from Siliguri, north of Calcutta, to the romantically situated mountain resort of Darjeeling. It was built in 1879–81, on the 0.610 m (2 ft) gauge, and at the time was considered quite an incredible feat of railway engineering. Today it could be regarded as a top tourist attraction, but still more remarkable is the fact that it remains steam-worked, and by a type of saddle-tank locomotive first introduced in 1889!

The engineer who surveyed and built this railway resorted to every known device to gain height, because a summit level of 2,255 m (7,407 ft) above sea level, at Ghum, was unavoidable. He used spiral locations, 'Z' type reversing stations and long gradients of 1 in 25, with sections as steep as 1 in 20 but unlike the mountain railways of Europe there were no rack sections. And up from the jungle lands of Siliguri, round the bewildering spirals, the little trains pound along, with two men riding on the buffer beam to put sand on the rails to check any slipping. The track climbs high above the jungle and the cloud level into the clear blue sky, where there are breathtaking views of the eternal snows of the main Himalayan range. As traffic developed and the line prospered; more and more of the little 0-4-0 saddle-tank engines were bought, all of identical design, until by 1927 there were no fewer than 34 of them in service. It is no wonder that railway enthusiasts from all over the world make the long and not easy journey to Siliguri, to ride up to Darjeeling.

When the summer seat of the Imperial Government was established at Simla, in the northern mountain regions of the Punjab, work on a narrow-gauge railway from Kalka was started in 1899 and completed in 1903 on the broad-gauge network of the former North Western Railway. The respective altitudes of Kalka and Simla are 657 and 2,078 m (2,154 and 6,819 ft) and 'as the crow flies' the distance is only 48 km (30 miles). But the intervening distance includes some of the most jumbled and erratic mountain wilderness one could possibly imagine. It is badly affected by landslides and subsidences during the monsoon season, and to get anything like a stable track the engineers had to take a very meandering course round the hillsides, to such an extent that the distance by the railway from Kalka to Simla is no less than 96 km (60 miles). There are no reversing stations, and no spirals – just one continuous hard grind. Today the line is worked by diesel power; but some of the 'K' class 2-6-2 tank engines were still at Kalka in January 1975. In the days of the North Western Railway they were painted black, but those remaining were finished in the standard style of the Northern Railway, with the side tanks half black, and half red-brown.

Quite distinct from these two railways leading into the foothills of the Himalayas, but equally fascinating, is the narrow-gauge line from Mettupalaiyam to Ootacamund in the Nilgiri Hills, in South India, usually known as the Ooty Line. This is unique in India in that the traction is partly adhesion and partly by rack, on the principle developed for certain through routes in Switzerland, where gradients of exceptional severity are encountered in the course of a journey that can be worked by adhesion over much of the total mileage. The distance by rail is 46.25 km (28¾ miles) and the difference in altitude is from 326 m (1,071 ft) at Mettupalaiyam to 2,203 m (7,228 ft) at Ootacamund. The rack sections are inclined at 1 in 12½, and the adhesion stretches 1 in 25 – which is steep enough!

The powerful steam locomotives of the 'X' class, introduced from 1914 onwards, were built in Switzerland and include the same principle of operation as those formerly used on the Brünig railway. They are of the 0-8-2 tank type, four-cylinder compounds, with all four cylinders outside. The high-pressure cylinders drive the ordinary 'road' wheels, and when working adhesion only the engine operates as a two-cylinder simple. On the rack sections working is changed over to compound and the low-pressure cylinders drive the rack pinions. The machinery looks very impressive in operation, when seen from the lineside, with a great proliferation of rods, wheels, cranks and rocking shafts all in rapid actuation. The locomotives are painted in a handsome blue livery, of a basic colour like that of the Caledonian Railway of Scotland. The scale is much larger than that of the 'hill' railways in the north, with metre-gauge track, and these locomotives weigh no less than 48 tons. On the upward journey to 'Ooty' the locomotives push their trains from the rear.

Japan

In the period of recovery after the terrible earthquake of 1923, which caused such catastrophic damage in Tokyo and Yokohama, and inevitably much serious disruption and destruction on the railways, much important modernization work was started. Even before the earthquake disaster, however, the Japanese railways had advanced a long way beyond their early habits, which in casual ways and a total inability to hurry made them something of a curiosity to visitors from countries which, by the end of the nineteenth century, had trains regularly topping 130 kph (80 mph) in their daily running and intense commuter services. The technical foundations were sound enough with two famous English engineers, W M Smith, and R F Trevithick, successively acting as Locomotive Superintendent. The second of these two was a grandson of the great Cornish pioneer of steam traction, Richard Trevithick, and was the first man to build a locomotive in Japan.

In other respects, however, there were hampering legacies from the early days such as roundabout sharply curving routes, built thus to minimize constructional costs

but a hindrance when the management in the first years of the twentieth century wanted to put on faster trains. There was also the rail gauge, which had originally been fixed at 1.067 m (3ft 6in) to lessen costs; and the structural clearance limits did not eventually permit of huge locomotives like those now running in South Africa, also on the 3ft 6in. Tunnels were frequent, and fine civil engineering work in bridges and station layouts was amply evident.

At the same time the Japanese railways, more perhaps than any others in the world, had a constant task in taking every possible precaution against earthquake damage. Of course the terrible occurrence of 1923 was altogether exceptional; but when the backbone of the main island of Honshu is a chain of not-so-extinct volcanoes anything can happen. The risk of earthquake damage is something that the Japanese railways have just got to live with. There is in constant readiness an organization for rapid attention to 'incidents', in the same way as precautions against air-raid damage were highly organized in all the belligerent countries in World War II.

Below. A freight train climbing into the hills on the Nippo Line, Kyushu, and approaching Aoidate The locomotive of the 'C57' standard light 4-6-2 class had worked the Royal Train on the previous day.

British influence was strong in the early days and it is not surprising that many of the earlier locomotives were built by English and Scottish firms. However they did include certain distinctive features specified first by W M Smith and then by Trevithick. Around the year 1910 Japanese locomotives had begun to have a definite 'family look', and this is to be seen in the several interesting types of the pre-1914 period preserved in the fascinating 'live steam' museum at Kyoto. Examples of two vintage classes were still in revenue-earning service in Japan in 1973. One of these was the massive '9600' class 2-8-0 freight engine, the first introduction of which dates back to 1913. Japanese locomotives of that period had a neatness of outline that revealed their British genealogy, though already in order to give easier accessibility many of the accessories were being mounted along the running plates. Another long-lived class of their period is the '8620' 2-6-0 of 1914 – a fast mixed-traffic type – which by its very length of service of nearly 60 years displays its excellence of design and general usefulness.

Today, in the main island of Honshu one finds the most extreme contrasts in railways that it is possible to imagine. The original 3ft 6in gauge main line from Tokyo to Shimonoseki, generally following the coast, is electrified throughout, and has been much upgraded to permit faster running, carrying all the freight traffic and long-distance passenger trains to the remoter parts of the country that involve overnight journeys and sleeping cars. The electric locomotives are painted in gay colours and immaculately maintained; but such a railway, however efficiently run, could not hope to meet the needs of a country now so highly industrialized along its east coast. and which has thrown off its traditional leisurely habits to become a nation of the greatest hustlers in the world – and incredible travellers. Even before World War II plans were in gestation for an entirely new and much straighter main line between Tokyo and Osaka, but it was not until 1964 that the new Shinkansen line, roughly paralleling the ancient Tokaido trail, was brought into service.

'New' indeed! Nothing like it had ever been seen previously on the railways of the world. An entirely new route was engineered, on the 1.435 m (4ft 8½in) gauge, cutting

so straight through every obstruction, mountains and valleys alike, that a speed of 210 kph (130 mph) could be maintained without a break from end to end. There is a breath-taking splendour in its engineering; in the magnificent electrical technology that enables the entire railway, 515 km (320 miles) of it, to be regulated from a single control room near Tokyo, and the exact position of every train seen at any minute. Every fifteen minutes from 6 am one of these Hikari, or lightning trains, leaves Tokyo for Osaka, each one with a cruising speed of 210 kph (130 mph), and the procession continues without a break until 9 pm—each one carrying, on an average, a *thousand* passengers. And a similar procession is winging its way northwards to Tokyo.

The central mountain chain that forms an almost continuous backbone from north to south in the island of Honshu provides a stiff obstacle to those sections of the railways that have to provide cross-country communication with the west coast, and there are many picturesque locations where steam locomotives can still be seen fighting severe gradients against a rugged mountain background. When modernization of the steam locomotive stock began in the 1930s, a range of new designs was worked out, all having a 'family likeness', but an entirely new look. While applauding its technical excellence that 'new look' was at once gaunt, angular and starkly functional. The new classes came eventually to include large batches of the 2-6-2, 4-6-2, 2-8-2, and 4-6-4 types, not only very sound in their basic design, but manufactured with precision and remarkably smooth and quiet in their operation.

The 'C58' class of 2-6-2 is essentially for light branch lines, and they could be seen working in the mountain passes in North Honshu. One of the most noticeable characteristics of the standard steam locomotive is the grouping together under a single elongated casing all the mountings on the top of the boiler, thus to include the sandbox and steam dome, leaving only the chimney, safety valves and the electric generator as separate projections. The generator is mounted just ahead of the cab and is an important accessory, because operating regulations require that all trains should run with headlights on even in the brightest sunshine. Another external feature is the 'boxpok' type of cast-steel driving-

Left. One of the veteran '9600' class 2-8-0s No. 69665, on a freight train on the Hohi line, in Kyushu, and passing a display of blossom on the cutting side.
Above. A pair of veteran '8620' class 2-6-0s toiling uphill on the Hanawa Line, in Northern Honshu, in a snow covered landscape.

Above. Two of the standard 'C58' class 2-6-2 engines seen broadside on, in wintry weather on the Rikuto Line, in Northern Honshu. *Left.* The Niseko Express, from Hakodate to Sapporo, in the northern island of Hokkaido, double-headed, with a 'D51' general purpose 2-8-2 leading a 4-6-4 of Class 'C62'.

wheel centres – quite unlike the usual form of spoked locomotive wheel.

To see Japanese steam operating in its most colourful and spectacular form one had to travel to the northern island of Hokkaido, for it was there that the largest of all passenger locomotives of the JNR saw their last regular service, on the express trains between Hakodate, the ferry terminal, and Sapporo, the capital city. The 'C62' class, of the 4-6-4 type, are very large and impressive engines. One of them can be seen in steam at the museum roundhouse in Kyoto, but enthusiasts from all over Japan used to travel north to see and photograph them as they thundered over the mountain route between Oshiamambe and Otaru – often two of them to a train, and on some heavy duties one sometimes saw triple heading. It was said that the waiting room of Kamimcha station, on the line, was always crowded with railway enthusiasts anxious to photograph a pair of 'C62' engines in action.

This section of line provided exceedingly colourful action for those who ventured north in the winter months. The climate in Hokkaido is severe, with heavy snowfalls. As late as April the mountain tops can still be covered, and in the deep gullies on the hill sections of the railway there may be many places where the deep drifts have not entirely melted away. Locomotives working in these conditions were equipped with two headlights, usually one on each of the smoke-deflecting plates so as to get the best possible lookout ahead during snowstorms. The express service between Hakodate and Sapporo is now operated by multiple-unit diesel trains, very smartly coloured, but without the emotional appeal of a noisy, black, smoke-belching steam locomotive.

The term 'smoke-belching' is no idle phrase where steam-locomotive operation in Hokkaido is concerned; for the Munhoran main line, following the sea coast and then turning inland through the important junction of Numanohatta, is an important coal-train route operated by one of the most numerous of the Japanese standard steam-locomotive classes, the 'D51' 2-8-2, of which more than 1,100 were built. It should be explained that the prefix letters in Japanese locomotive numerology denote the number of coupled axles. 'C' has three coupled axles, whether the actual type is, for example, a 2-6-2 (C58), a 4-6-2 (C57) or a 4-6-4 (C62). The 'D51' has four coupled axles, and was first introduced in 1938. Engines of this class were to be seen in most parts of Japan where steam-operated freight trains ran.

In Hokkaido they were doing a great deal of very hard work. Watching them from the lineside there were certainly some interesting features to be noted. For example, there was the extraordinary quietness

of their running. With locomotives engaged in heavy freight service one is accustomed to a certain amount of noise and clanking, particularly when drifting with the regulator closed; but these 'D51s' were going about their jobs like so many sewingmachines. The Japanese railwaymen are always warning visitors not to be caught unawares when one of them is approaching, in almost complete silence. But what they lack in noise they make up for in full measure in the sight of their exhausts. You will never – repeat never! – see so much black smoke thrown out; and while this can often be the delight of the photographer, if the wind happens to be blowing the wrong way one can secure nothing more than a headlight and a vast black cloud.

In the southernmost island of Kyushu, as in Hokkaido, the intense industrialism of the east coast of Honshu is left far behind, and in the beautiful country south of Beppu the railway runs through a succession of enticing coastal scenes, rich farmland, and the limitless expanse, in many places, of the rice fields. The use of steam was diminishing, when I was in Kyushu, but in the far south at Miyazaki, there is a photographer's paradise. The station and yard are interesting and there are excellent viewpoints from which trains crossing the long viaduct over the estuary of the River Oyodo can be photographed, but it was at Miyazaki also that we saw the Japanese Royal Train. It had not long previously arrived and the engine was still carrying its decorations. They consisted of two national flags arranged crosswise on the front of the smokebox and the traditional gilded chrysanthemum just above the centre of the buffer beam. The engine itself, a 'C57' class Pacific, was of course superbly cleaned up, with many additional embellishments and everything that could be polished not merely polished but *burnished*.

The railway system on the island of Kyushu is connected with that on the mainland of Honshu by a tunnel under the Kammon Straits, between Moji and Shimonoseki, and some through express trains are run. In the early 1970s work had started on the extension of the high-speed Shinkansen line from Okayama to an eventual deep-level tunnel under the Kammon Straits, and as far into Kyushu as Hakata. One fears however that when the novelty of very high speed has worn off somewhat, journeys by the 'bullet trains' will lose some of the fascination of train travel. Between Okayama and Shimonoseki quite half the total mileage will be in tunnel, bored deep into the mountain range of Honshu. The speeds are planned to be even higher than on the original section between Tokyo and Osaka, up to 258 kph (160 mph); but with long stretches in tunnel the effect on a passenger intent upon sightseeing will be rather confusing.

Australia

Steam traction has practically disappeared on the various state railways of Australia, and entirely so in New Zealand, so far as regular services are concerned. The history of the railways could be called chequered due in part to the diversity of rail gauges. For example New South Wales adopted the British 4 ft 8½ in or 1.435 m, while Victoria and South Australia decided upon the Irish 1.600 m (5 ft 3 in) with inevitable confrontation, and age-long inconvenience of interchange at the state boundary. Then there was the pioneering of long, single-tracked lines into the seemingly limitless 'outback'. How these railways are now being gradually connected up is one of the greatest romances of modern transport, even though the traction is diesel, except on the commuter lines of Sydney and Melbourne.

In all the states there are railway museums, some no more than in the assembly stage; but in the vicinity of Adelaide, Brisbane and Melbourne there are magnificent collections of historic locomotives. The Australian climate is a great

advantage here, because these large and impressive assemblies are out of doors. In addition to these static exhibits a number of historic locomotives have been preserved in full operating condition and are used frequently for special trips sponsored by the Association of Railway Enthusiasts or the Australian Historical Railway Society. For the most part these trips have the enthusiastic backing of the railway administrations in the various states. Some of them involve long mileages and a wealth of careful organization beforehand.

Originally the locomotive colours in most of the states were black. That of New South Wales was inspired by the style of the London and North Western Railway, and exemplified today on the splendid little 2-4-0 *Hardwicke*, preserved in the National Railway Museum of Great Britain, at York. There had been a green livery prior to 1890 in New South Wales, of which a superb example can be seen on the old outside-cylindered 4-4-0 preserved on a pedestal at Canberra. But for 'Old English' splendour in locomotive liveries that of the Victorian

Railways up to the turn of the century had few equals, even at home in Great Britain. The Victorian steam locomotives preserved in the open-air museum at North Williamstown, near Melbourne, have a rather watered-down version, retaining the bright green, it is true, but with plain black and white lining instead of a gorgeous array of red, yellow and brown, with much ornamental brass and copper work.

It was curious that while Victoria turned to plain, unadorned black in the last years of steam traction, Queensland, South Australia, and Western Australia went gay with bright new colours. The tank engines working the Brisbane suburban services, for example, were painted sky-blue, and in

New South Wales

Left. New South Wales: the 'AD60' class Beyer-Garratts were the most powerful locomotives on the standard gauge in Australia. Of the number supplied, only one remained in working order in 1975, here seen broadside-on, working a special train.

Top. New South Wales: the preserved 'C32' class 4-6-0 No. 3203 with a special train in 1975 on the Sydney to Melbourne main line near Menangle Park.

Above. New South Wales: one of the very famous 'C32' class 4-6-0s, originally 'P6' and dating from 1890 at Clyde, near Sydney, on a special trip in 1975.

Western Australia the fine new main-line engines introduced in the 1950s were painted in a handsome shade of leaf green. Examples of all these colourschemes have fortunately been preserved including one of the big Queensland Beyer–Garratts in 'Derby red'. When from 1925 onwards South Australia suddenly decided to double the haulage capacity of its main-line locomotives, the enormous new engines built in England began life in plain black; but in their later years they were 'dolled up' to some extent, with the running-plate valences painted green and the smokebox fronts painted aluminium colour. The enginemen nicknamed them 'Palefaces'!

The New South Wales Government railways had a distinguished history of locomotive development, from the Scottish inspired 'P6' class 4-6-0 of 1891 to the massive 'C38' Pacifics of 1943. These latter engines were still in main-line service in 1969, and it was still possible to ride behind one of them on the Newcastle-Flyer service from Gosford northwards. Apart from enjoying a hard steam ride, with speeds up to 112 kph (70 mph), it was very interesting to find that the enginemen worked through from Sydney to Newcastle, although half the mileage is electrified. They took the electric locomotive from Sydney, and then at the halfway point would be prepared to work either steam or diesel for the rest of the journey. This was most probably the only instance anywhere in the world of enginemen not only 'swopping horses', but swopping the form of motive power as well. The route includes the crossing of the supremely beautiful Hawkesbury River, with its numerous creeks and only the oyster beds to dispel any momentary thoughts an Englishman from the West Country might have that he was back in Cornwall.

The Victorian Railways, like those of Great Britain, were worked almost to death in World War II, and afterwards recovery was made under a plan known as 'Operation Phoenix'. It included the purchase of many new steam locomotives among which were the very powerful 'R' class 4-6-4s, for heavy express passenger work. A concession towards colour was made on these engines. While unlined black was still the basis, the running-plate valences and the small smoke-reflecting plates on each side of the smokebox were painted a vivid pillar-box red. An order for 70 of these engines was placed with the North British Locomotive Company of Glasgow; but they never really fulfilled the task for which they were ordered. The change to diesel traction began very soon after their first introduction and to get full money's worth out of the expensive new power, the diesels had to be allocated to the longest and hardest duties.

Until comparatively recently Victoria and South Australia were the only two states with a common boundary to have the same rail gauge, and for a long time the 'Interstate Express' was the only train by which one could travel from one state capital to another without having to change between Melbourne and Adelaide. The train of today, enormously heavier but not much faster, is the 'Overland'; but although it is well patronized very few of its passengers could tell you much about the intervening country because the journey is done through the night. The frontier station of Serviceton, where the locomotives and crews of the Victorian railways hand over to those of South Australia, is itself something of an enigma. In earlier days the only people likely to get out would be smugglers arrested when interstate customs were imposed; and the station was provided with dungeons for the safekeeping of these miscreants.

In the last stages of the long run from

Left. New South Wales: a 2-8-2 tank engine on the Richmond Vale Railway, an industrial serving the coal industry. At the time the photograph was taken, in August 1975, the locomotive, No. 10 *Richmond Main* was 64 years old, and still in original condition.
Below. New South Wales Government Railways: the first five of this class of thirty 'Pacifics', dating from 1943 were partially streamlined and painted green. The rest were black. Engine No. 3801 pictured here in South Australia in 1972 is preserved in working order, for special trains.

Victoria

South Australian Railways

Serviceton to Adelaide South Australian locomotives had to work their hardest in climbing the severe gradients of the Mount Lofty Range, with the incessant curvature. It was for taking trains like the 'Overland' that the 'Palefaces' were built. There were, nevertheless, other parts of the South Australian railways where such heavy locomotives could not be used and were in fact not needed by the ruling gradients, and a very elegant 4-8-4 design was brought in during World War II, semi-streamlined and incorporating some of the most advanced techniques of the day. The form of streamlining on these engines had its inspiration from some gigantic express locomotives of the Pennsylvania Railroad; and for the first time in South Australia they were all named. The first to be put into traffic was named after the Governor, Sir Malcolm Barclay-Harvey, himself a railway enthusiast and author of a fine book about a colourful little railway in his home country, the north of Scotland, running from Aberdeen up to Elgin and also working the Royal Deeside line to Ballater. This engine is now preserved in full working order.

The railways of South Australia began with the 1.600 m (5ft 3in) gauge, linking up with those of Victoria at Serviceton, but events elsewhere led to the introduction, within the one state, of a second gauge. When railways began in Queensland and Western Australia the territories were so far removed from other railway activities that little chance was foreseen of their eventually linking up,

and as cost was a major consideration in those developing lands the decision was taken in both states to adopt the 1.067 m (3ft 6in) gauge. In South Australia there were remote tracts where railways were needed, but not to the extent of having the spacious 5ft 3in of the interstate main line; and so these feeder lines were also built on the 3ft 6in gauge. In the museum just outside Adelaide preserved examples of the small 3ft 6in gauge locomotives can be studied alongside an enormous 'Paleface', and its heavy freight equivalent. But there is also a 4-6-0 of the 4ft 8½in or 1.435 m gauge. Three gauges in the one state? – and that 4-6-0 looks suspiciously like a standard New South Wales design. How did this come about?

At the end of the nineteenth century the British Government in London was anxious to bring the hitherto independent colonies into a unified federation, in the same way as had been so successfully achieved in Canada. At first Western Australia stood out against the project. She was isolated from the rest not only by great distance, but also by the vast extent of the intervening desert land, where there were no trees, no vegetation, no animals, no people – absolutely nothing. Recalling the curiously similar situation of some 30 years earlier in Canada, where British Columbia, separated from the rest by the great barrier of the Rocky Mountains, had resisted the idea of being included in the Confederation,

Above. Victorian Railways: a spectacular view of a 'K' class lightweight 2-8-0, No. 184, en route for Ballarat, in 1971.
Left. South Australian Railways: the preserved 4-8-4 *Sir Malcolm Barclay-Harvey* on a special from Adelaide to Truro in August 1975.

145

Queensland Railways

the Imperial Government made exactly the same proposal to Western Australia as they had done to British Columbia: if Western Australia would join, a railway would be built to connect it up with the others. Western Australia agreed, and the Commonwealth came into being in 1901. The promise of a railway meant constructing a line across the utter 'nothingness' of the Nullarbor Plain. The word 'nullarbor' means no trees – but there was nothing else either, particularly water. The line was to be built under Commonwealth auspices, and there arose at once the question of the gauge. At Kalgoorlie, the western end, there was the 1.067 m (3ft 6in) gauge of Western Australia; at the eastern end the 1.600 m (5ft 3in) of South Australia. By chance, wise beyond anything that was foreseen at the time, the Commonwealth railways decided on the British and New South Wales standard of 1.435 m (4ft 8½in). And so, for a period that lasted for more than 50 years, there was a 'break of gauge' at both ends, and trains on three gauges running into the South Australian station of Port Pirie.

It is an amazing journey from Port Pirie westwards across the Nullarbor Plain. In 1969 we came up from Adelaide in a 5ft 3in gauge train, and there, late in the afternoon, transferred to the 'Trans', as railwaymen then called it. This was to be our 'home', our travelling hotel for nearly two days. After the sun had set in a cloudless sky and

we drove on into a darkness punctuated only by the flashing brilliance of the stars, it seemed that we were indeed going out into the blue. Soon after sunrise next morning, we stopped at Cook for servicing and change of engine crew. We were able to look ahead down a single line of rails, disappearing in a perfectly straight line into the far distance across a limitless expanse of dwarf scrubland. Believe it or not, the line is absolutely straight for 478 km (297 miles) across this incredible 'nothingness', with the soft bluish-grey of the scrub mixed with the dun colour of the sand under the dazzling brilliance of the cloudless sky. Soon we were running at 90–96 kph (55–60 mph), and kept this up steadily for mile after mile. As we approached the next station objects began to appear like the first sight of ships at sea – the tops first, literally over the curve of the earth's surface. When we travelled the new standard-gauge line had been built from Kalgoorlie to Perth and we did not have to change on reaching Western Australian metals. Since that time the standard-gauge link east of Port Pirie has been completed and the magnificent 'Indian –Pacific' express runs through from Perth to Sydney entirely on this 4ft 8½in gauge.

If one wishes to recapture something of the pioneering spirit of Australian railways one must ride 'The Ghan' to Alice Springs. It runs over a line north from Port Augusta that was part of a companion to the Nullarbor

Above. Two out of the three gauges at Port Pirie: at left a South Australian 1.600 m (5ft 3in) gauge 'Pacific' No. 621, and at right a New South Wales standard gauge 4-6-0 No. 3642, Engine No. 621, now named *Duke of Edinburgh*, is preserved in full operating condition.
Right. One of the maroon-painted 'C17' class 4-8-0s of the Queensland Railways on a rail-tour up the Monkland-Brooloo branch in April 1975.
Previous pages. On the 1.067 m (3ft 6in) gauge in South Australia. A pair of 'T' class 2-8-0s, Nos. 186 and 199, of 1903 vintage on an A.R.H.S. special from Peterborough to Quorn in 1970.

route, providing a continuous south-to-north link and eventually reaching Port Darwin. But although construction started from both ends the link-up was never made and the line from the south got no further than Alice Springs. Before the railway came transport was entirely by camel and the name of the only passenger train is derived from the Afghans, who led the camel caravans over this desert country. Even now that diesel locomotives have replaced steam locomotives, and the 'Ghan' has dining cars throughout its long journey, the trip is not to be lightly undertaken. To travel from Port Augusta to Alice Springs and back takes five days.

In steam days, on 3ft 6in gauge, the 'Ghan' was hauled by locomotives of Queensland design, distinguished among all other Australian locomotives by the ornamental sandbox on the boiler top, between the chimney and the dome. In Queensland itself locomotives of this type are now little more than treasured museum pieces, though at one time they were used on specials over the highly scenic line from Cairns, at the terminus of the long main line up from Brisbane, to Kuranda and the Atherton Plains. Climbing the gradient from Cairns the line passes on a slender trestle almost within the spray of a spectacular waterfall. Kuranda station is one of outstanding beauty. It is not far removed from a halt among a profusion of tropical ferns. There

cannot be many railway stations that are a popular tourist sight; but Kuranda is certainly one of them.

One would not ordinary expect to find interesting locomotives on iron ore railway lines but there are two major instances of this in Western Australia. It was the need for mass transport of ore from the great deposits at Koolyanobbing to the refinery at Kwinana, beside Fremantle on the Indian Ocean, that justified the building of the standard-gauge line from Kalgoorlie to the west coast. Today the railway acts like some gigantic conveyor belt, 500 km (310 miles) long, from the mines to the refinery, and over it thunder at 80 kph (50 mph) trains of 96 cars, hauled by three 3,300 horsepower diesel locomotives, with a trailing load of nearly 10,000 tons. To stand at the lineside in the beautiful Avon valley and see one of these trains roar past—half-a-mile long, and headed by the three blue and white locomotives — makes one realize that steam does not hold the monopoly on excitement and colour.

If the diesel-operated ore trains on the State railway are colourful, what can be said of the Hamersley Iron Railway, up in the north west? The standard-gauge line west of Kalgoorlie is a general purpose railway, carrying the Trans-Continental 'Indian–Pacific' express, fast local railcar services, grain in large block loads in addition to iron ore; but Hamersley, again connecting huge

mineral deposits with the port of shipment at Dampier, was built as a single-purpose 'conveyor belt', set in the stark, barren, but intensely colourful land of the north-west. For the entire landscape is the red colour of iron ore, and this amazing railway, 293 km (182 miles) of first-class heavy main-line track, was built to carry a payload of 15,000 tons per train. When the line was first opened, to the new mining centre of Tom Price, these trains represented a gross trailing load of 18,000 tons, in 152 cars. But with the opening of the extension to Paraburdoo some trains are made up of no less than 186 cars. Because the gradients are generally in favour of loaded trains no more than three locomotives are required for this tremendous load of 22,000 tons. The locomotives sport a vivid colourscheme of bright blue and yellow, in startling contrast to the prevailing red of the countryside and the dazzling white of the salt pans near Dampier. On the extension line from Tom Price to Paraburdoo, which was only completed in 1972, the newly excavated cuttings, some of them very deep, showed up the many brilliant colours of the varying strata of naked rock, providing an amazing background to the passage of these heavy trains.

Before the building of the standard gauge line westwards from Kalgoorlie, the Western Australian Government Railways were an exclusively 1.067 m (3ft 6in) gauge system and some extensive modernization of

steam motive power took place after World War II. The operating conditions are severe, not so much in their demands for high or long-sustained outputs of power, but in the terrain, and in the characteristics of the coal available in large quantities in the south-west of the State. A high proportion of the total railway mileage permitted no greater axle loads than 10 tons and yet powerful new locomotives were needed. The indigenous coal burns slowly, with a long flame, and fireboxes of specialized proportions were needed to burn this to the best advantage. Another basic requirement was to minimize the emission of sparks. In the hot summers, the whole countryside is highly susceptible to bush fires and every precaution had to be taken to lessen the chances of these being started by locomotives. So that while providing every incentive to rapid combustion of a somewhat reluctant burning coal, this could not be done by the easy expedient of a sharp blast and instead spark arrestors had to be fitted.

All these requirements were successfully incorporated into the new 4-8-2s introduced in 1951. They were built in England by Beyer, Peacock and Company, a firm which had a distinguished record of vast mechanical engineering exports in the Beyer–Garratt articulated locomotives. In the Western Australian 'W' class 4-8-2s their designing experience and ingenuity was taxed considerably. Externally, the new

engines were distinguished by a handsome
new livery of pale green, whereas previous
steam locomotives in the State had been red-
brown. Inside a notably neat and compact
outline was packed a wealth of locomotive
'know-how' that resulted in a remarkably
successful traffic unit. The 'W' class was
followed by a much larger version, having
the 2-8-2 wheel arrangement, for working
over those sections of line where larger
locomotives were permitted. Although
designated for freight duties, these also
had the smart colourscheme in light green.

The two locomotives set aside for the
present 'tourist' run in the south of South
Island have a long history of hard and noble
work on the main lines of New Zealand, and
this makes the 'Kingston Flyer' the object
of much affection by all railway lovers. The
New Zealand railways have been served
by many notable locomotive designs, but
none better for their size and weight than the
'Ab' 'Pacifics', introduced in 1915, and
eventually multiplied to a stud of 152. Today
these two working survivors, kept in exhibition condition with everything that can
be polished simply glittering, take turns to
roll their train placidly over the 61 km (38
miles) from Lumsden to Kingston in 80
minutes; and the class as a whole will be
remembered for the 30-odd years when they
were the mainstay of the New Zealand
railways motive power stud.

Above left. One of the most characteristic sights
in North Queensland are the immense fields of
sugar cane, and 0.610 m (2ft) gauge railways
are used to bring the crops to the main line
stations. Here, a little 0-6-0 named *Melbourne*
brings a load from Trebonne, near Ingham.

Top. 'The Ghan'—en route to Alice Springs, in
the days when that train was steam hauled. The
locomotive is one of the Queensland-type 4-8-0s,
working on the 1.067 m (3ft 6in) gauge.
Above. Queensland Railways: one of the 'B18¼'
class 'Pacifics' at Caboolture, on a special to
Gympie, on the Brisbane–North Queensland
main line.

South Africa

Down at the Cape, almost in the shadow of Table Mountain, there is a big locomotive depot, Paarden Eiland, where many steam, diesel and electric locomotives are serviced. Capetown was the birthplace of railways in Southern Africa and from that once remote British colony the prospect of a great trunk line to the north was evolved – not at the outset, it is true, because there was at first little reason to extend communications from the Cape of Good Hope over the barren mountain ranges to the north and across the great inhospitable Karoo desert. It was the discovery of diamonds at Kimberley and then gold in the Transvaal that transformed the whole situation and gave to the 'Cape Government Railway' and its sister enterprise in Natal a strong commercial, as well as a colonizing objective, and both extended their tracks towards the mineral riches of the interior. Both railways also assumed a strong strategic significance when war broke out at the end of the nineteenth century.

At first there was no call for speed. The railways were built where nothing save the primitive tracks of the trek wagons had previously existed. After some preliminary building on the 1.435 m (4 ft 8 in) gauge the sub-standard gauge of 1.067 m (3 ft 6 in) was chosen to save expense and the rails followed the contours of the ground, often on a meandering alignment. But once the great drive to the north was under way, Cecil Rhodes, then Prime Minister of the 'Cape of Good Hope, proclaimed his great vision of Imperial development, with a Cape to Cairo' railway, with his personal slogan; 'The railway is my right hand, and the telegraph is my voice.' Nowhere previously had railways been built in such conditions of torrid heat, waterless countryside and a primitive and often hostile native population. The pioneers who took railroads across the American continent had to fight off the attacks of Indians, but in South Africa the tribes often fought among themselves with the utmost ferocity. It was difficult to get a railway built when reliance had to be placed upon the native population for much of the

and placed on a pedestal at the south end of Kimberley station. Seventy years ago and more, there were many more staging points for locomotives on the way south dictated by their limited fuel- and water-carrying capacity; but the modern conception of economonical steam operation was to work the longest mileages possible, even if it meant a change of engine crew intermediately, and to do this on the more southerly sections of the South African railways meant the development of certain new techniques in engine design. It was not only a case of working over longer distances. Increased luxury of accommodation meant heavier carriages and longer trains so that locomotives had to be larger as well as capable of running longer mileages in one continuous assignment.

To meet these requirements the tremendous '25C' class locomotives were introduced. These were not only very large in themselves but they were fitted with special tenders in which the exhaust steam was condensed back into water, and used again. In this way the water carried in the tanks enabled the locomotive to run much further without replenishment. Of course the equipment necessary to effect this saving in water was expensive and required so much space that the tenders containing it were larger than the engines, enormous though the engines were; but the economies of operation over the desert sections of the great north-to-south main line were such that this high investment was justified. Economies apart, these engines present a mighty spectacle in the stark, arid countryside, whether hauling seemingly endless freights or prestige passenger trains like the 'Orange Express' or the 'Blue Train'.

Out in the midst of the High Veldt is one of the most remarkable railway centres in the world, De Aar Junction. It is as though the railway activities of Carlisle or York had been set down in the heart of the African wilderness. One reads of towns that have been created by the railway, with great manufacturing plants set up; but De Aar is not one of these. It is a junction, pure and simple, but also like Carlisle and York in the days of British steam, a major staging point for locomotives. Hardly any train, passenger or freight, passes De Aar without changing engines. The line that comes up from the southeast, originating at Port Elizabeth, is nowadays not the main route from that area to the Transvaal, while the fourth line, although the only route into South-West Africa and its capital city of Windhoek, is again secondary to the main 'Cape to Cairo' line—to use Cecil Rhodes's name for it. The line to Windhoek is perhaps the one more beset by water problems than any other in South Africa and its train service is now entirely operated by diesel locomotives.

But the centre of the action is in the locomotive sheds. In this, also, De Aar

Top. One of the condensing '25' class 4-8-4s leaving Orange River, with a heavy freight from De Aar to Kimberley. This is South Africa's busiest steam main line with about'30 trains in each direction daily.
Above. Two '15F' 4-8-2s of the South African Railways on a heavy freight train in rugged country near Karee.
Above right. Two of the huge 25C condensing 4-8-4 locomotives near Kloofeind on the Kimberley–Bloemfontein line with a heavy freight train in April 1970.
Previous page. One of the huge condensing '25C' class 4-8-4s leaving Nelspoort on a northbound goods.

labour force. The traveller of today, riding one of the luxurious trains of the South African Railways northward from the Cape, needs little imagination to picture what things were like in construction days when De Doorns is left behind and the ascent of the Hex River Pass begins. The line is now electric and the smart red-brown locomotives take their heavy trains steadily up the gradient; but it is no wonder that the South African railways developed their steam locomotives to gigantic proportions – 3 ft 6 in gauge notwithstanding.

It was not only a matter of sheer strength to lift trains up the steep gradients. Once the high inland plateau of the Great Karoo desert was attained there was the question of water, which steam locomotives used in plenty. As if to accentuate as vividly as possible the striking development of locomotives in South Africa, one of the early engines of the Cape Government Railways has been restored to its original condition

stands alone. At most of the large steam depots on the South African railways there is interesting mixture of the vintage and the huge modern locomotives. Most of the veterans are kept in very smart condition by staff to whom steam seems to be the very breath of life. At each of these depots there are high galleries on to which loaded coal wagons are propelled to discharge supplies into the bunkers from which locomotive tenders are recharged. At Paarden Eiland, Port Elizabeth, and at great depots in the Transvaal, work is found for the veterans in pushing the loaded coal trucks, two or three at a time, up on to the high galleries. At De Aar, however, no veterans were to be seen when I was was there last, and the great main-line engines were doing the pushing. Watching a huge 4-8-2 – '15F' class, or even a '23' – charging up the slope I half wondered if the slender steel lattice-work of the gallery would stand the weight of such a great thundering locomotive!

The line northwards from De Aar over the High Veldt to Kimberley is one of the real racing grounds of the modern South African Railways. The maximum speed permitted with steam is 88 kph (55 mph), but a prestige train such as the 'Orange Express' or the 'Trans-Karoo Express' coming through a country station with fifteen or sixteen cars on, hauled by one of the giant '25' class 4-8-4 locomotives, with the sun blazing down from cloudless blue African skies, is a marvellous sight, especially when

the platforms are thronged with gaily attired native women waiting for the next stopping train. The freights are all fitted with continuous automatic brakes and can also be run at passenger speed. Some of them are made up to enormous lengths and require *two* of the monster engines. A double-header fighting a heavy gradient is always a stirring spectacle, but two Class '25s' in tandem doing 50 mph across the open veldt with a coal train is a sight and sound to remember!

Away from this great main line that leads north from Capetown to the cities of the Transvaal one meets that astonishing locomotive phenomenon, the Beyer–Garratt articulated. It was conceived some 60 years ago for railways where the going was tough and over the years it was developed and enlarged to colossal proportions to work on some of the most colourful and spectacular railways in the world. Two predominating conditions govern most routes where the Beyer–Garratt excels: first, that the track can bear no more than a limited axle load and, secondly, that it includes many sharp curves and steep gradients. In some areas only one of the conditions is present; but both are combined in full measure on the celebrated 'Garden Route', never far from the southern coast of South Africa, between Capetown and Port Elizabeth.

Eastbound, one journeys through the night. On the main 'Cape to Cairo' line the train was electrically hauled as far as Wellington, and there, for the 'Garden Route', one

of the Beyer-Garratts took over. Before turning in for the night the opportunity was taken to ride on the open platform between two coaches, and for a time to watch the engine's powerful headlight illuminating the track ahead, through a beautiful wooded country. There were many curves, the beam of the headlight swung from side to side, but no game was to be seen that night. The Beyer-Garratt type consists essentially of two separate engines fed from one enormous boiler. Each engine has its own chassis and machinery, and the boiler is carried on a cradle suspended from the fore and aft engine units. The 'drive' is applied to a large number of axles so that the weight on any one does not need to be heavy, and the articulation from there being, in effect, is in three separate sections–front engine, boiler cradle, rear engine enabling the complete locomotive to negotiate quite sharp curves with ease.

On the 'Garden Route' there are many sharp gradients to be surmounted as the line makes its way across the valleys and intervening ridges running down to the sea between Mossel Bay and George. But then the really spectacular part of the journey begins – the ascent of the Montagu Pass. While waiting at George one can look up the mountainside and see, hundreds of feet above, the steam of another train. It is so high up it looks like a toy. At first the line makes a complete U-turn and we begin the climb looking back along the coast the way

we have just come, towards Mossel Bay. The higher we mount the more magnificent the view becomes, but our driver and fireman have little chance for sightseeing. The hillside becomes increasingly wild and rugged; there is always the chance of boulders or other obstructions on the track and, as this is a hand-fired engine, the fireman is shovelling continuously for a while. We are marshalled with the cab end of the central cradle leading. There are several tunnels to pass through; the line is single-tracked, and in the confined space the exhaust gases and steam from the chimney can be unpleasant, if not actually dangerous. But the chimney is behind us as we climb and with the windows in the carriages shut for the tunnels all is well.

Now, at no more than about 24 kpn (15 mph) we are turning into a truly harsh and barren mountain pass. Little by little the wonderful sea view is cut off and the roar of the exhaust beat is flung back at us from stark, almost vertical rock walls. It is interesting to hear that the front and rear engines, though not mechanically connected in any

Above. On the Rosemead–Graaf Reinet line Cape Province: one of the powerful branch line '19D' class 4-8-2s on a freight train near Erin, No. 2714.
Right above. The Port Elizabeth–Cape Town express climbing to the summit of the Montague Pass. The locomotive is one of the 'GMA' class Beyer–Garratts, which work the train over the very steeply graded section between Oudtshoorn and Mossel Bay. The auxiliary water tank attached to these engines can be seen ahead of the leading coach.
Right below. One of the GEA class Beyer-Garratts, 4-8-2 — 2-8-4 type, leaving Oudtshoorn on the run over the Montague Pass to Mossel Bay.
Following pages. One of the lightweight branch 2-8-4s of Class '24' on the morning goods train from Knysna to George passes the mouth of the Kaimaans River.

way, are exhausting in unison. Sometimes if there is a momentary wheel slip in one or other of them the beats go out of step and there is a distinct syncopated effect; but very soon they fall into step once again, to provide a single thunderous beat.

For the lighter and branch line workings the South African Railways have two very interesting and thoroughly modern types of fourteen-wheeled steam locomotives, the '19D' 4-8-2 and the '24' class 2-8-4. There are still many hundreds of miles where the largest main line engines are prohibited, on account of their weight, and the '19D' is the final development of a long and successful series of 4-8-2 designs dating back to 1910, when the first of them, built in Great Britain was put to work in the Cape. Following the formation of the Union of South Africa all the former independent state railways were amalgamated to become the South African Railways, and it was over the tracks of the former Cape Government Railway with its heavy grades and severe curves in the Hex River Pass that the first 4-8-2s worked. Development of the design was continuous to 1947, when the '19D' was introduced. The later engines of this class, which I have seen working in many parts of Southern Africa, have enormous tenders of the Vanderbilt type, that weigh nearly as much as the engine. The water tank is cylindrical and carries no less than 28,400 litres (6,250 gallons).

While the '19D' class was designed for routes on which the maximum permitted axle-load is 14 tons, there are many purely branch lines on which the restriction is still more severe. One of these is the very picturesque coastal route eastward from George, in Cape Province. While the main line to Port Elizabeth turns inland and toils up the tremendous climb of the Montagu Pass the branch continues rarely out of sight of the sea, and here the 2-8-4 engines of the '24' class are used. They are 'lightweights' in every sense, designed for tracks with a maximum axle-load limit of 11 tons. The '24' class, one hundred strong, were built in Glasgow by the North British Locomotive Company, and represent a highly skilled piece of engine designing. One of the most interesting features, to reduce weight, was the incorporation of a one-piece cast steel frame, that included the side frame members, cross-stretchers, smokebox saddle and cylinders all in one single casting. It is a design practice that became common enough in the later years of steam locomotive production in the USA, but the South African '24' class were the first built in Great Britain to be so distinguished. Many of these locomotives were still at work in different parts of Africa in the late 1960s at least. Today, of course, the 'winds of change' are affecting the South African Railways. It is a major point of policy to change over to electric traction, where possible. There are ample reserves of coal in the country for

generation of electricity, and it is a matter of making the necessary capital available. In the meantime the steam locomotives are not getting any younger. The great firms in Europe from which the South African Railways previously obtained their steam power are no longer building steam, and spare parts are becoming increasingly difficult to get. So, certain sections are being turned over to diesel traction, particularly the lines across desert country, south and west of De Aar Junction. The giant '25C' class 4-8-4s, with condensing tenders, designed specially for the near-waterless sections of the Cape main line south of De Aar are being transferred to the sections north to Kimberley and Bloemfontein, and are having their condensing gear removed.

It was in Natal that the Beyer–Garratt first won its spurs. When first introduced, designers of orthodox engines looked upon it as something of a freak, a rather improbable conception. In the USA, as mentioned elsewhere in this book, the Mallet form of articulation was well established for slow-haul heavy-grade work and on the Natal section of the South African Railways, where there is a very long and severe incline from Durban up to the Cato Ridge, some very large Mallet articulated locomotives, built in Scotland, were securely entrenched and held in high favour. There was healthy competition, however, between various British firms in the locomotive-building business, and Beyer, Peacock's of Manchester, who had acquired the manufacturing rights for the Garratt type of locomotive, secured an order for one experimental unit, for trial in Natal. So, just as Shap and the wild mountain country of the Settle and Carlisle line in England had been and continued to be the scene of momentous locomotive trials, the great climb from Durban into the Drakensberg Mountains witnessed a battle of railway giants in South Africa.

The contest proved a triumph for the Beyer–Garratt type of locomotive and it brought to the fore a young South African engineer, W. Cyril Williams, who was nominated invigilator on these important trials. He wrote a report so heavily in favour of the Garratt as to earn a reproof from his chief mechanical engineer — so firmly was the Mallet type held in high favour. But Williams stuck to his guns and in a further prolonged series of trials the superiority of the Garratt was clearly obvious. Williams thereupon left his employment on the South African Railways, sailed for England where he walked into the office of *The Railway Gazette* in London. Granted an interview with the Editor he said simply: 'I've come to sell Garratts.' Eventually he did sell many million pounds' worth, and nowhere more successfully than to his first employees, the South African Railways.

Around Johannesburg, 'The Golden City', the railway tracks are often bordered

by the conical golden-coloured spoil heaps of the mines. The frequent winds send yellow dust flying over all the equipment; it gets into every crevice and makes the gasketing of vital machinery more necessary here, perhaps than in torrential rain or the sandstorms of desert lands. But the spoil heaps of the Reef add a distinctive and colourful touch to the lines on which set out express trains to still more distant parts of Africa. Rhodes's 'Cape to Cairo' line skirted the western frontiers of the two Boer republics, and from Kimberley made its way through the protectorate of Botswana to Mafeking. After the South African war this became an important junction, where a line westwards from Johannesburg joined the 'Cape to Cairo' route.

This cross-country line through the north-western Transvaal was another one that presented steam locomotive operators with water problems. The economic situation here was not such as to justify using the great '25' class 4-8-4s with their condensing tenders, and instead a class of very large Beyer–Garratts was introduced, to which was attached a huge auxiliary water tank. These engines were used on the through express trains between Johannesburg and the cities of Rhodesia. The Beyer–Garratts work on the 205 km (128-mile) section between Krugersdorp (Johannesburg) and Zeerust, where the ruling gradient is as steep as 1 in 40, and where there are only three places intermediately where a locomotive can get water. At Krugersdorp the line is nearly 1,850 m (6,000 ft) above sea level, and it descends at one point to little more than 1,070 m (3,500 ft). This is indeed railroading in the raw, where sharp curves, steep gradients, and desert conditions are all combined. The working here makes such demands for steam that the engines are mechanically

stoked; no one man could shovel coal at the rate these Beyer–Garratts consume it on such duties.

Rudyard Kipling wrote about 'romance bringing up the nine-fifteen'; but if ever there was a line steeped in romance it was that which Cecil Rhodes saw as eventually running from 'Cape to Cairo', as anyone who has read George Pauling's *Chronicles of a Contractor* will realize. 'Georgie Porgie', as Cecil Rhodes called him, the gigantic, supremely colourful civil engineer, who built many hundreds of miles of the 'Cape to Cairo' railway, has left a monument as enduring as the Pyramids, and nowhere more so than in the continuation of the line northwards from Bulawayo to the crossing of the Zambesi river, at the Victoria Falls. Only once, and then no more than briefly, does the scenery become spectacular; but there is history and atmosphere in almost every station name, and the farther one drives north from Bulawayo the greater are the chances of meeting nature in the raw. The 'stations' are mostly no more than passing places where two long trains can pass each other, and the appearance of the countryside is epitomized by the station name Igusi – more correctly Gusu, in Sindebele – which describes the sandy, scrub-covered land thereabouts.

From Sawmills, the next important station, lying in a pleasant valley, the line climbs once again to the low bush country and runs dead straight for miles, and it is here that one can meet wild life in earnest. Not infrequently elephants stray on to the line, and are sometimes hit, with gory consequences, by the big Garratt locomotives. I was coming up from the Victoria Falls one moonlight night on an engine of the Mail, and we saw a large herd of elephants making their way through thick bush, and immediately afterwards as we were ap-

proaching a little station, round a curve, the driver clutched my arm and said, 'Look.' There, drinking at the foot of the water column was a lioness. She made off as soon as our headlight picked her up, but not long ago there was a real wild-life disaster on this same line, when a freight train going at full speed ran into a whole pride of lions, and killed four of them outright. Riding on the Garratts can be an exciting business on the 'Cape to Cairo' line!

The great spectacle is of course the viaduct over the gorge of the Zambesi river beside the Victoria Falls. The midpoint of this magnificent bridge is now an international frontier. Cecil Rhodes himself never saw the Falls, but the stupendous sight they present, together with the curtain of spray that is always rising, appealed so much to his imagination that he decreed the 'Cape-to-Cairo' line should not only cross the gorge at a point where passengers could see the Falls in all their glory, but near enough for the carriages to be bathed in the spray. Today, unfortunately, no passenger trains cross the bridge and visitors clad in water-proofs walk to the rain forest, to be drenched by the spray.

Railways since 1945

Post-war gloom In World War II most of the belligerents had repeated the railway organizational measures of World War I. An exception was the USA, where the railways were not taken under government control but merely coordinated in a semi-voluntary way. Physical destruction was much greater than in World War I, thanks to the development of the bomber. The main effect of bombing was in the disruption of railway work rather than in the damage caused. In Britain, less than a 1,000 railwaymen and passengers were killed by bomb attack. The most war-damaged railways were those of France, Holland, Russia and perhaps Italy. In the two first-named, the railways were bombed by both sides and sabotaged by their own resistance movements. In Russia the ebb and flow of the struggling armies was accompanied by the thorough destruction of railway facilities by each side in turn as it retreated. Traffic increased greatly everywhere, partly because of the demands of war and partly because the railways' competitors, motor transport and coastal shipping, were seriously restricted by fuel shortages and enemy attacks. Traffic reached a peak in 1944 in North America which in the case of passenger traffic would never be surpassed. In the USA, 1944 freight traffic was 82 per cent greater than in 1918 and passenger more than double. As elsewhere during the war, the fastest trains were withdrawn from American railroads, and passenger services were not expanded to handle the increased traffic. The result was overcrowding and slow transits which had a bad and longlasting effect on the public's opinion of railway travel. In North America, congestion was less severe than in World War I, partly because lessons had been learned and partly because the inter-war technique of Centralized Traffic Control (CTC) was applied to lines facing wartime pressure. CTC is the control of train movements over perhaps hundreds of miles of track from one central control office, whose personnel operate all signals and switches by remote control and can see train movements presented as lights on a panel. This technique makes it easy to arrange train meets on single-track line; in fact these meets are timed so accurately that sometimes both trains can reach the double-track crossing station simultaneously, and pass without either stopping. One key line on which CTC was installed early in the war was the Canadian National's single-track line from Moncton to the main wartime port of Halifax. This line was Halifax's only rail connection with the rest of Canada and the USA, and after the installation it could handle 50 trains each day. Such a capacity was certainly needed, for one sailing of the troopship *Queen Elizabeth* would require 28 special trains.

In Europe there were wholesale transfers of rolling stock. The Hungarian State Railway, for example, became a key link between the Axis powers and the Russian Front, and to help it handle the extra traffic the Italian Railways handed back locomotives of Austrian, and therefore familiar, construction which had been transferred as reparations after World War I. Special wartime locomotives were also designed and built in large numbers. Most numerous of these was the German *Kriegslok* 2-10-0, built in thousands in Europe and left behind on the railways of countries which had been occupied by the Germans. After the invasion of Normandy, the US standard wartime 2-8-0 and the British 'Austerity' 2-8-0 were used in large numbers by continental railways, and some, especially the *Kriegslok*, are still in service.

Of the German-occupied territories, eastern France and the Netherlands were possibly the worst damaged; so damaged in fact that the Dutch and French railways often found it possible after the war to make a clean start and, rather than spend resources on the restoration of old facilities, build completely new installations. When Holland was liberated the railways were left with 334 locomotives, 80 electric multiple unit trains, 36 diesel electric trains, 233 passenger cars, and 1,073 freight cars, compared to the 1939 stock of 865 locomotives, 430 electric trains, 82 diesel trains, 1,908 passenger cars, and 30,453 freight cars. Much of the missing equipment was eventually returned from Germany, but by no means all and by no means promptly. Destruction of facilities, especially workshops, was on the same scale, and much catenary and substation equipment had also been taken by the Germans. Maintenance of Dutch railways had virtually ceased in 1944 when, after a message from London, Dutch railwaymen ceased work, leaving the German army to operate the railways. In the first post-war months a few new steam engines of pre-war design were acquired, and great use was made of British 2-8-0 'Austerity' locomotives, but in the long run advantage was taken of the destruction to electrify far faster than would have been the case otherwise. In some fields, like car building, modernization began simultaneously with restoration, with all-steel vehicles becoming standard.

Elsewhere in formerly occupied Europe, restoration had top priority; highway vehicles had almost disappeared in many countries, so the railways had an even greater burden of responsibility. Trains were infrequent and confined to really essential traffic required to avert famine and to restart basic industries. Improvization was essential; so, for example, Chapelon's celebrated 4-8-0 passenger locomotives could be seen hauling heavy coal trains in Northern France. In Central and Eastern Europe the Germans left behind large numbers of their *Kriegslok* 2-10-0, and these formed the basis of railway operation in some areas, notably Austria. However, those *Kriegslok* units left in Eastern Europe were largely appropriated by the Russians. The Russians also removed much of the railway equipment they found in their zone of Germany (subsequently known as the German Democratic Republic). A complete electrified system was taken, on double-track lines one track was removed so that the rails could be sent to rehabilitate Soviet railways, and some single-track lines were lifted entirely for the same purpose. Workshop equipment was also taken. Single-track main lines can still be seen in the GDR, the missing track never having been restored; however, with CTC some of these singled sections have been found adequate.

In western Germany the advancing Allies were able to make almost immediate use of the railways, for the Germans usually left their locomotives behind them when they retreated. Locomotive power had not been scarce in Germany during the war, and many new locomotives had been put into store for future use. Cabsides of most engines were plated with 15 mm (⅝ in) steel as a protection against low-flying aircraft attacks. Apart from clearing up rubble and restoring damaged installations, the Allied railway battalions were not worked hard, for it was found that German railwaymen carried on their duties quite contentedly under military supervision. However, various shortages meant that only really essential trains could be operated. In the following years, when the Germans recovered direction of their railroads, they too began to steadily increase the mileage worked by diesel and electric traction, although there was not, nor could there be, a premature scrapping of steam locomotives. The division of Germany into two republics meant great changes in the direction of traffic flows, the east-west lines naturally losing much of their importance. However, German railways, partly for strategic reasons and partly because of the pre-1918 independence of the various states, had never been based on the capital in the same way that French main lines radiated from Paris, so it was not hard to adapt to the new traffic flows. West Germany's main lines became the Hamburg–Bremen–Rhineland–Munich and the Hamburg–Hanover–Munich routes.

Railways all over the world faced difficult times in the post-war years. In the more developed countries it was the re-emergence of a strengthened competition which was the main threat to the railways' future. The motor truck, which now tended to be less a one-man enterprise than a part of a big trucking company, took from the railways much of their most profitable traffic, high-value manu-factured articles for which railway freight rates were high. However, it is true that the trucks also took traffic which was unprofitable for the railways, short-distance and small-size consignments. A rational division of traffic would have been achieved if the trucks had been confined to the latter kind of business, allowing the railways to concentrate on the business for which they were most fitted, the carriage of large shipments over long distances. To some extent this did happen, but to very different degrees in different countries. Some European countries legislated to prevent trucks taking an excessive bite from the railways' traffic, but found it technically or politically impossible to do what was economically rational, that is, to levy on trucking companies a fair charge for highway and policing services. Truckers received these free while the railways paid about a fifth of their income on track and signalling. In America any legislation tended to favour the trucking industry rather than the rail-roads; the latter were not even free to regain business by lowering their charges. This meant that trucks operated over distances far longer than their technical characteristics justified; what was economically irrational from the social point of view had become commercially attractive from the truckers' point of view.

In many countries, especially the USA, the Netherlands, Germany and Japan, the long-haul and bulk traffic, for which the railways were very suited, was attacked from a different direction, by coastal and inland shipping. Here geography was the deciding factor, and there was little competition which the railways could describe as 'unfair'; at least not until they made efforts to recapture that traffic, when shipping interests sometimes succeeded in preventing them reducing their rates. In the passenger field there was a divergence between what happened in the countries of great distances, like North America and Australia, and what happened in Europe. In the big countries the aeroplane had begun to erode the railways' passenger traffic well before the war, ever since Douglas had introduced the DC-3 aircraft in the mid-1930s. However, it was precisely in these long-distance countries that passenger services were least profitable for the rail-ways, partly because the traffic flows were not dense and partly because long-distance trains with their sleeping, lounging and dining accommodation carried fewer passengers than shorter-distance trains. So it was not long after the wartime peak of passenger traffic that the railways began to lose passengers and to withdraw passenger services. Attempts, sometimes successful but more often not, were made to retain certain services with new rolling stock, and the long-distance passenger train still exists in America and Australia, but most travellers move by automobile or aircraft. In the European countries, however, the picture was different. Faster and more comfortable trains, and skilful public relations, enabled most systems to hold their passengers; some railways even achieved an increase, and Europeans in general never came to regard train travel as something old-fashioned or eccentric, as happened in America.

What was particularly worrying for railways was the declining share of freight traffic which they carried. In the post-war decades there were some railways, the British, for example, whose freight traffic declined absolutely (British railways carried 303 million tons in their peak year of 1923, 268 million in 1948, but 202 million in 1969). There were other railways, like those of North America, in which freight traffic increased but at a much smaller rate of increase than the total freight traffic carried by all forms of transport (in Canada, for example, railway freight ton/miles doubled between 1913 and 1970, but the Canadian economy developed much faster than that). Moreover, the traffic left to the railways was usually the low-valued (and therefore low-

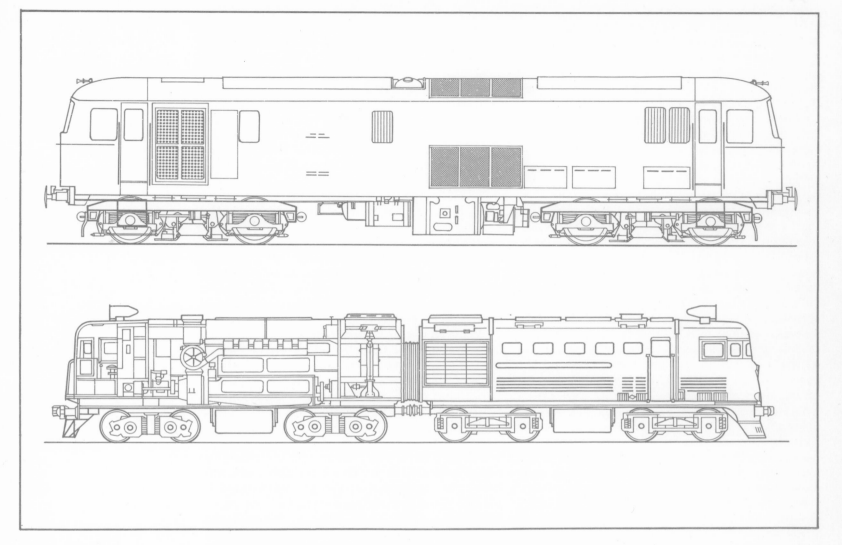

charged) traffic; freight revenues therefore suffered more than freight traffic. However, this gloomy picture was not universal. There were still countries like Russia, China, and India where economic development was still at a state when ever-increasing amounts of bulk traffic were requiring carriage and when road transport was still insignificant. The railways of these countries faced a more palatable kind of difficulty, that of handling fast-increasing traffic with a minimum of resources.

In the western world the railways could be further divided into those which in the three post-war decades seemed to cope with their problems and create modern systems organised and operated on rational principles, and the railways of Britain and America which, for a time and each in their own characteristic way, became travesties of competent railway management. In Britain the railways and road haulage firms in 1948 joined the airways as nationalized corporations. There were many good arguments for railway nationalization: Britain's railways were run-down and needed massive capital investment which could only be supplied by the state, competition between rail and road needed to be supervised so that each form of transport would be used for those tasks for which it was most fitted, railway transport was perhaps too important a social service to be in private hands, and bringing the railways into one organization promised further economies of scale, as, for example, through standardization of equipment. In general, most of the hopes placed in nationalization were disappointed. The new undertaking was only ostensibly subject to the much-vaunted 'public account-

ability' while at the same time it was vulnerable to government intervention, which became progressively more frequent. The government appointed a top management which was undistinguished, and then discouraged the rare initiatives of this management by a series of controls and imperatives which, taken together, were unworkable. It was two decades before clear minds were applied to railway problems. In those 20 years British Railways was organized and reorganized, centralized and decentralized, as successive governments came to power with new policies. Trains were painted in a variety of exciting new colours. Capital was wasted on a new and unnecessary range of standard steam locomotives. Coordination of rail and road not only did not take place, but was avoided; in Britain the first major railway electrification and the first motorway were undertaken simultaneously and ran parallel, and sometimes in sight of each other. While large sums of public money were invested unwisely, good capital investment projects were started, halted, and restarted because the government would sanction capital expenditure only on a one-year basis. Finally, as on many US railroads, management decided on dieselization, undoubtedly advantageous, as a cure-for-all-ills, which it could never be.

In the USA government intervention was never quite the problem which it became for British Railways, but it was nevertheless damaging. Enterprising railway management was rare in the USA, and it was all too often discouraged by bureaucratic intervention. For example, the control over railway rates exercised by the Interstate Commerce Commission meant that a railroad which introduced more

efficient equipment might be prevented from reducing its freight rates accordingly, on grounds of 'unfair' competition. Railways which wished to withdraw unprofitable passenger services were prevented from doing so; where high taxation levied by a state made passenger services impossibly costly, the same state could refuse to permit the railroad to withdraw them. In the meantime the federal government built a network of super-highways that enabled truck operators to offer faster services at lower cost, US Army engineers installed lock systems, dredged and otherwise improved inland and coastal waterways, and both Federal and state governments financed the building of city airports. These handouts of the taxpayers' money to the railways' competitors were accompanied by high taxation of railway property. It could happen that a city or state would agitate about the need for a smart new railroad station which, when it was built by the railroad, would be taxed at a higher valuation by the same local authorities. However, the greatest harm caused by outside intervention was to labour relations.

Reductions in the labour force Developing railway technology in the first half of the twentieth century had made it feasible to reduce the labour force. This did occur; indeed, from 1940 to 1975 the US railroads cut their labour force from one million to half a million, even though freight traffic increased during that period. However, there was scope for much greater reduction than this. But the railway trade unions, able to influence the votes of hundreds of thousands of workers in elections, particularly local and state elections, had much greater political power than railway managements. Many states were induced to pass 'full-crew' laws, which in effect meant that railroads in those states were required to employ far more men than were really necessary. In general, railroad managements were reluctant to face the strike action entailed by a confrontation with the railway unions. The latter, apart from successfully insisting on high levels of manpower, also were able to impose high wage rates. When strikes did occur, or were threatened, the Federal government intervened to impose settlements which would only damage the railroads' commercial prospects; in the 1946–1952 period, because of labour troubles, the US government three times took over the railroads under its emergency powers, the duration of one such takeover being almost two years. The big test came with dieselization and the railroads' wish to dispense with locomotive firemen as steam engines were phased out. From 1959 to 1963 there was argument, threatened strike action, congressional and court intervention until in 1964 an arbitration award permitted the elimination of firemen on most non-passenger trains. However, when the two years were over the dispute was rekindled, and many railroads were forced to reinstate their firemen.

The firemen issue did arouse public interest, and the accusations of 'featherbedding' levelled at railroaders, did intensify public antipathy towards the railroads. Featherbedding indeed there was, and examples were not hard to find because they were universal. Here is just one: to run a fast passenger service from Denver to Chicago (1,670 km or 1,034 miles) on a $16\frac{1}{2}$ hour schedule, eight locomotive drivers and eight firemen had to be employed, with crew changes about every 100 miles. Moreover, with what was called 'overtime', these eight crews collected $10\frac{1}{2}$ days' basic pay. In olden times 100 miles had been an average day's work for a locomotive crew, and in the mid-1970s, when trains might cover that distance in less than a couple of hours, it was still regarded as the standard distance entitling locomotive men to one day's pay.

One US railroad did eventually insist on freedom of management, and its experience was revealing. The Florida East Coast Railroad refused to pay a wage increase accepted by other US railroads, on the grounds that it could not find the money out of declining revenues. Later, it refused to recognize long-imposed work-rules. For a few days the railroad was brought to a standstill by the strike of its operating staff. Then a few trains were gingerly operated by its supervisory staff. Soon, new employees, non-union, were hired. The Railroad was supported by local business interests, but not by other US railroads or by the government, although the Supreme Court upheld its right to revise working practices. The strikers resorted first to picketing and then to violence. Hundreds of acts of sabotage or violence were committed, including the removal of rails, pot-shots at the cabs of diesel locomotives, and tampering with switches. The Kennedy administration tried to persuade the Railroad to accept the unions' terms, while the administration's FBI did less than might have been expected to arrest saboteurs. But in 1964 the extremists among the strikers made the tactical error of dynamiting two trains while President Johnson was in the vicinity. This time the FBI did take action and quickly arrested the culprits. The strike went on for years, but was increasingly irrelevant. The Railroad closed three out of its four locomotive workshops, sold off surplus locomotives, scrapped four fifths of its buildings, reduced its yards, and applied CTC to permit the single-tracking of much former double main line. These reductions were made possible without deterioration of service because the Railroad had introduced completely new working procedures, more in keeping with modern railroad technology. No longer, for example, were three successive five-man crews required to work a train from Miami to Jacksonville; one two-man crew (driver and conductor) was found to be enough. Main-line engine crews no longer refused to handle switching work en route. From 1963, when the trouble started, to 1973, the work force fell from 2,100 to less than 1,100. In 1976 the strike finished; the unions had lost and the Florida East Coast Railroad was profitable, efficient, and well appreciated.

In the post-authoritarian age, there was a genuine problem in ensuring that railway workers would put into society as much as they drew out of that society. In America there was little attempt to solve this problem because too many influential interests refused to acknowledge that it existed. In continental Europe, especially in those countries which had known the psychological shocks of defeat and destruction, railway workers were less distrustful of managements and more willing to sacrifice today's possibility for tomorrow's prosperity. There were, it is true, frequent railway strikes in some countries, notably Italy and France, but these were short and almost ritualistic. Between strikes railwaymen worked hard and intelligently, with an apparent pride in their job.

Even in Britain, where labour relations were

generally poor, unions did not push their demands to a point which would bring railroads to bankruptcy, as happened in the USA, where the first Class I railway to go out of business (the Ontario & Western) did so in the mid 1950s. In Britain, the railway unions extracted conditions and wage rates which did at certain periods mean that the money paid out in wages was not fully returned by the value of the work performed. But in general the self-interest of railway union leaders was not unenlightened. When in the early 1960s the British taxpayer began to resent the never-ending government financing of the railways' deficits, at a time when British Railways' revenue was in decline, the unions did not obdurately oppose economies in the use of manpower. It was clearly seen that rational use of labour was necessary for the railways' survival and unions acquiesced in an orderly reduction of manpower in exchange for a share in the financial gains of such a rationalization. It was not until the mid-1970s, partly because there were several competing railway unions, that pay claims sometimes became unreasonable in relation to the work done and to the railways' revenues.

The delicate question of the number of men required to operate a non-steam train gave some insight into the rational use of manpower by different railways. In the USA even a locomotive moving without a train was required to take a 5-man crew with it. In Britain a fireman was no longer required outside the small hours unless the run was longer than two hours or 100 miles. On the SNCF 2-man locomotive crews were required by the unions but railcars and multiple-unit electric trains could be operated with one man in the cab plus a train conductor with access to the driver's position. Switching locomotives within station limits could also be single-manned. In Germany all trains except those with an average speed of more than 90 km/h (55 mph) could be driven by one man, provided the conductor had the means to stop the train in emergency. In Ireland there was one-man operation. Italian State Railways were equipped for one-man operation but two were used 'as a step to reduce unemployment'. In Spain there were two men in the cab. In the Netherlands only one man was required in the cabs of electric passenger trains. In Sweden, short trains could be crewed by one man (no conductor being necessary), passenger trains of less than 30 axles and not running more than six consecutive hours could be driven by one man. In Norway electric trains were single-manned.

In countries of the Soviet bloc the railway trade unions cooperated fully with government policies. Their task was largely that of explaining such policies to their members and ensuring that the latter confirmed. This sometimes meant that working conditions, including safety measures, were not always commendable. On the other hand, it gave Soviet and eastern bloc railway managements greater freedom of management than their British or American counterparts.

The growth of diesel and electric systems
During the first post-war decade, when railway service in most countries of Western Europe seemed so slow to rise from its wartime trough, one of the few sources of optimism was France, where the SNCF was steadily electrifying its main line south from Paris through Lyons to the Mediterranean.

Work started as early as 1946, literally when the rubble was still being cleared, and electric services from Paris to Lyons were inaugurated in 1952. France had extensive experience of electrification before the war with, in particular, two electrified main lines from Paris to the south-west. These had been converted at 1,500 volts dc, and the same system was chosen for the first post-war project. Power for the Paris–Lyons scheme came from hydro-electricity generated in the Alps. Sub stations were remotely controlled and placed (according to the capacity of their rectifiers) at intervals of 9 km (5½ miles) or 14 km (9 miles). One result of the electrification which captured the public eye (and not only in France) was the acceleration of passenger trains, but the more important benefits were less obvious, except to railwaymen. Under steam traction there had been speed and load restrictions west of Dijon, because of long gradients. This had, in effect, meant a restriction of line capacity with much through freight traffic being passed over the parallel but less suitable secondary main line through Nevers. Electrification, with the provision of locomotive power which could be relied on for consistent hill-climbing capacity, eased this problem, and a further innovation, *banalisation*, finally eliminated it. *Banalisation* was a train control technique, permitting both tracks to carry traffic moving in the same direction. Thus at peak periods, when there was usually a definite one-way trend of traffic, the underemployed track would be changed to what was formerly called 'wrong-line working' for a period. Technically, there was nothing spectacular in this procedure, which could be described as treating a double-track line as consisting of two single-track lines under Centralized Traffic Control. Operationally, however, this was a great step forward, and avoided the need to convert double-track to quadruple-track. Meanwhile, as the electrification was carried out, other improvements were made. Centralized Traffic Control enabled signal boxes to be reduced from 39 to 19, flyover junctions were built to speed the entry to Paris and the passing of Dijon and Macon, and alignment was improved to permit higher maximum speeds. Taking advantage of electrification work to make other improvements would be a regular feature of future electrifications, in France and elsewhere. Electrification therefore came to mean not simply a new method of traction, but almost the provision of a completely new railway.

By the end of 1952 the *Mistral* passenger train from Paris to the Mediterranean had become one of the world's best-known trains, for it ran over the 511 km (317.5 mile) electrified section from Paris to Lyons in 4¼ hours, with a stop at Dijon. In later years, as the electrification progressed towards Marseilles, the *Mistral* stayed in the headlines. Quite apart from speed, the electrification brought economic improvements. With the replacement of hundreds of steam locomotives by fewer electric, traction costs were reduced in many ways (not the least being the elimination of the daily procession of trains from Northern France carrying locomotive coal).

It was over the Dijon–Lyons section that French engineers conducted the first of their high-speed experiments. Using one of the CC 7100-type electric locomotives built for this line, pulling three

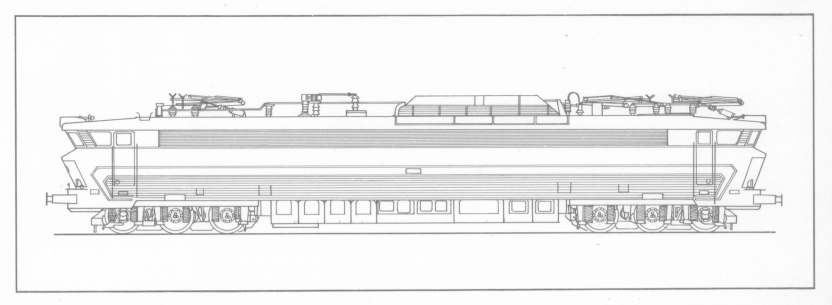

Class 18 electric locomotive of the Belgian State Railways. This is a multicurrent design, able to work on Belgian 3,000-volt dc, Dutch 1,500 volt dc, French 25,000 volt ac, and German 15,000-volt ac systems. This class was built by the French Alsthom Company in 1973. Similar locomotives (Class 40100) have been built for the SNCF.

cars, successive tests were made on a section of straight track until, on 21 February 1954, a world record of 243 km/h (151 mph) was achieved. Subsequent tests were carried out on the Paris–Bordeaux line, where alignments were more favourable, and in March 1955 two successive tests, in the final days of a series, produced maximum speeds of 431 km/h (205 mph) first by CC 7107 and then on the following day by the newer BB 9004. Although at the time the SNCF denied that these exploits were 'stunts', in a sense they were, for such high speeds would not have been attainable in normal conditions. Indeed, even with modifications, the pantographs melted at the high speeds, and the tests had to be carried out at low temperatures, when the copper overhead wire would be suitably tense. Nevertheless, stunt or no stunt, the tests did provide information which would be useful a decade later, when high-speed trains became a commercial proposition. Perhaps more important, the astonishing speed record of 1955 did much to encourage those who, in otherwise gloomy times, believed that the passenger railway still had a future, despite cars and aeroplanes.

Elsewhere in the world electrification continued, but less spectacularly. The Netherlands, war-devastated like France, electrified fast and retired its last steam locomotive as early as 1958. But it was the diesel locomotive which made the most dramatic progress in the post-war decades. By 1957, only one of the Class I US railroads, the coal-hauling Norfolk & Western, still made great use of steam traction, and even the N & W would shortly change over to diesels. Most North American railroads dieselized faster than consideration for optimum advantage would have warranted. Sometimes the wish to appear progressive, to be able to announce an 'all-diesel' railroad was responsible for this haste; sending almost-new steam locomotives to the scrapheap could seem very progressive and decisive to those who did not stop to ask themselves how much those steam locomotives were worth. However, this should not be regarded as a criticism to which only railroad managers were liable, for airline managements behaved in precisely the same way when the time came to consider a changeover from propeller to jet propulsion. In general, the world's railways could be divided into those which for one reason or another eliminated their steam fleet as soon as possible, once the decision to dieselize was

taken (these included most of the North American railroads, Britain and the USSR) and those which slowly dieselized, retaining the newer steam locomotives in the meantime (France, Germany, and Italy were prominent among these). Among the advantages of the latter policy were the avoidance of premature writing-off of steam locomotives, the maintenance of a stable diesel locomotive industry with a steady stream of orders, rather than inflicting a boom-and-slump sequence generated by a rushed dieselization scheme, and the opportunity of learning from mistakes in time to avoid really large-scale blunders.

Time was certainly needed to consider the optimum mix of electrification and dieselization; while electrification was best fitted for heavy-traffic lines, which could justify the heavy capital expenditure on lineside equipment, the exact division between electrification and diesel territory depended very much on a careful study of local circumstances. What happened on the best-ordered railways was that the obvious candidates for electrification were converted first and the first diesel locomotives were allocated to lines which would be electrified later. When this second group of lines were electrified, the diesels would be sent to the next most heavily-trafficked lines. With variations, this process was adopted in France, Germany, Italy, Russia, India, South Africa, and several other countries where, for the most part, it is still continuing; India and South Africa still operate many steam locomotives, and so, to a limited extent, do other countries. In North America the diesel had very little competition from electrification; in fact the advent of the diesel persuaded some companies which had electrified difficult sections to replace electrics with diesels. British Railways' motive power policy was eccentric. After nationalization in 1948, its new management decided to introduce a completely new range of steam locomotives and then, a few years later, decided to dieselize rapidly and completely all lines not electrified. Some kind of record was perhaps achieved in the short interval (seven years) between the building of the last new steam engine and the running of the last steam train, and also by the variety of diesel types ordered. Ignorant, perhaps, of the fact that General Motors had made a success of the diesel largely by producing only one or two types which were sold without any modification, the British decided on a policy of 'let all flowers bloom' (all

British flowers that is, for the most experienced diesel locomotive builder, General Motors, was deliberately excluded). The result was a bonanza for British locomotive builders (followed by the ruin of two of the best-known in the inevitable aftermath) and the saddling of British Railways with a fleet of diesel locomotives that was heterogeneous.

The post-war years witnessed the granting of independence to several former colonial territories. Of these, India was the biggest and the only one to have a really substantial railway network. Although run-down during the war, Indian railways were remarkable among colonial lines for their high engineering standards, and when India embarked on her 5-year industrialization plans the railways could rely heavily on this built-in reserve capacity to handle the increased traffic flows. After a period

Java witnessed much capital investment of which by no means all arrived at the intended destination. During the Japanese occupation and the subsequent liberation war, the railways suffered badly, even though by some kind of gentlemen's agreement the opposing Dutch and indigenous forces sometimes allowed trains to run unhindered between their respective zones. Rehabilitation of the railways was patchy. The main lines received German 2-8-2 steam locomotives and, later, German and American diesels, together with all-metal passenger cars. However, the secondary lines are still operated on rather less than a shoestring, with old and badly-maintained rolling stock running over threadbare track. The war did end one problem, however, for the Japanese solved the Javan gauge problem by transferring all the 1.435 m (4 ft 8½ in) gauge equipment to China,

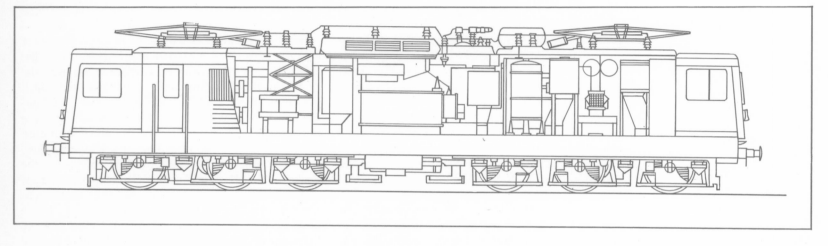

during which Indians appointed to the highest managerial positions were to some extent learning their jobs, various improvements were introduced. Some of these were technical, and others social. Among the latter were the progressive introduction of fast third-class-only long-distance passenger trains, and the opening (sometimes more ostensible than real) of railway operating jobs to all, irrespective of caste. Among the technical innovations was the introduction of a new standard range of more powerful locomotives (under British rule there had been fairly strict standardization. The new locomotives carried this further with, basically, just four types: a passenger and a freight design for each of the two main gauges). To ensure that the railways, with little investment in double-tracking and new lines, could carry the increasing traffic in coal and minerals, new high-capacity 4-axle freight cars were introduced. In subsequent decades electrification of some main lines was carried out and, more recently, a start has been made in converting narrow and metre-gauge routes to broad gauge, a very long process. After starting with a big steam locomotive works in the late 1940s, Indian Railways have since provided themselves with further production units and now build their own electric and diesel locomotives as well as passenger and freight cars. Their steam locomotive works eventually changed to diesel and electric locomotive production, but steam engines are expected to remain in service well into the next century.

Another colonial territory with a developed railway network was Java, the most prosperous of the former Dutch possessions in the East Indies. As the most developed part of the new republic of Indonesia,

leaving 1.067 m (3 ft 6 in) as the standard gauge.

Another big territory which could almost be described as ex-colonial was China, whose first railways had been built by foreigners in search of 'spheres of influence'. After the Chinese revolution of 1911, itself partly incited by controversy about who should own and operate China's railways, there was a disturbed period of gradual nationalization, civil war, Japanese occupation, and civil war again. Finally, in 1949, a strong government was installed, committed to massive economic development. With its emphasis on basic industries this economic policy assured the Chinese railways of an important role. At first there was much Russian assistance; the Chinese Eastern Railway through Manchuria, once part of the Trans–Siberian, was operated by Russia until 1952, and served as a training ground for Chinese railwaymen learning from Russian example. The Russians also assisted in setting up railway workshops; a steam locomotive of essentially Russian design is still being built in China. After the Russians left the Chinese were able to carry on alone, building their own diesel and electric locomotives and laying thousands of miles of new track.

In the USSR railway development was held at a level somewhat behind the rate of industrial growth. This meant that traffic density was high; by the early 1960s the Soviet railways, possessing about only one tenth of the world's railway mileage, carried half of the total freight traffic moved by the world's railways. The first post-war 5-year plan was largely devoted to repairing wartime damage and neglect, but in the 1950s there was opportunity for improvement. However, not all opportunities were taken. Like railway managements elsewhere, the Russians

A 7,200 hp thyristor-controlled electric locomotive built in the German Democratic Republic. This locomotive (class 250), is intended mainly for freight services; the prototype appeared in 1974.

did not see why methods which had worked before the war should not be continued after it. But unlike western managements, they lacked the spur of competition to force them to look around for better ways of performing their tasks. Highway transport had been neglected in the Soviet Union, where there were few hard-surfaced roads, and the inland waterways were a hindrance only insofar as they absorbed capital investment which would have been better utilized by the railways. In any case, at a time when the main problem was not finding traffic, but in handling it, waterway 'competition' was not competition at all, but useful load-shedding. So the Soviet railways handled their growing traffic, not so much by electrifying or dieselizing, but by building enough steam locomotives to provide two engines for the heavier mainline trains. This, even in Russian conditions, was not the most economical solution of the problem, but it was not until after the death of Stalin that out-of-date concepts could be safely abandoned. Then, basing itself largely on French experience, the Soviet Ministry of Transport embarked on large-scale electrification of main lines. At the same time, using at first designs based on American practice, there was a really massive production of diesel-electric locomotives. A Soviet passenger train was soon listed among the world's fastest; this was the *Avrora* between Moscow and Leningrad which covered 318 km (198 miles) of the journey at 138 km/h (86 mph). Thus, at a time when in many developed countries doubts were being cast on the railways' ability to survive even as freight carriers, in Russia, China, India and other countries committed to rapid growth, the railways evidently had a future as well as a past.

Towards a new railway system The inability of many railways to make a profit in the face of new competition meant that by the mid-1950s it became fashionable to predict an early end of railway transport; the steel wheel running on the steel rail was condemned as obsolete. Over the last two decades, however, there has been a change of attitude. This stems from two new factors: there were technological advances in rail transport which promised to do much to provide better service and reduce costs and, secondly, it was realized that the elimination of railways would create enormous problems, so governments began to examine transport problems and decided to make it easier for railways to perform those tasks for which they were best suited.

Typical of the new attitudes was the so-called Beeching Report on British Railways, published in 1963 and acted upon in subsequent years. Among its recommendations was that the railways should be allowed to shed loss-making operations, such as the running of stopping passenger trains and the maintenance of branch line services. By cutting out loss-making activities, there would be more resources available for improving those services which had a promising future, particularly longer distance freight and passenger services. By reducing the railway mileage to about 12,800 km (8,000 miles) a reduced but better-utilized network would be created. The network in fact was only reduced to about 17,700 km (11,000 miles) because line closures aroused great opposition, especially when it was realized that the British Railways management was not always correct in its assessments of which lines were the least promising. Subsequently British Railways

received greater freedom in fixing its charges; it could, within limits, actually bargain with individual shippers to obtain higher revenue. In the late 1960's however, it became clear that most of the economies obtained from withdrawal of services were absorbed by rather higher wages. The concept of 'cost-benefit' then came to the fore; it meant that a railway line's viability was no longer to be judged by its profitability, but by its financial result taken in conjunction with the value of the benefits it conferred on society. This opened the way for subsidy of loss-making services maintained for social reasons. Commuter services were a first beneficiary of this attitude, and financial responsibility for some was taken over by local authorities; the railway was a far cheaper way of moving workers into and out of a town but it was nevertheless unable to avoid heavy losses, for season ticket fares were low and rolling stock and facilities had to be maintained for just a few hours work each day.

Each in their own way, the railways of other western countries benefited from similar changes of government attitude. In Canada there was the inevitable Royal Commission, which decided that it was unfair for Canadian railways to carry on loss-making service without public subsidy, while the government of Ontario decided to halt the building of a new expressway into Toronto, and instead to institute its own commuter rail service over the tracks of the Canadian National Railways. In France, 1971 saw the amendment of the 1937 agreement which had led to the formation of the SNCF. From 1971 the French National Railways were to have freedom of management, especially in financial matters, and equality of opportunity was to be imposed on all forms of transport (a provision which benefited the railways, which were more regulated than other forms of transport). In 1973 the governments of both Britain and Germany admitted that if railways were to provide the required level of service they could hardly make a profit, and therefore sums had to be made available to them for investment.

In the USA, events took a different course. There was a trend, encouraged by the government, towards the merger of railways. The Chesapeake & Ohio took over the Baltimore & Ohio and the Western Maryland, the Norfolk & Western absorbed the Nickel Plate and the Wabash railroads, and the old James Hill empire was reconstituted when the Great Northern, Northern Pacific, and Burlington united to form the Burlington Northern. These three amalgamations produced stronger and bigger companies which were allowed by the labour unions to eliminate some, but by no means all, of the duplication of facilities in their territories. Other very desirable mergers did not take place, however, sometimes because labour pressures made the potential economies seem unattainable, or because the partners could not agree on terms. In the eastern states, where there was a longstanding duplication of railway lines and very strong competition from the air and highway, individual railroads seemed likely to follow the path into insolvency taken by the Ontario & Western in 1957. In 1961 the New Haven Railroad, connecting New York and Boston, went bankrupt and was absorbed into the Pennsylvania Railroad. The Erie and Lackawanna railroads merged in the vain hope of avoiding bankruptcy, and so did the two one-time trend-setters of the American railroad industry, the New York Central and the Pennsylvania, forming for a time the Penn Central Railroad. But these changes were insufficient. Freight services remained very vulnerable to highway competition, even though for the most part they ran over distances which in European conditions would have made them the undoubted preserve of rail transport. Freight trains were delayed where they passed from one system to another, and the high cost of labour made it essential to run as few trains as possible; the resulting long trains meant that services were infrequent and facilities such as yards were of excessive size and even then could not handle traffic efficiently. In 1970 Penn Central went bankrupt, joining several other eastern railroads in a like predicament. More than half of Penn Central's costs were for labour.

This railroad crisis was one which the government could not ignore, and the eventual result was the creation of Conrail (Consolidated Rail Corporation) which was essentially a nationalized railway even though every effort was made to hide this fact from a public long schooled to regard the word nationalization with suspicion. Conrail united into one organization the seven eastern railroads: Penn Central, Boston & Maine, Erie-Lackawanna, Lehigh Valley, Central of New Jersey, Reading, and the Lehigh & Hudson River. In order to provide some competition, two profitable railroads, the Southern and the Chesapeake & Ohio, were invited to take over 2,000 miles of track formerly belonging to the bankrupts. However, because of a dispute over work rules, the SR and C & O only accepted this offer under pressure. Conrail's prospects were hopeful; elimination of duplication would be feasible over the long term though, in the short term, it was not possible to reduce the labour force to a size (about half) which railway technology really warranted.

Earlier, another nationalization in all but name had overtaken the long-ailing US passenger train. Most railroads, anxious to shed loss-making passenger trains, were only too willing to cooperate in this. Like Conrail, the National Railroad Passenger Corporation (AMTRAK) was called, delicately if inelegantly, a 'quasi-non-governmental-organisation'. It was formed in 1971 and operates almost all non-commuter passenger trains, using the tracks of those railroads which agreed to participate. Most of its early locomotives and passenger cars were handed down by the companies which formerly operated them, and were in a generally poor condition. Moreover, it often happened that the passenger cars of one railroad could not run on other railroads because of

size or equipment variations. In recent years, therefore, AMTRAK has been ordering new cars and locomotives. In general, AMTRAK has been a success. It has not been profitable, and will probably require government financial support for several years. But it has achieved the other objectives of the government by ensuring the continued existence of the passenger train and in fact winning back passengers to rail transport. Interestingly, it has increased first-class travel faster than the lower-fare coach class. About half of its traffic comes in the so-called North-East Corridor (Washington–New York–Boston). Between New York and Washington its 'Metroliner' high-speed multiple-unit electric trains have won back significant traffic from the airlines. On this 366 km (224 mile) route their three-hour schedule is very competitive with the airlines, given the time needed to reach the airports over frequently-congested highways.

However, private enterprise passenger trains still exist in the USA. The Southern Railway, one of the few US railroads under energetic management, decided that although its passenger trains might not run at a profit, at least they could bring credit to their company. The SR therefore did not join AMTRAK, but continued to operate an excellent passenger train between Washington and New Orleans. A new private enterprise in the passenger train business is the Auto-Train Corporation. This borrowed the European idea of transporting holiday makers with their automobiles by train, the passengers moving in passenger coaches and the automobiles in special automobile cars originally designed for carrying one of the railways' fastest-growing traffics, new automobiles moving from factory to distributor. Auto-Train acquired its own locomotives and trains, and concentrated on making its patrons' journey enjoyable, insisting that its own staff, and not railroaders, should deal with the passengers. Its first service, from Virginia to Florida, was immediately popular and promised to show a profit. Other non-traditional solutions to US railroad problems were the taking-over by local interests of lines or services formerly operated by bankrupt companies. The Michigan Northern (394 km or 246 miles) is an early example of this operation; the state of Michigan leased the track from its owner, the ill-fated Penn Central, and the Michigan Northern operated it under contract to the state. It was non-union, paying union rates of pay but imposing its own work rules. Elsewhere, several cities have taken over, or at least subsidized, commuter services. The State of New York both owns and operates the outer-suburban Long Island

A thyristor-controlled locomotive of British Rail. This unit, built in 1975, is basically of the 87 class, introduced for the West Coast main line; it was built in British Rail workshops with the assistance of GEC.

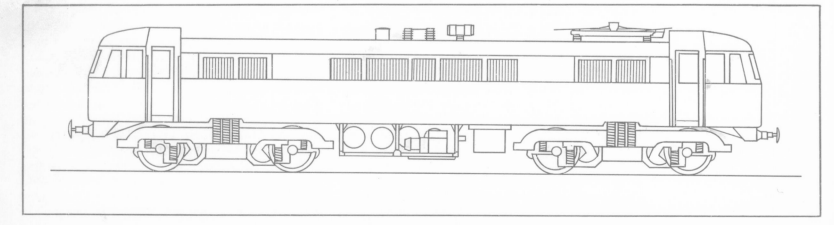

Railroad, and most of its suburban services are operated by its Metropolitan Transportation Authority. Locally-financed or operated commuter services have also been witnessed in Britain and continental Europe. In Britain, local passenger authorities attempt to coordinate and operate all forms of commuter transport and similar schemes have long been accepted by certain French and German cities. One of the world's oldest railways, the St Etienne to Lyons line (59 km or 37 miles) now has a subsidized commuter service of 14 trains each way, formed by new stainless steel cars financed by the local authorities; and this is just one example of what is becoming a widespread European practice.

The European railways encountered airline competition later than the US railroads, and were therefore better-prepared. They had the advantage that typical inter-city distances were suited to a continued role for the railways, and that in the first post-war decade the national airlines were more interested in the longer international routes than in internal services. The first major step by the railways to safeguard their passenger business came with the introduction of the Trans-European Expresses (TEE). These were designed to forestall airline competition on international routes inside Europe, that is, to attract precisely the businessmen clients whom the airlines were tempting. The new TEE trains were usually fast diesel sets, very comfortable, with hostesses and meal service, and charging a supplement as well as the first-class fare. Distinctive colours for the train sets was one feature of the skilful publicity for these trains, whose success was due, however, not so much to publicity but to their truly excellent and convenient service. In the beginning the various railway undertakings were each encouraged to design their own TEE diesel trains; some of these were successful but others less so. The TEE appellation was later extended to cover trains which did not cross frontiers but which maintained the standards (and the exclusivity) of the TEE concept. On many routes TEE traffic has grown so much that full-size trains are used. Between Paris and Brussels, for example, there are now six TEE trains each way. These trains are of 15 cars (750 tons), hauled by a 6,000 hp electric locomotive of French design, capable of working on four different electrification systems (although in this service only two systems are encountered). These trains leave at times to suit the business man, in the morning and evening, and cover the 310 km (193 miles) in 2 hours and 20 minutes (132 km/h or 82.5 mph).

In Britain, where airline competition was similarly late to develop, there was an initial introduction of one or two TEE-style Pullman multiple-unit diesel trains, but these were not especially successful. In general, subsequent British policy was to raise the speeds of all trains and to provide ample first-class accommodation on all of them. The Pullman idea did survive, however, notably in a couple of business trains on the newly-electrified line from London to Manchester and Liverpool. The British passenger fare structure was more complex than its ostensible two-class division suggested. Apart from high first-class fares, there were usually high second-class fares payable for travelling on the most convenient trains, and several low second-class fares, described as cheap tickets, which could be used on other trains.

The US railroads had experimented with various types of multiple unit diesel trains in the 1950s, but with little commercial success. However, the Budd rail diesel car was a great cost-saver on secondary routes. This was a successor to the old gas-electric railcar, and could be purchased in several configurations with varying proportions of passenger, mail, and parcels space. Secondary line operation by railcars was already a tradition of European railways, and this continued. Germany re-introduced the railbus for branch lines, and British Railways as part of its modernization plan acquired a great variety of diesel train sets. However, more spectacular advances in the passenger field came with the new high-speed trains.

Broadly, the high-speed trains were of two categories: improved versions of conventional trains and trains employing completely new concepts. Among the former, the SNCF's *Aquitaine* from Paris to Bordeaux is an outstanding example. In 1970 this was equipped with stainless steel cars of TEE standard, stable at high speeds, and the schedule for the 576 km (360 miles) was set at four hours. This represented an average speed of 144 km/h (90 mph), and the SNCF had eight other return services averaging more than 128 km/h (80 mph). Other countries had similar although not perhaps quite so superlative services. In Germany and Britain the fastest trains tended to be scheduled at average speeds up to 120 km/h (75 mph), although these, especially in Germany, made more frequent stops than the fastest French trains. Perhaps Italy provided the only real rivals to the SNCF trains in comfort and speed. The *Vesuvius Arrow* between Naples and Rome averaged 140 km/h (87 mph) over 208 km (130 miles). In Russia there was the *Avrora* service between Moscow and Leningrad, but the comfort of this train could not compare with the best western European trains.

Using conventional rolling stock, and with a minimum of track upgrading, some railways decided that even faster services could be run. A new series of German electric locomotives (Class 103) was introduced, capable of 200 km/h (125 mph). This was given high-speed trials and also used to accelerate certain inter-city services. However, the extra expense entailed by the higher speeds was not really justified by the commercial advantages, so interest in Germany, as in France, turned to the construction of entirely new railways, designed from the start for high speeds. In Germany, while some existing lines were to be upgraded for high-speed running, completely new lines were also planned, notably from Hanover southwards towards Munich, and from Cologne down the Rhine to Stuttgart and Munich. Work has already started on this new project, but is unlikely to be finished before the mid-1980s, by which time the DB's market research experts forecast a doubling of passenger traffic and a sizable increase in freight (which means that new railways would be needed in any case). The new track will be designed to accept trains running at up to 300 km/h (185 mph), while the upgraded lines will accept 200 km/h (125 mph). In France the first of the new high-speed lines will be the Paris–Sudest, which was authorized in 1974. This will run parallel to that traditional main artery of French railway communication, the Paris–Lyons route, and it is expected that electric multiple-unit trains will be used to

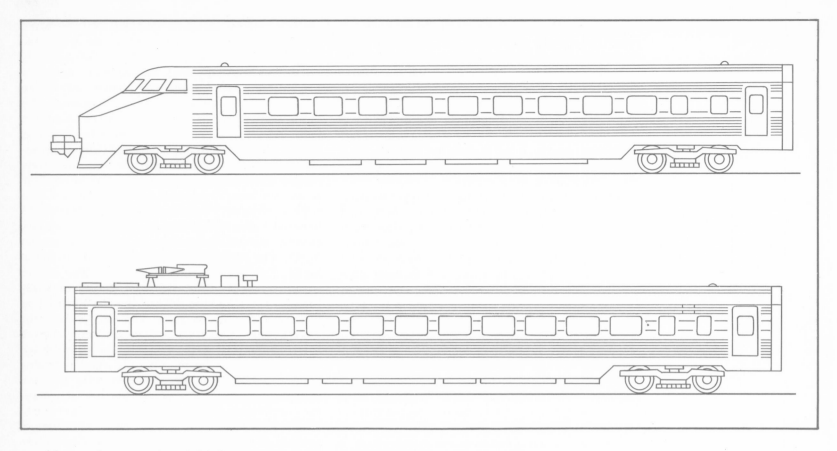

Prototype ER200 high-speed electric multiple unit train of Soviet Railways. Currently on trial between Moscow and Leningrad, this 14-car train is designed for speeds up to 200 kph (125 mph).

provide services running initially at 250 km/h (155 mph), and faster later. This route, again, is one on which passenger traffic has been steadily increasing year by year and its construction will allow freight service to be handled on the existing line while most passenger traffic will move by the new route. Meanwhile in Italy the new Florence to Rome *direttissima* will probably be the first of the European high-speed routes to be completed. This differs from the French scheme in that conventional electric trains will be used, and 250 km/h (155 mph) will be the maximum speed, curves will be of a minimum 3,000-metre radius in place of the French 3,200-metre, and the new line will be used for freight services as well as passenger. Belgium and Switzerland are also considering high-speed lines and it is quite likely that by the end of the century western Europe will have a network of these new railways. Elsewhere, the Soviet railways are modernizing the Moscow-Leningrad main line. This, one of the oldest Russian lines, was built with easy gradients and is dead straight for most of its length; it is therefore suited to a fairly economical upgrading to permit speeds of up to 200 km/h (125 mph).

Inspiration for these high-speed projects came from the success of the New Tokaido Line in Japan. This was the first step in a planned creation of an entirely new trunkline network which would be of the 1.435 m (4 ft 8½ in) gauge rather than the standard Japanese 1.067 m (3 ft 6 in). The first 514 km (320 mile) section was opened in 1964 between Tokyo and Osaka. It was a double-track route with very easy gradients and curves, and intended for fast passenger services only; freight and stopping passenger trains were concentrated on the old 3 ft 6 in line. Electric multiple-units, the so-called 'bullet trains', were used, at speeds up to 210 km/h (130 mph), and extra fares were charged. Despite the extra fare, the trains were a real success and heavily patronized. It appeared that internal airline competition could not beat this new railway com-

petition, even though the railway fares were only slightly lower than airline fares. However, the airlines have since improved their schedules with the introduction of jets and, moreover, access from city to airport has been eased, so that city-centre-to-city-centre time by the airline is now not much more than two hours, compared to the bullet trains' three hours and 20 minutes. It would seem that on the Tokyo to Osaka route the railway will maintain a good share of the traffic, but on the longer distance services the future is less certain. Indeed, the original plan for over 6,880 km (4,300 miles) has been criticised in some quarters on this basis, although even with air competition the new lines should be valuable for inter-city links of up to 300 miles. The Osaka line has since been extended, and on the full length of the line from Tokyo via Osaka to Hakata (1,180 km or 735 miles) the bullet-trains average 170 km/h (106 mph) and run every half-hour. These lines are exceptionally efficient, as indeed they ought to be, carrying one type of traffic in bulk over long distances; it has been estimated that an employee of the New Tokaido Line produces nine times the revenue generated by the average railway employee. One unexpected costly item of the new line has been track maintenance, and it is likely that future new lines will be laid not on stone ballast, but attached to a continuous belt of concrete. Such concrete rail-beds were tried in the late 1960s in Germany and elsewhere in anticipation of the need for very robust track when high-speed trains are operated.

The operation of high-speed trains called for the application of the most advanced signalling systems. At speeds over 200 km/h (125 mph) the chances of a driver missing a conventional visual signal increase rapidly and trains at such speeds usually need longer braking distances. Some degree of automatic control was therefore required, and this was already available in further developments of the track-circuiting principle. Instead of trains merely indicating their presence by short-circuiting a weak current in one of the rails, it was found possible to pass electric pulses through the rails which could be picked up by the locomotive, the pattern of the pulses being varied to create a code. For example, a particular coded pulse could not only indicate that a speed reduction to a given speed was required, but could also itself actuate the required changes in the locomotive's control system. In other words, the automatically operated train was a full possibility, and a number of the world's railways have operated experimental driverless trains with success.

Where a comparatively simple and regular operation is to be carried out, automation is fairly easy and in fact does not need modern track pulses. Since 1926, for example, a narrow-gauge tube railway operated solely for carrying mail bags between stations and sorting offices has been working automatically beneath London. Several recent underground railways have also been equipped for automatic operation, although in these cases a trainman is carried. The Times Square shuttle of 1964 was one such line and part of the Paris Metro and London's Victoria Line are similarly equipped. In San Francisco the Bay Area Rapid Transit system employs fully automatic trains, with even the opening and closing of doors being effected without human intervention. Trains are controlled by a Centralized Train Control installation which is itself operated by computers. Drivers are carried on the trains, but they have no real function apart from reassuring nervous passengers and being on hand if the unexpected should happen. There are also a few mining railways, where operations are repetitive, which are operated automatically. In general, there is no technical reason why trains should not be operated automatically, although there are good commercial and human reasons why the driverless train has not yet triumphed.

A cheaper alternative to the building of new high-speed routes is the design of trains which can run at high speed over existing tracks. Design problems are more complex in this case, and the maximum speeds may be somewhat slower, but such trains are cheap and bring the benefits of high speed earlier than the construction of super-railways. One of the first examples were the electric *Metroliners* built for the New York to Washington service of the former Pennsylvania Railroad. Although they encountered many troubles in their early days (the intended maximum speed of 255 km/h [160 mph] was soon found to be impracticable), and although they were not really much advanced beyond the conventional train, they succeeded in winning back passengers from the airlines. The British High Speed Train (HST), introduced in 1976, is a far more sophisticated design. This is another multiple-unit train, powered by diesel electric engines in the end units, and intended for a speed of 200 km/h (125 mph). Before introduction, some realignment of track was undertaken, but this was not substantial. The first service operated by these trains was between London and Bristol, a route facing competition from the private automobile moving over a motorway. Some criticism was expressed on the wisdom of investing many millions of pounds in order to shave a quarter-hour from passenger schedules, but early indications were that whatever the economic arguments might be, the HST was a step forward in fostering a favourable public opinion towards passenger train travel. The HST was expected to be followed by a true high-speed train, the Advanced Passenger Train (APT). This, already running in prototype form, had such novelties as a suspension which kept the wheel flanges away from the rail, even on curves, to reduce friction, and a tilting body to absorb centrifugal forces on curves. Tilting bodies were not new; the Chesapeake & Ohio Railroad, the SNCF, and the US-built turbo-trains of the 1960s had tilting bodies, but these were passive. However, starting in Germany in 1968, an active tilt was developed, in which power was applied to the pivoted bodies so that the tilt could be initiated before the centrifugal pressures were felt, thereby subjecting passengers to much gentler forces. The APT has this active tilt, and can therefore run at high speeds over routes whose curves have not been eased in anticipation. A train mid-way between the HST and APT is the Canadian LRC, which began trials in 1974. This differs from the HST in that the two end power units are closer to true locomotives, and the train can be operated without the rear locomotive unit, thereby giving greater flexibility in the choice of train size and power provision. The coaches, but not the power cars, are tilting, and great use is made of lightweight alloys (the leading member of the consortium of companies behind this project is the Aluminium Company of Canada). The diesel-electric power cars were designed and built at the Montreal Locomotive Works. Both the main Canadian railways are interested in this train and high speeds have been reached on trial so often that an aggrieved Department of Transport issued an instruction that future record-breaking runs were to be notified in advance.

Whereas Britain and Canada in their high-speed train projects were satisfied that diesel-electric traction was adequate, other designers pinned great hopes on the gas turbine. From 1964 American-built turbotrains appeared on the New York–Boston and Montreal–Toronto runs. These had passively tilting bodies, and engines derived from aviation practice. They put up some good performances but were subject to more breakdowns than could be tolerated in railway service. The Canadian units were withdrawn for modification, and re-installed later, but could still not be regarded as really successful. The French were more fortunate with their several designs of gas turbine train. The French railway equipment industry had been highly successful since the war. The forward-looking policy of the SNCF enabled progressively more advanced items to be designed, tested, and produced, this process creating a stock of experience and also a stream of orders from foreign railways, impressed by the 'shop window' provided by the SNCF. So when it was decided to investigate the possibilities of building a train powered by gas turbines for providing fast services on lines insufficiently busy to justify electrification, the prize was not just orders from the SNCF, but a further batch of orders from abroad too, and the continued reputation of the French as leaders in applied railway technology.

Gas turbines had been tried before on various railways. Their great advantage was their low weight per horsepower, and their great problem was that they only worked efficiently at maximum power. In railway service maximum power is not normally required except at starting and perhaps up steep gradients. This is why the only railway to make substantial use of gas turbine locomotives (strictly speaking, gas turbine electrics) was the Union Pacific Railroad, which had heavy trains to be pulled over long heavily-graded routes in the foothills of the Rockies. However, a high-speed passenger train, so designed that to maintain high speed the engines would have to deliver maximum output for most of the time, was also a promising field for gas turbine propulsion. The French began with a train powered by a gas turbine at one end and a diesel at the other, but later shifted to all-turbine propulsion.

The first regular service of these turbotrains commenced in 1970 on the Paris to Caen and Cherbourg line. Their introduction was accompanied by a wholesale revision of the timetable; hitherto the usual SNCF pattern of long trains leaving in the morning, at midday and the evening had been operative. The turbotrains, while offering a much faster service, had only 188 seats compared to the 800 seats of the conventional trains. Therefore a frequent service was required to handle the traffic. Such a fast and frequent service (supplemented by conventional trains at weekend peaks) attracted an additional clientele; just as British Railways discovered when their London to Manchester electrification led to faster and more frequent trains, new passengers were attracted who were not drawn from other forms of transport, but were people who would otherwise have not travelled at all. In the case of this first route to offer turbotrain service, passenger carryings increased by one fifth almost immediately. The success of these ETG trains led the SNCF to introduce the RTG type, in which the diesel engine at one end was replaced by a second turbine. This RTG, consisting of five cars (one more than the ETG), had a maximum speed of 200 km/h (125 mph). It was not long before foreign interest was aroused. Two 5-car trains were ordered by the American AMTRAK for the Chicago–St Louis service, and performed so well that four more were ordered, with another seven to be built in the USA under licence. This was by no means the first time that foreign equipment had been acquired for American railroads; in the 1950s some German diesel-hydraulic locomotives had been tried by the Union Pacific and the Rio Grande railroads, but maintenance costs had been high. American equipment had always been rugged and heavy, to withstand hard use and rough maintenance. Possibly the success of the French turbotrains had some connection with the fact that they were owned and operated by AMTRAK, which did not belong to traditional American railroading. Another export outlet for the turbotrains was Iran, which spent some of its oil income on railway modernization. The Iran order, however, is also a reminder of one drawback of the gas turbine, its rather high fuel consumption. After the rise of world oil prices in 1973 the gas turbine, despite much lower maintenance costs compared to diesel engines, and its low weight, became somewhat less attractive from the commercial point of view.

Although several railways in western Europe now derive more revenue from passengers than from freight, the reverse still holds true in most countries, and especially in North America. The most potent technique for regaining the high-value freight traffic from the highways has been the door-to-door service obtained from the use of demountable containers or 'piggyback' services. Piggyback, which won early acceptance in North America and France especially, is the carrying on railway flatcars of road semi-trailers, which begin and end their transits on the highways. A feature of this service is that the railways' nominal competitors, truck operators, can use this service for their own semi-trailers, reducing their costs by so doing. This enables the railways to draw back some of the revenue lost to highway competition. A notable example of this is in Australia, where transcontinental truckers use the Trans-Australian line for the long haul over the Nullarbor Plain, their drivers travelling on the piggyback train in passenger cars. The time saved by this, and the consequent reduced wage-bill, makes this very worthwhile for the truck operators. Piggyback, however, does involve the carriage of the semi-trailer's wheels, which in itself produces no revenue and on some railways creates height clearance problems. From this point of view the container is more acceptable, even though it requires lifting gear at each terminal to move it between railway flatcar and highway flatbed truck (piggyback only requires a loading ramp). In the early years, in North America, full value of the container idea was not obtained, because different railroads adopted different sizes and types of container; this meant that a given container could only be received or despatched by those railroads which had adopted that particular system. This drawback still exists, but is being alleviated following the adoption of a world standard (ISO) for container dimensions and tie-down arrangements. This standard was adopted largely at the initiative of shipping companies, intent on making the best use of their expensive container ships, and of European railways. Among the more noteworthy of the container movements thereby made possible is the traffic from Britain and the continent to Japan, much of which travels in container ships and container trains via the Trans-Siberian Railway. In internal services, British Railways made an early success of so-called liner trains, which were regular fast trains of specially designed rolling stock, carrying containers only. The term 'liner train' has also been applied to non-container trains offering regular fast transits between (usually) two points. Freight trains of this type now travel at much higher speeds. The Santa Fe Railroad's *Super C* averages about 110 km/h (70 mph) over 337 km (205 miles) of its trip and one or two other US and Canadian railroads have freight trains scheduled at over 97 km/h (60 mph). In Europe the fastest freight train is the SNCF's *Provence Express*, which averages over 97 km/h (60.3 mph) over 712 km (443 miles), touching 140 km/h (87 mph) in places.

For bulk traffic not suitable for container handling some railways, and in particular British Railways, have offered trains of specialized rolling stock 'in captive service'; that is, reserved for the use of a particular customer making regular shipments. A typical operation is the carriage of oil products from refinery to distribution point. The rolling stock carries the name of the shipper, which provides gratifying publicity for the latter. In France, a particular effort has been made to provide major industrial plants with their own railway siding. This is a very old practice in all countries, but in recent decades has tended to disappear. Not so in France,

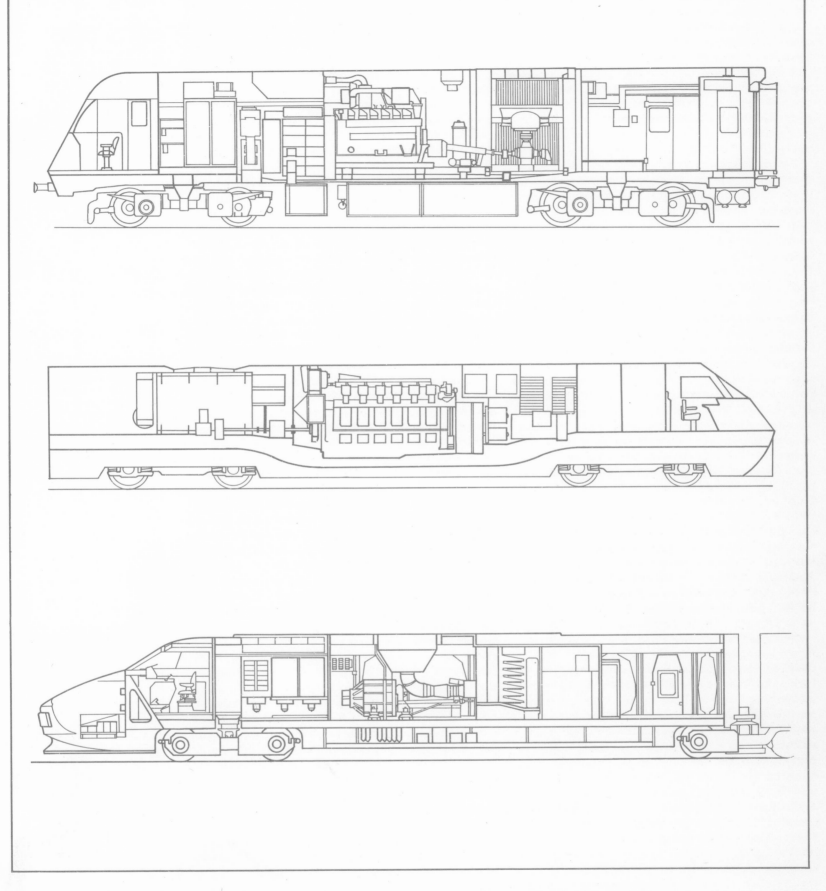

however, where nine tenths of railway freight traffic now either arrives or departs from a private siding.

For bulk traffic the unit train has become widespread. Basically this again is an old idea, being the regular conveyance of one commodity between just two points in a train reserved for that purpose. This speeds transit and allows more intensive utilization of the rolling stock. In Britain the so-called 'Merrygoround' services are a notable case; these carry coal from mine to power station in special rolling stock which can be loaded and unloaded while the train is travelling very slowly. With loops at either end of the journey there is no need for the train to come to a complete halt; trains are not held up for hours or days in yards, as once used to be the case. In America very heavy unit trains are used by some railroads which have regular coal shipments. The first heavy long-distance unit train in the USA was introduced by the Santa Fe Railroad in 1970. This was a 3,540 km (2,200 mile) round trip between New Mexico coalfields and California, with the 11,000 ton trains taking four days to complete the cycle. With such long trains, diesel locomotive units are inserted halfway down the train, connected by remote control to the leading locomotive. This distributes the pull down the train, easing the strain which otherwise might break conventional couplings. The Canadian Pacific Railway operates a similar train through the Rockies, carrying export coal towards Japan; here the 100-car trains are entrusted to ten locomotive units. Another railway similarly handling very heavy coal trains, again mainly for export to Japan, is the Queensland Government Railways, which operates the heaviest trains (10,600 ton) ever seen on the 1.067 m (3 ft 6 in) gauge.

Other aids to efficient freight operation are the application of roller bearings to some specialized freight cars, thereby reducing the danger of over-heated axleboxes. For the prompt detection of these 'hotboxes' some railways have installed line-side hotbox detectors, sensitive to any heat emitted by a passing freight car. For the efficient use of freight cars (and to provide what shippers have for decades been asking for), electronic systems feeding into computers can provide information of the whereabouts of any freight car within the system. In Europe, it is expected that there will be an inter-national scheme embracing both western Europe and the nations of the Soviet bloc, and a few other nations besides. All freight cars in these countries have been renumbered in an international scheme, and these numbers are capable of being scanned and recorded by lineside electronic apparatus. Also, the introduction of an automatic coupling is imminent in Europe. This has been delayed somewhat by the decision to make it compatible with the Russian system, but the end result will be that truly auto-matic couplers, which not only join the cars' draw-bars but also automatically join the cables and pipes of the braking and control systems, will be a feature of all freight cars in Europe. Presumably Britain may be late in joining this scheme, given the postponement of the railway Cross-Channel Tunnel and the archaic design of the average British freight car, which makes it unsuitable for operation in European conditions.

While European and American railways are en-grossed with applying the very latest technology, the conventional railway is still expanding. Contrary, perhaps, to the general belief, thousands of miles of new railway are being laid each year. Such con-struction is not confined to rapidly developing economies, like Russia and China, but is also taking place in newly-rich countries, in poor but potentially rich African countries beginning a politically inde-pendent life, and wherever there are raw materials worth exploiting. Australia provides a good example of the latter, with long railway lines being built in Western Australia to tap ore deposits. Notable among the new African railways is the Tanzania–Zambia Railway (the Tan-Zam). This 1,860 km (1,160 mile) line links landlocked Zambia with the Tanzanian port of Dar es Salaam. Opened in 1975, it was built with Chinese capital, by Chinese engineers, and largely by Chinese manpower. Rolling stock and locomotives are Chinese-built, although the designs still show Russian influence. This line is of 3 ft 6 in gauge, conforming to the Zambian standard but incompatible with the metre-gauge of Tanzania. Of the railways planned by newly-rich countries, those of Iran are perhaps the most ambitious, with thousands of kilometres of new route being surveyed. One new line will connect with Pakistan Railways, making it possible to travel by rail from Turkey to India or, via Russia, from Calais to Calcutta. In the USSR the biggest project is the Baikal–Amur Railway, which will run north of the Trans-Siberian from Lake Baikal to the Pacific through some of the most difficult terrain ever pene-trated by a railway; steep gorges, permanently-frozen subsoil, volcanic tremors, flash floods, and landslides are all being faced and, in one way or another, surmounted. An interesting point about this railway is that its primary purpose is to trans-port oil from new oilfields in Central Siberia; a pipe-line was considered, but rejected on the grounds that it was almost as expensive as a railway and, unlike a railway, could carry only one commodity and offer nothing for the development of the intervening territory.

Apart from new lines, electrification is still spreading. Even some US railroads are looking at the possibilities of electrification, and the Canadian Pacific expects to electrify its route through the Rockies, which now carries a heavy coal traffic. Over the last two decades 25,000-volt ac current at in-dustrial frequency has been the preferred system. This was made a success by French engineers, although pre-war German research paved the way. The first big electrification on this system, in which capital costs are much lower, was in eastern France between Valenciennes and Thionville. Subsequent French electrification was carried out on this system, so that while the south and south western lines are on the old 1,500 volt system the northern and eastern lines are at 25,000 volts. This is quite a common situation in other countries which began their electrification before the development of small 'solid state' rectifiers enabled current to be supplied at the high voltage and converted on the locomotive itself to low voltage dc for the traction motors. For through workings on routes where the system changes, locomotives have been built which can work on up to four different systems.

However, as with all railway technology, electri-fication practice is still capable of further develop-ment. There is already a railroad functioning at the full industrial voltage of 50,000 volts. This is the 125 km (78 mile) Black Mesa and Lake Powell line in northern Arizona. This new line has many, though not all, of the features which seem most likely to distinguish the railways of the 1980s. It carries coal from mine to power station in unit trains which make three round trips daily and consist of 77 cars, each carrying 120 tons. The trains, hauled by three 6,000 hp electric locomotives, are loaded while travelling at about .8 km/h (.5 mph) and dump their loads at a speed of about 5 km/h (3 mph). They run on track welded into long lengths and laid on con-crete crossties. The locomotives are automatically driven, although one 'observer' will always be carried. In its own specialized way, this line showed how productive a well-run and carefully planned railway can be. It is owned and operated by a consortium of electric power authorities; traditional railroaders have no place in it.

The United States

In no country of the world was the superseding of steam more rapid or more ruthless than in the USA. At the end of World War II the diesels swept in everywhere, and large numbers of powerful steam locomotives with a great deal of service still left in them were scrapped. The diesels, the majority of which were at first of General Motors standard design, were painted in bright, distinctive, and often garish colours; their goings and comings lacked the tremendous atmosphere of steam, particularly because in the USA heavy working on mountain gradients was frequently accompanied by highly spectacular exhausts of black smoke. The great locomotives of the New York Central, the Milwaukee Road, the Norfolk and Western and the Union Pacific – to mention only four – were in a long and distinguished line of descent from some of the most colourful engines that have ever run the rails, any-

where in the world. Not even in Great Britain, in the spacious days of the nineteenth century, were locomotives so gaily and fancifully adorned as the early American 4-4-0s. Although running in a wealth of different styles and a great diversity of colouring, the 4-4-0 with outside cylinders, a huge closed-in cab, and very often a colossal 'balloon' stack designed as a spark arrester, was so generally typical and so universal as to be called the American type.

While the slaughter of more modern locomotives was in progress before the advancing diesels, it was fortunate that a number of those old warriors was preserved, some in good enough condition still to be safely steamed. None of them surely appeared in more spectacular guise than old '144' of the Canadian Pacific, which steamed so many miles in Canada during the filming of the television serial *The National Dream*.

In the USA itself, one of the most historic events in the history of railways is now commemorated out in the high country at Promontory, Utah, where the gangs building the first Trans-Continental line across America, working from east to west, met on 10 May 1869, and the last spike was one of gold. The section of line has actually been superseded by a diversion having an improved location, and the opportunity has been taken to erect the most fascinating memorial, with two locomotives representing the converging construction gangs of the Central Pacific and the Union Pacific Railroads, which came cowcatcher to cowcatcher at the driving of the last spike.

From this dramatic start the Union Pacific developed into one of the greatest of American railways. It came to possess, in the famous 4-8-8-4 'Big Boys' of 1942 the largest and heaviest steam locomotives ever built, and now it has some of the largest-ever diesel electrics. Its route through to the West over the Wyoming hills is actually one of the easiest so far as gradients are concerned, though Sherman Hill provided tough enough going for the big 4-8-4 passenger locomotives to need double-heading, with maximum-load trains. The modern steam locomotives of the Union Pacific, like those of most other American railways, were painted plain black and were an impressive sight blasting up Sherman Hill or bringing up great express freight trains from the west through the stark, rocky wilderness of Echo Canyon, Utah.

The Union Pacific 'Big Boys' were of the 'Simple' Mallet articulated type, which was to North America what the Beyer–Garratt has been to the countries of the British Commonwealth. The true Mallet was a compound, with the low pressure cylinders driving the leading engine unit; but in later years most articulated locomotives of the basic Mallet form of construction were 'simples'. Mallets consisted of two separate engines beneath one colossal boiler. The rearward engine was carried on the main frames, while the forward one was on a truck that could swing from side to side, and thus give a degree of road flexibility to what would otherwise have been a very long locomotive. The Garratt, on the other hand, had the engine units fore and aft, and the boiler carried on a central cradle, forming a three-piece articulation. In America the Mallet was originally a slow-speed, heavy freight and mineral hauler. Supporting of the front part of the boiler on the articulated front engine unit was not a very certain job, and when the speed reached around 48 kph (30 mph) the riding became very rough, if not actually dangerous. This instability did not matter so long as Mallet locomotives

Previous page. Ancient and modern, side by side on the Atchison, Topeka and Santa Fe: a preserved Consolidation 2-8-0, with balloon-type smoke-stack, alongside one of the latest diesel-electric locomotives.
Above. A beautifully restored example of the 4-4-0 type, outside the Mount Clare Works of the Baltimore and Ohio Railroad, Baltimore, and named *William Mason*, after one of the most celebrated U.S. locomotive builders of the mid-nineteenth century.
Left. May 10, 1969 was the Centenary of the famous Golden Spike ceremony at Promontory Utah, where the construction gangs of the Union Pacific working westwards, and of the Central Pacific working east met, and the last spike in the first Transcontinental railway across America was driven in. Although the present main line does not now run over this location, the Centenary was marked by the creation of a National Memorial, in which a length of track was relaid, and two vintage locomotives were restored and repainted to represent the *Jupiter* of the Central Pacific, in the foreground, and the '119' of the Union Pacific, facing it. The ensemble together with a small exhibition building forms one of the most original kinds of railway museum to be found anywhere in the world.

were used for toiling along at about 15 to 25 kph (10–15 mph) with endless trains of coal or iron ore.

But on the Union Pacific in particular something considerably larger than the conventional 4-8-4s and 4-12-2s was needed for the fast freight and express fruit trains, and much study was given to the methods of supporting the front part of the boiler of these articulated locos and equalization of the weight carried on the front and rear engines. As a result of this research a simple 'articulated' with the 4-6-6-4 wheel arrangement was designed for the Union Pacific, which was not only an extremely powerful locomotive, but which was quite steady at speeds of more than 96 kph (60 mph). They were indeed used on passenger trains up to speeds of about 130 kph (80 mph). The experience gained with this type led to a series of notable express freight 'simple' Mallets being introduced on a number of American railways, notably the Denver and Rio Grande Western, on the Norfolk and Western, and on the Chesapeake and Ohio. The Norfolk and Western retained the 2-8-8-2 type with compound expansion for its heaviest mineral hauls. None of these locomotives was, however, as enormous as the Union Pacific 4-8-8-4 'Big Boys'.

For the heaviest express passenger service on routes that included hill climbing as well as much fast level running the 4-8-4 type represented the climax of American steam. Again the Union Pacific had a splendid design, which is shown in the picture on page 81, while on the neighbouring Denver and Rio Grande Western, cutting through some of the most rugged mountain country in the whole of North America, even large 4-8-4s were not enough to handle the heaviest trains without an assistant engine. Both routes west from Denver, that through the Moffatt Tunnel, and the highly spectacular 'Royal Gorge' farther to the south, provided some of the most colourful railroading imaginable.

Still farther south, the Santa Fe set its final series of 4-8-4s some of the greatest feats of endurance, combined with maximum sustained demands for power, ever attempted with steam traction. On the very heavy sleeping-car expresses from Chicago to Los Angeles these great engines worked throughout over the 1,985 km (1,234 miles) between La Junta, Colorado and Los Angeles, being manned successively by *nine* different engine crews. These engines were oil-fired. In the eastern states the changeover to diesels did not come quite so rapidly. The coalfields were near at hand, and on the New York Central in particular engines of the new 'Niagara' class, 4-8-4s introduced at the close of World War II, were tested rigorously against diesels to compare running costs, fuel consumption and availability. It was always claimed that diesels did not require so much time between trips for servicing as did a steam locomotive. The

New York Central did not immediately accept this and considered that with a well-designed modern steam locomotive equally good figures for availability could be achieved. Although the first cost of a diesel was more than double that of a 'Niagara', the diesels showed up to advantage; but ultimately other factors intervened and the diesels took over on the New York Central as everywhere else.

One of the great problems with very long locomotives like the various articulated types was that of steam beating down and obscuring the driver's view ahead. The chimneys were so small and the boilers so large that except when blasting up heavy gradients, with the exhaust going sky-high, smoke and steam tended to cling to the surface of the boiler. On routes with lengthy tunnels often with no more than a

driver had to walk along to the 'cupboard' on the boiler, they earned the nickname of 'Mother Hubbards'. There was, on some railways, an even more cogent reason for doing this. The use of soft coal, or even of lignite necessitated very large and wide fire boxes and it would have been difficult to fit a conventional cab within the limits of overall width. In another respect they must have been awkward engines to manage. The efficient operation of a steam locomotive requires close cooperation between driver and fireman, and on a 'Mother Hubbard' this cannot have been easy with the fireman on his own at the rear end. Nevertheless, engines of this type were used for some years on some of the fastest trains in America, the 'Atlantic City Flyers' of the Philadelphia and Reading Railroad, between Philadelphia and Atlantic City.

single-track bore, conditions in the driver's cab could become unpleasant, and there was sometimes even the danger of asphyxiation. On the Southern Pacific operating the important north-to-south route from Portland through San Francisco to Los Angeles, the largest locomotives were all oil-fired and as there was no need to have immediate access to the fuel, they turned their Mallet articulated engines back to front, as it were, having the driver's cab at the leading end and trailing the tender containing the oil and water supply behind what, in a normal locomotive, was the leading end. This not only gave the enginemen a clear lookout, but also put them well ahead of the exhaust steam when passing through the many tunnels on the route through the Sierras over Donner Pass.

The problem of smoke beating down was a troublesome one on American railways even before the nineteenth century was out, and it was solved on some of the eastern lines by putting the driver in a cab by himself, halfway along the boiler. Very quaint these engines looked, and as the

The engines on these trains had the 4-4-2 wheel arrangement and because of this high-speed assignment the type became universally known as the 'Atlantic'. Loads were increasing to such an extent in the USA that larger engines were needed with six, and then eight, coupled wheels and in the country of its birth the 'Atlantic' type was not long in vogue. But it was widely adopted in Great Britain and France, and through the British influence its use became extensive also in India. Some of the most powerful American 'Atlantics' were developed on the Pennsylvania Railroad. The first of these were also built as 'Mother Hubbards'; but it was the 'E6' class – rather

Above. Norfolk and Western: one of the enormous Class Y6b Mallet compound 2-8-8-2s on a westbound empty coal train in the New River Gorge.

stumpy, and not very elegant to look upon – that had nevertheless a distinguished record of performance. When the very fast *Detroit Arrow* was put on in the early 1930s, at first with a light load, the train was worked by 'E6' Atlantics in preference to the much more powerful 'K4' Pacifics used on all other Pennsylvania express passenger services.

It was not until the 1940s that the Pennsylvania built anything larger than 'Pacifics' for its numerous, heavy, and very fast express trains. Except in crossing the Allegheny Mountains, between Pittsburgh and Harrisburg, the gradients east of Chicago and St Louis were easy and the need was for sustained high steaming at speeds of 120–135 kph (75–85 mph). The great rival of the Pennsylvania, particularly on the prestige first-class service between New York and Chicago, was the New York Central and this line developed the 4-6-4 type, which provided the greater carrying capacity of a four-wheel truck beneath the huge fireboxes needed. The NYC trains, like the *Empire State Express* and the *Twentieth Century Limited* often loaded to more than 1,000 tons–more than double that of the *Flying Scotsman*–and speeds over 130 kph (80 mph) on level track were a daily requirement. At times of the heaviest traffic the *Century* as it was always known, sometimes ran in three or four sections. It is sad to think that nowadays passenger traffic by rail in the USA has dwindled to such an extent that there is no through service from New York to Chicago by the former NYC route. Only the *Broadway Limited*, following the former Pennsylvania route provides a fast overnight service between the two cities. In their day, the 4-6-4s of the New York Central were among the finest express passenger locomotives in North America.

Heading once more towards the mountains, it is interesting to recall that the Denver and Rio Grande Western, which today provides an important link in the east–west chain of communication across the USA, began its existence as a narrow-gauge line. In the first place it was not conceived as an east–west route at all. The 'Western' in its name was added later. The original plan was for a narrow-gauge line from Denver to the Rio Grande in the far south, which forms the international frontier between the USA and Mexico. But the railway from Denver never got anywhere near the Rio Grande. Instead, discovery of mineral wealth in the Colorado Rockies led to branches being built westward into the mountains, all on the narrow gauge; and in those fastnesses there took place some of the most exciting railway operations imaginable. Much of the original narrow-gauge mileage is now closed, but happily some sections have been preserved as tourist and railway enthusiast attractions, and visits to them **are extremely popular. The summer service**

over the 73 km (45¼ miles) from Durango to Silverton features in the *Official Railway Guide* for North America, and is operated by the Denver and Rio Grande Western Railroad itself; but part of the section east of Durango, over the Cumbres Pass is operated by the Cumbres and Toltec Scenic Railroad under a leasing arrangement with the states of New Mexico and Colorado.

The old main line to the west, which began with its junction with the standard **gauge at Salida, went over the Continental Divide at the Marshall Pass, on through Gunnison and then over Cerro Summit with** its fearsome curves and gradients of 1 in 25, is now closed; but the tales told of old-time operation on that line still linger in the Colorado Rockies. There were speed restrictions, it is true; but when a cargo was needed in a hurry, livestock for example, it was no unusual thing for a driver definitely to be instructed to disregard them all and get through as quickly as he could. Most of

the drivers needed little encouragement, and tales are told by some of the conductors (guards in British Railway parlance), that one could tell by the look in the eye of one old Boomer that 'he was gonna run like hell'. From this one must not imagine that the *actual* speeds were very high by ordinary railway standards; it is just that they were breathtaking on such a track and in such a terrain. A record run made in 1894 with a stock train over the 130 km (80 miles) from

Above left. Denver and Rio Grande Western: an astonishing location on the narrow gauge line descending eastbound from the Cumbres Pass, Colorado. This 70-car freight train is so strung out round a bend that the 2-8-2 locomotive was photographed from the caboose of its own train! *Below left.* Silverton, Colorado, a station on the same line.
Top. The glamour and colour of the vintage 2-8-0, No. 40, makes a perfect period picture on the narrow gauge in Colorado, at Central City.
Above. Along the track of the Denver and Rio Grande Western a pair of ex-Rio Grande narrow gauge 2-8-2s make ready with an excursion train for Antonita at Chama, New Mexico.

Above. Chicago, Milwaukee, St. Paul and Pacific: a westbound local train pulling out of the old Milwaukee station, Chicago, in 1952, hauled by Pacific locomotive No. 196.
Right. New York Central: the 'Empire State Express', eastbound from Chicago to New York leaving Dunkirk N.Y. hauled by one of the celebrated J-3-a Hudson class 4-6-4 locomotives.
Far right. Chicago, Milwaukee, St. Paul and Pacific Railroad: In 1952, Pacific No. 165 leaving Chicago with a semi-fast passenger train.

Ridgeway to Gunnison gave an average speed of 29 kph (18 mph). Today the Silverton passenger train takes 3½ hours for the 73 km (45¼ miles) from Durango.

Both on this line and on the Cumbres scenic line the locomotives are of 2-8-2 type, of relatively modern design and although operating on the 3 ft or 0.91 m gauge they are very heavy and powerful units – not in comparison with the latest standard-gauge steam locomotives in America, but certainly in relation to those elsewhere in the world. They were introduced in 1923–5 and took over the hardest duties from an assortment of very picturesque old warriors. But even these new engines, which weigh as much as a 'Royal Scot', could not manage loads of more than 230 tons on the gradients of the Marshall Pass; and since the traffic people had to work 600-ton trains at times it needed three of the latest engines, two in front and one pushing in rear.

With very few exceptions American steam locomotives were painted plain black. Towards the end of the 1930s, when the first high-speed diesel railcar trains were being introduced, a few selected steam locomotives were streamlined, more for publicity effect than anything else, and some were painted in startling colours. The Chicago Milwaukee St Paul and Pacific, for example, put on the spectacular 'Hiawatha' trains between Chicago and Milwaukee, which had to run at 160 kph (100 mph) in everyday service. Special high-speed engines were built and these had the silver-coloured streamlined casings adorned with orange and crimson bands. The New York Central was more restrained in the streamlined 4-6-4s put on to the *Twentieth Century Limited*, but the Southern Pacific went very gay with the semi-streamlined 4-8-4s built for the Daylight Expresses, between Los Angeles and San Francisco, having broad red and orange bands below the centre line of the boiler. Everything above that was black, except that the conical smokebox front was painted aluminium colour.

However, when the general introduction of diesel-electric locomotives began after World War II, the railways of America took on an entirely new look. In steam days when nearly everything was black one could just recognize some of the more distinctive of the company locomotives by their silhouettes; but the great majority of what we now call the 'first generation' diesels came from one manufacturer, General Motors, at their great plant at La Grange, Illinois. It was no accident that they all looked alike. The overriding policy of the firm was to sell a standard product and no other. The story is told of one railway administration wishing to buy a large batch of diesel-electric locomotives, but requiring certain deviations from the standard General Motors product to suit their own circumstances. The manufacturer stood rock solid. It was 'standard or nothing' and they refused

to take the order! In one respect, however, General Motors did make a concession. They did not take the line of one English railway manager, who once said he did not mind what colour the locomotives were painted as long as it was black; and so, on the new diesels the railways of America suddenly became strikingly distinguishable from each other by the adoption of gay new colourschemes. Some indeed went to the extent of having different colours for the freight and passenger locomotives.

The diesel revolution on the American railways was of course greatly regretted by all lovers of the steam locomotive, and there were business interests who felt that strict technological and economic factors were not considered with the impartiality necessary in the making of so important a

transition. But apart from anything else the diesels had an overwhelming advantage over steam. Locomotives of each kind might have an equal hauling capacity with a fast train at 96–130 kph (60–80 mph) on level track or easy gradients; but get into the mountains, and there are plenty of very severe inclines in North America, and at below 32 kph (20 mph) the diesel will have twice the tractive power of the otherwise equivalent steam locomotive. It was because of this that when the Canadian Pacific first introduced diesels they put them on to the divisions in the Rocky Mountains, where the climbing speed of both passenger and freight trains was usually no more than about 32 kph (20 mph), not on the fast stretches across the open prairies. The other factor is of course the capacity for doubling up the

power at the head-end without the need for additional engine crews. Two, three or as many as five locomotives can be coupled together and through the electrical controls operated by one man and his co-driver. On the Canadian Pacific, for example, on the Beaver Hill, British Columbia, in steam days, the heaviest westbound trains needed four locomotives, each with its own crew. Now as many as *nine* diesel-electric locomotives are controlled by a pair of men.

Left. Union Pacific Railroad: a special excursion leaving Denver, hauled by steam 4-8-4 locomotive No. 8444, with diesel-electrics following.
Below. A dramatic location on the Union Pacific main line to the west: Weber Canyon, Utah. One of the largest ever diesels, No. 6929, of 6600 horsepower, coupled to *three more* diesels hauling a maximum tonnage freight train.

The decline in railway business, which has affected so many countries all over the world, has been especially severe in the USA, and although there has always been strong resistance to anything savouring of nationalization, it has been necessary to provide substantial support recently in the form of Federal funds. In 1970, by Act of Congress, the National Railroad Passenger Corporation was set up to support the operation of a basic network of inter-city passenger trains. The routes chosen for operation under the auspices of AMTRAK were aimed to eliminate the duplication of service and competitive lines which, admirable in an era of boom demand, had led to the near-bankruptcy of certain of the individual railway companies. It is under this regrouping, for example, that the Pennsylvania route between New York and Chicago was chosen for support, with the 'Broadway Limited' running now under AMTRAK colours.

As appropriate to the new set-up, so far as the principal passenger services are concerned, the locomotives and coaching stock on AMTRAK-sponsored trains are now painted in distinctive colours. The new style in grey, blue and red on the diesel locomotives is most attractive but it is imposing a degree of nationwide standardization whereby, for example, the 'San Francisco Zephyr', the 'Hiawathas' of the Milwaukee Road, and the 'Empire State Express', run in the same colours as the Coast Daylight/Starlight, from Seattle to Los Angeles, or 'The Broadway Limited'. But it is better to have trains with a standardized colourscheme than no trains at all; and that catastrophe could easily have happened in the USA!

Above right. Denver and Rio Grande Western: This is one of the routes not included in the Amtrak network, and the splendid train 'Rio Grande Zephyr' is powered by locomotives in the railroad's own colours rather than those of Amtrak. The photograph is taken at Grand Junction, Colorado, where the two routes westward through the mountains link up.
Right. The 'Amtrak look': the 'San Joaquin' express takes the Southern Pacific inland route from Los Angeles, serving San Francisco, and continuing north to Seattle.

Canada

There is no greater romance in the development of railways than that of the Canadian Pacific. The whole question of colonizing the vast, uncharted territories of the west was political dynamite in mid-Victorian times, and there were many in England seeking immediate financial reward who deplored the deployment of any effort in Canada when riches seemed more readily to hand elsewhere, in India for example. In Canada itself far-seeing statesmen urged the welding together of the scattered colonies into a single confederation; but while this project was generally accepted in the east, and welcomed as a means of bringing together areas hitherto under the warring British and French influences, on the west coast the isolated colonies of British Columbia and Vancouver Island saw no reason to be associated with Ontario, Quebec and the Maritimes. Yet in Eastern Canada it was felt that the very isolation of the colonies on the west coast, shut off by the great and unexplored barrier of the Rocky Mountains, rendered them dangerously susceptible to non-British influences, and liable to absorption by the United States. So an offer was made that if they would join the Confederation of Canada a railway would be built through the mountains, and across the prairies to connect them with the centres of population in the east. The western provinces agreed, and the famous document was duly signed, in Ottawa in July 1870, stating that the railway would be built in ten years.

It was a fantastic commitment. At that time the railways reached no further than 282 km (175 miles) west of Montreal, and some 4,350 km (2,700 miles) of virtually unknown country lay between the 'end of steel' and the Pacific Coast. Romantic though the story of the ensuing years now appears one can be very sure that it never looked that way to those who were involved in it in the fifteen years between the signing of the agreement in 1870 and the driving of the last spike at Craigellachie, British Columbia, in 1885. The political implications, and the so-called 'Pacific Scandal' led to the downfall of one government, while the constructional work, whether in high-speed 'mechanized' track-laying across the prairies or in the adventures of the surveyors in trying to find ways through the Rockies, and the Selkirks, involved feats of endurance almost without parallel. And

the picture of that little Balloon-stacked 4-4-0 No. 148, standing on the breathtaking trestle viaduct epitomizes the entire story. It was no wonder that that colossus of a general manager, William Cornelius Van Horne, confined his comment to two words when he first rode a locomotive over the western part of the line: 'My God!'

The Canadian Pacific came to possess many splendid steam locomotives in later

Below. Canadian National Railways: the 'U-1-d' class 4-8-2 No. 6043, which ran the last scheduled passenger train to be steam hauled, from the Pas to Winnipeg on April 25, 1960. Now preserved in Assiniboine Park, Winnipeg, Manitoba.
Bottom. Canadian National Railways: an historic double-headed combination on an east-bound freight passing through Toronto in April 1952. The leading engine is a 2-10-2 of Class T-I-C, built in 1920 for the Canadian Government Railway. The second engine is a modern 4-8-4.

years, and the passenger types were distinguished by having the cab and tender panels painted in a rich Tuscan red. Appreciation of this led to a change in locomotive colours on the Victorian Railways, in far Australia. Until the early 1900s these latter had been decked in a typical nineteenth-century English colourscheme, of bright green, with brown underframes of a plethora of polished brass and coffee work; but when a new Commissioner arrived from

Canada he instituted a change to the Tuscan red of the Canadian Pacific. Apart from museum pieces in Ottawa and elsewhere, the famous livery of the CPR can be seen in all its glory on a working engine on the British Columbia Railway, and in the most colourful surroundings imaginable. The main line of the former Pacific Great Eastern, now the British Columbia Railway, runs from North Vancouver at first beside the mountainous fiord of Howe Sound, to Squamish, and over this section steam hauled trains are operated with one of the famous 'Royal Hudson' type 4-6-4s of the CPR, so named from the part played by one of this class in working the Royal Train during the visit of King George VI and Queen Elizabeth to Canada in 1939. The engines of this class all carried the crown, by Royal permission, but the preserved working engine now carries the name 'British Columbia' over the front buffer beam.

The second great trunk line across Canada, the Canadian National, dates from 1922, after a Government grouping and amalgamation of a number of immensely long single-tracked lines that had been built with more enthusiasm and 'wishful

Left. A fascinating re-enactment: the Canadian Pacific preserved 4-4-0 with two restored period cars was used during the filming of the television serial 'The National Dream', and is here seen on a branch line in the Rockies where some of the original-type timber trestle viaducts still remain.
Right. Canadian Pacific Railway: a Pacific No. 2471, splendidly adorned with the Tuscan red panels, leaving Windsor Station, Montreal, with a commuter train in April 1952.
Below. The British Columbia Railway passes through some of the most beautiful scenery in the West of Canada, and happily some of it, beside Howe Sound is within easy reach of Vancouver. It is along this line between North Vancouver station and Squamish that seasonal excursion trains are now being run, steam hauled, and using the magnificent 'Royal Hudson' 4-6-4 locomotive, formerly of the Canadian Pacific Railway.

hoping' than sound business acumen, and had become bankrupt, or nearly so, in the process. But they had been vitally needed in World War I, and the Government had taken financial responsibility for them. On amalgamation into the new Canadian National system the route mileage was no less than 22,000 or 35,400 km! At once a great rationalization and 'streamlining' of services began under the wise and kindly leadership of Sir Henry Thornton–a man who carried out his reorganization with such tact, and consideration for the entire staff that he soon became one of the best-loved of all railway managers. His programme was accompanied by the introduction of enormous new steam locomotives, of which a number are fortunately preserved. Most of these are static open-air museum pieces, enthroned on pedestals at the lineside, or in public parks; and examples may be seen at Winnipeg, Capreol, Sarnia and Jasper. The huge 4-8-2 locomotive in the Assiniboine Park at Winnipeg was the very last steam locomotive to work a regularly scheduled passenger train, on the remote line running near to the western shores of Hudson Bay between Winnipeg and The Pas.

While it is good nevertheless to be able to view these engines, and study their splendid physical and engineering proportions it is still better to see them in full action, and for operating special excursion trains Canadian National maintains in first-class working order one of these eight-coupled giants. In 1971 one of the largest ever of the 4-8-4 type, No. 6218, completed her service life. After being superseded by diesels in ordinary traffic, this engine had been retained for special trains; but there are many factors that preclude the indefinite extension of the life of a steam locomotive, and in 1971 the time had come to say 'no more' for the old faithful 6218. Nevertheless so much interest, enthusiasm and a modest increase in revenue had accrued from the running of steam hauled special trains that Canadian National made a survey of the preserved static locomotives to find out which, if any, could most readily be put back into working order to replace 6218. The choice fell on a 4-8-2, No. 6060, which had hitherto been on show at Jasper, in the Rockies. Though not quite such a powerful engine as No. 6218, she had the advantage of being one of a class that had some colour in its painting style. The running plate valences and the tender panels are in a pleasing leaf green; and now, No. 6060, magnificently restored, is running steam hauled specials on Canadian National.

Today all main line traffic in Canada, passenger and freight alike, is worked by diesel-electric locomotives, and these are of two broad types. The first are of the familiar 'first generation' 'nose-cab' design, that became so familiar, in a great variety of colourschemes in the USA after World

War II. In Canada both the 'Big Two' have changed their locomotive liveries in fairly recent years. The Canadian Pacific naturally included its Tuscan red in the colourscheme on its first diesels, but when under a major re-grouping of the business activities of the great organization the Canadian Pacific Railway became 'CP Rail' a change in colour symbolical of the new image was made, and the locomotives are now red and white. These same general types can be seen also in the distinctive colours of the Ontario Northland, and the black and white of Canadian National.

Far more numerous, now, than the 'first generation' type, are the less-aesthetically styled but supremely utilitarian 'road freight' type, with their walkways along the outsides. These have been adopted by all the Canadian railways, including mainly mineral lines like the Quebec, North Shore and Labrador,

Top. The Dübs 4-4-0, of 1882, now working on the 'Prairie Dog Central' line, being prepared for the day's work in her berth beside the Canadian National station in Winnipeg. Built in Glasgow for the Canadian Pacific she was sold to the City of Winnipeg Hydro Department in 1918 for use on their private line between Pointe du Bois and Slave Falls. She was retired in 1962 and put into store until taken over by the Prairie Dog Central.
Above. Canadian National: eastbound express for Montreal leaving Toronto, hauled by semi-streamlined 4-8-4 locomotive No. 6402, built 1936, by the Montreal Locomotive Works.

the British Columbia, and the Algoma Central–all with highly distinctive colourschemes – as well as by the 'Big Two'. On heavy express passenger trains one often sees a *posse* of four diesels, two of the 'nose cab' type leading and two 'road freights' coupled to them. In such service speeds up to 150 kph (90 mph) are often called for.

Index

The publishers would like to thank the following individuals and organizations for their kind permission to reproduce the photographs in this book:
AFIP endpapers; W. J. V. Anderson 7, 19, 20-21, 26-27, 28 above, 28 below, 29 above, 29 below, 30, 31 below, 32 above, 32 below, 50 above, 57 above, 60-61, 62, 63 above, 63 below, 64 above, 64 below, 64-65, 66 above, 66 below, 68, 73, 75, 76-77, 77 above, 78-79, 79 centre, 102 above, 152-153, 157 below, 158-159, 160 above left, 160 above right; ANP-FOTO 97, 98-99; Douglass Baglin 151 above; Bildtjänsten Sverigehuset 105 above; Yves Broncard 6; Camera and Pen International 104; Derek Cross 55, 56 below; Deutsches Bundesbahn 24-25; F. Dumbleton 58-59; C. T. Gammell 17, 52-53, 67 above; 70, 71 above, 72-73, 74; 79 below, 109 above, 129 above, 129 centre, 129 below, 130, 131 above, 131 below, 132-133, 154 below, 155; V. Goldberg 178 below, 181 above, 181 below, 186 above, 186 below, 188-189; Victor Hand 184; J. M. Jarvis 106-107, 108 above, 108 below, 109 below, 178 above, 179, 180 above, 180 below, 182-183, 182 below, 183 below, 187 below, 189 above, 190 below; Keystone Press Agency 10 above; L. G. Marshall 134; E. Milne 142-143, 144-145, 148; S. A. Mourton 140-141, 141 above, 141 below, 142 above, 145 above, 146-147, 149, 150, 151 below; O. S. Nock 8 above, 8 below, 187 above, 190 above; Nordisk Pressefoto (Peer Lauritzen) 101, 104-105; D. Rodgers 9 above, 16, 49, 54 above, 54 below, 56 above, 57 below, 67 below 69 above, 71 below, 77 below, 154 above, 156, 157 above; Rapho (Larrier) 14, 14-15, (Jean Poitier) 10-11; Santa Fe Railroad 177; SNCF title, 9 below; Brian Stephenson contents, 12 below, 13, 22-23, 23, 100; H. Vematsu 135, 136-137, 137, 138 below, 138-139; Union Pacific Railroad 185; C. Whetmath 51, 79 above, 102 below, 102-103; J. S. Whiteley 18, 31 above, 58, 69 below, 110-111, 112 above, 112 below; D. Wilkinson 50 below.